THE

EVERYTHING

GET-A-JOB

BOOK

From resume writing to interviewing to
finding tons of job openings

Steven Graber

Adams Media Corporation
Holbrook, Massachusetts

TO LAURA

Editor: Heidi E. Sampson
Research: Thom Blackett, Marcie DiPietro

Acknowledgments
I would like to thank Mark Lipsman for his thoroughness and insightful suggestions;
Heidi Sampson, Thom Blackett, Will McNeill, Linda Spencer, and Marcie DiPietro for
their ideas and support; and my entire staff for all of their hard work.

An Everything Series Book.
"Everything" is a trademark of Adams Media Corporation.

Published by Adams Media Corporation
260 Center Street, Holbrook, MA 02343. U.S.A.
www.adamsmedia.com

ISBN: 1-58062-223-2

Printed in the United States of America.

J I H G F E D C B

Library of Congress Cataloging-in-Publication Data
Graber, Steven
The everything get-a-job book : from resume writing, to interviewing,
to finding tons of job openings / Steven Graber.
p. cm.
Includes index.
ISBN 1-58062-223-2
1. Job hunting. I. title.
HF5382.7.G69 2000
650.14–dc21
99-046343

This publication is designed to provide accurate and authoritative information with regard to the subject matter covered. It is sold with the understanding that the publisher is not engaged in rendering
legal, accounting, or other professional advice. If legal advice or other expert assistance is required,
the services of a competent professional person should be sought.
— From a *Declaration of Principles* jointly adopted by a Committee of the
American Bar Association and a Committee of Publishers and Associations

Illustrations by Barry Littmann

This book is available at quantity discounts for bulk purchases.
For information, call 1-800-872-5627.

Visit our exciting Web site at http://www.careercity.com

Contents

CONTENTS

Preface

Welcome to the wonderful world of job searching! On the list of all-time pleasurable activities, job searching ranks up there with looking for a place to live, buying a car, and having root-canal work. Yes, it's a dirty job, but everyone's got to do it.

This book can help. Finding a job involves learning certain job-search skills and polishing them to a high degree. This book takes you through each step of the process, beginning with the all-important self-assessment: what are you looking for, and what do you have to offer? Unless you know, you may not get what you want. You also need to know the basics of job winning: planning, organizing, and the best ways to look for jobs.

Because most jobs aren't advertised, one of the most important parts of the job search is networking. Networking brings you in contact with people who refer you to people who refer you to people. . . . And once you know where you want to apply, you need a well-written, sharp-looking resume. You'll learn how to put together a resume that conveys your strengths convincingly, including a whole chapter of resume samples.

These days, even the best paper resume isn't good enough. You need a resume that can be scanned into a database, and even that isn't enough—you may need to be able to submit your resume by e-mail. In Chapter 6, you'll learn how to prepare an electronic resume for scanning and for e-mailing to on-line databases, news-groups, and directly to companies.

Many job seekers mistakenly think a cover letter is just another piece of paper that accompanies a resume, saying "Enclosed please find my resume." Chapter 7 tells you why a well-written cover letter is crucial and how to turn out a concise yet attention-grabbing letter. You'll find these techniques illustrated in a chapter of sample cover letters. Chapter 9 shows you how to say "thank you" gracefully to the various people who help you along the way. It also includes samples of a few more letters you may need to write.

Because looking for jobs is a big time-eater, knowing where to look is half the battle. Expand your options and save time with Internet and CD-ROM job searches. You might also want to try an employment agency—you'll find a chapter on them which includes

information on executive recruiters, temp agencies, and permanent placement agencies.

Eventually, you'll be called for an interview. Once you've made it to this stage, you need to do in-depth research on the company at which you're hoping to be hired. Chapter 13 tells you how, and the interviewing chapter gives you advice on what to say and not say at the interview. If the company uses computer-assisted job interviews, you can learn about them in Chapter 15.

Finally, you receive the job offer, perhaps even multiple job offers! What do you say to the recruiter? While holding the phone in one hand, turn to Chapter 16 with the other to find out.

Remember: These are skills you'll use throughout your career. The more polished you are, both on paper and in person, the better your chances of landing the job you want.

CHAPTER 1

Self-Assessment

Where exactly does one begin a job search? Before wading through the help-wanteds or buying new stationery, it helps to focus on two big questions:
What do you want?
What do you have to offer?

What Do You Want?

One of the biggest mistakes job seekers make is to start looking for a job before they're really ready—even before they have a well-defined goal. Setting goals is critical in all areas of your life, but especially when it comes to obtaining a job. You need to define your objectives clearly. Setting your job objectives is also known as career planning, which has become a field of study in itself.

A Good Match

Time and again, career counselors report that one of the most common problems job seekers run into is that they don't consider whether they're suited for a particular position or career. Keep in mind that, on a daily basis, you'll spend about as much time in your job as you do sleeping—so it's important to know you'll enjoy the work. If you're thinking about becoming an elementary school teacher, be sure you enjoy spending a great deal of time with children. If you want to be an accountant, ask yourself if you're meticulous and like detail-oriented work. If you want to work for a daily newspaper, be sure you can handle a fast-paced, high-pressure environment.

A Job and a Lifestyle

Bear in mind, too, that you're choosing not just a job but a lifestyle. If you decide, for example, that your goal is to be a management consultant for an international firm, chances are you'll be spending a great deal of your time in an airplane—so you'd better like to fly!

Think about geography. Do you want a career that would require you to live in a large city, such as an urban engineer? Or would you rather live in a less populated, rural area?

Think about compensation. Which do you feel is more important: to make a lot of money or to be fulfilled by your work?

Think about your work schedule. If you want a job where you have a flexible schedule, this will have a big impact on the type of job you choose. If you're ambitious and achievement-oriented, that's likely to mean that you'll spend some time burning the midnight oil.

Think about how fast you want to advance. Some careers and some companies offer a much greater chance than others to advance quickly. In some fields, the opportunities for advancement are virtually nonexistent.

Vocational Testing

One formalized way to focus in on your interests is to take a standardized interest inventory test. These are multiple-choice tests designed to help you figure out your likes and dislikes and determine which jobs are best for you. To give you an idea of the types of questions you might find on an interest inventory test, we've included ten questions that you should consider. Do they describe your job and career-related interests?

I enjoy:
- ❏ working with objects most of the time
- ❏ working with people most of the time
- ❏ working in an office or business environment
- ❏ doing scientific and technical studies
- ❏ doing routine or repetitive activities
- ❏ doing abstract and creative activities
- ❏ working with people in a helping role
- ❏ working with machines most of the time
- ❏ working for prestige and the admiration of others
- ❏ seeing concrete results of my work almost immediately

Although it's been said that you are what you do, think about this phrase reversed: You do what you are. Your personality, likes, dislikes, values, and goals should determine where you work and what you do, not the other way around.

Look at the big picture. Take a moment to see beyond whether you want to work in an office or outdoors and consider trying the

Job Counseling Services

The job counseling services offered by your city or town, which can be found in your local phone directory, can be a useful option in career planning. You can also contact The National Board for Certified Counselors at (910) 547-0607.

You may also wish to consult the *Adams Executive Recruiters Almanac*, which lists career counseling services in addition to executive search firms, employment agencies, and temporary help services. This guide may be found in bookstores, your local library, or your college career office.

exercise that's been given to many creative-writing students: Write your epitaph. It doesn't have to be a one-line composition. Write for as long as you want. But answer this question: "What do you want to be remembered for?"

Even if you feel you have a clear idea where your interests lie, and even if you're not entering the job market for the first time, try these exercises. Remember: You're not just looking for a paycheck. Use this time to figure out what's important to you.

What Do You Have to Offer?

Once you've thought about what interests you and what's really important to you, the next step is to think about the second big issue. Broadly speaking, what are your skills? Don't answer by guessing your typing speed; for now, think more broadly than that.

- ❏ the ability to understand and use words well
- ❏ the ability to do arithmetic quickly and accurately
- ❏ the ability to think geometrically
- ❏ the ability to see details
- ❏ the ability to make precise movements quickly
- ❏ the ability to coordinate your hand and foot movements with things you see
- ❏ the ability to work well as part of a team
- ❏ the ability to work well independently
- ❏ the ability to take a position and then defend it

If you've answered these questions, you're almost ready to start your search in earnest. Now's the time to use what you've learned about yourself to decide on the industry, job, and part of the country that appeal to you. One reason to do this is that it makes your job search easier; if you try to pursue too many different avenues, you'll only frustrate yourself. Having a well-developed plan based on objectives you've taken time to think about is easier on you—and will make you a stronger candidate.

The State of the Industry

Ask yourself whether the industry you're interested in is flourishing or dying. This isn't to say you should jump into a particular field just because it's doing well, but the growth in a given field will probably have a major impact on your career prospects some years down the road. If the industry is flourishing, it could mean many more exciting challenges and better opportunities—but it could also mean you've chosen a much less stable profession and will have to jump from one company to the next throughout your career. Sometimes it's a good idea to consider careers in industries that are slowing down or maturing, because they're more likely to have greater opportunities for advancement than industries that are booming and flooded with applicants. Sometimes an industry may be doing poorly in one geographical area but well in another. This is no reason to give up on that industry, but you may have to consider relocating.

Take into consideration whether the job function itself is flourishing or dying. Will the demand be increasing for the job, or is it slowing down? Again, you've got to consider not only what the competition will be like to get the job but also what the competition will be like to advance.

For Students and Recent Graduates

Choosing a Career

It can be helpful to focus on what you've been good at and what you've enjoyed doing in the past. Which classes were your favorites? In which ones did you find least cause for complaint? If biology rang your bell, how about working in a hospital lab? Maybe your natural proclivity for English could come in handy as an editor at a publishing company or as a copywriter at an ad agency. You may even decide you loved a particular subject so much that you actually want to be a teacher and pass that love on to others.

A Clear Direction

Employers like job candidates who have real interests and a clear direction. They know that if you're interested in a particular industry, company, or job, you're more likely to enjoy the position, perform well, and stay with the company.

Employers *don't* like to hear that you aren't at all discriminating—that you'll take whatever job they have available.

What Are Employers Really Looking For?

You may be surprised to learn that employers generally are not looking for just the best grade point average, the most clubs, or the most athletic letters. One of the most important things that employers *are* concerned with is the answer to a simple question: How long will you stay with the company?

Commitment

The average college graduate stays with his or her first employer for only nine months. Employers have concluded that most new young hires are unrealistic about what entry-level jobs entail and will soon leave in search of something "better." They're right.

This costs companies a lot of money, because training new hires is expensive. It's not surprising, then, that most companies—especially those with training programs—will be interested in whether you're likely to remain in that position.

Interest

How can you show a company you won't move on too soon? Your grades probably won't be a strong indication of this. You must display a true interest in the industry, in the job function itself, and particularly in that employer. Intelligently discussing current trends in the industry and showing that you're genuinely interested in the job are two great ways to communicate to an interviewer that you're a low-risk hire.

Consistency

Another way to demonstrate commitment is to stress only a small number of extracurricular activities that you pursued for an extended period of time; this shows that you didn't just participate in many different activities, jumping from one to the next. Although this may seem surprising, it may actually look better to an employer if you participated in only one activity during your college career than if you experimented with many. As long as the activity you highlight was something you spent a lot of time and energy doing, something you made progress in over the years, it will carry more weight than many activities you were only nominally involved in.

Remember, consistency is often more important to employers than excellence in school or outside activities.

Knowing What You Want

Additionally, you should show the employer you're likely to stay with the firm by making it clear that you know what you want. Although you probably don't know the precise title of the job you want, you must show the employer some particular interests and career direction. You should also show that you have a realistic feeling for what the job entails, that you understand what the pluses and minuses are in the position you're considering, and that you've decided, after making a realistic assessment of the job, that it's something you'd enjoy doing for a substantial period.

Maturity and Confidence

Another factor that employers weigh heavily is maturity. Many young graduates, in one-on-one situations with older adults, simply don't come across as being mature and confident enough for the professional world. Unfortunately, such judgments are often made based on a brief interview. Your references could help you in some cases, but your interview is going to matter much more. Chapter 14 will show you how to prepare for interviews and how to make sure you project yourself as a mature candidate who is ready to enter the business community.

Professionalism

Employers want to know whether or not you have a professional demeanor. This is difficult to define but is perhaps best understood as the ability to "fit in with others" in a given work group, adhering to their standards of communication, dress, and conduct. Professionalism is something you need to prove to employers as soon as you contact their firm. One of the ways you do this is by following a more or less accepted format for your resume. Your cover letter also needs to look professional. (We'll review the details later in the book.) In terms of dress, it is important to look like you will fit in at the company from the first glimpse. In your answers and presentation at the job interview, you

Be Realistic

Most important, make sure your career plans are realistic. You have to start somewhere. Accept that most entry-level positions are usually lower paying and less than glamorous. It will probably take you a number of years to achieve your career goals and advance to your ideal job.

Consider an entry-level job the first step toward attaining your long-term goals.

must convey that you know how to conduct yourself properly in a business setting.

Adaptability and Growth

Proving you can do a certain job is not enough. Companies, especially those hiring for management training programs, also want to see that you're going to grow within the company. Employers hope to use these programs to groom potential senior managers. You must assure them that you're capable of adapting to new positions within the company and that you can handle a good deal of responsibility.

That's Not All!

Punctuality is a sign of responsibility. It follows that you've got to be on time for the interview. What's more, you'll have to project the image of a business-oriented person by showing an interest in the industry and in the business world in general. To be sure, employers also want to see that you can perform the job function with a reasonably high degree of certainty. But because most students applying for an entry-level position aren't going to be able to prove their capabilities by citing previous work experience, elements like punctuality and business orientation are crucial in applying for that first job.

Persevere

Today's job market is competitive, and as a job seeker you face many challenges. However, if you recognize this fact and keep putting sufficient effort and energy into your job search day after day, you'll greatly increase the number of opportunities open to you and ultimately find the top-notch job you deserve. After all, your job search can itself be considered your first full-time assignment. Treat it as such, and you'll reap the rewards.

CHAPTER 2

Basics of Job Winning

11 INFORMATIONAL N...
BURNS RESEARCH A...
12 TOUR OF FACILITY
1 INTERVIEW WITH KARA H...
AT BURNS RESEARCH AGE...
2
3 Commute Home
* SEND THANK YOU NOTE
4 GO TO CAREER FAIR
5
6

SEND...

WWW.CAREERCITY.COM

9

...LL HEAD HUNTE...

INFORMATIONAL MEE...
...RNS RESEARCH AGE...
...F FACILITY
...EW WITH KARA H...
RESEARCH...

DATE:

TO DO   ACTION LIST

11 A.M. - 3 P.M.
INFO. MEETING, TO...
AT BURNS RESEARCH...

9 A.M.   WEDNESDAY
INTERVIEW WITH...
AT NARD INC.

THURSDA...

8 A.M.   FRIDAY
MEET WITH BILL M...
DIRECTOR OF CAREER...
AT BIG RED UNIV...
SATURDAY

Job Hunting While You're Still Employed

Job searching while you're still employed is particularly tiring because it must be done in addition to your normal work responsibilities. Don't overwork yourself to the point where you show up to interviews looking exhausted or start to slip behind at your current job. On the other hand, don't be tempted to quit your present job! The long hours are worth it. Searching for a job while you have one puts you in a position of strength.

Making Contact

If you must be at your office during the business day, you have additional problems to deal with. How can you work interviews into the business day? And if you work in an open office, how can you even call to set up interviews? Obviously, you should keep up the effort and the appearances on your present job. Maximize your use of the lunch hour, early mornings, and late afternoons for calling. If you keep trying, you'll be surprised how often you can reach the executive you're trying to contact during your out-of-office hours. You can frequently catch people as early as 8 A.M and as late as 6 P.M.

Scheduling Interviews

Your inability to interview at any time other than lunch might work to your advantage. Set up as many interviews as possible for your lunch hour. This will go a long way toward creating a relaxed atmosphere, but be sure the interviews don't stray too far from the agenda on hand. Lunchtime interviews are easier to obtain, however, if you have substantial career experience, and these are usually not standard practice for filling entry-level positions.

Often, you will find no alternative to taking time off for interviews, especially when your interview is not in close proximity to where you currently work. If you have to do this, try to take the whole day off in order to avoid being blatantly obvious about your job search, and try to schedule two or three interviews for the same day. (It's difficult to maintain an optimum energy level at more than three interviews in one day.) Explain to the interviewer why you might have to juggle your interview schedule. He or she should honor the respect you're showing your current employer by minimizing your days off and will probably appreciate the fact that another prospective employer is interested in you.

References

What do you tell an interviewer who asks for references from your current employer? Just say that while you're happy to have former employers contacted, you're trying to keep your job search confidential and would rather that your current employer not be contacted until you have a firm offer. Furthermore, once a potential employer has asked for your references, be sure to forewarn or remind those references that they may expect to receive a phone call soon.

Be Discreet

The days when employees dedicated their entire careers to a single employer are long gone. It's expected that people will change jobs several times during their careers, and it could be unwise to leave a position without having something else lined up. You shouldn't feel obligated to inform your current employer you're job searching until you're ready to give your notice. Revealing this information too soon could cost you your job. Remember, employers would rather lose you at their convenience than at yours.

To ensure that your job search is kept quiet, avoid telling any of your coworkers or colleagues of your plans. This may sound obvious, but it's a mistake that's too often made—at the expense of the job seeker.

If You're Fired or Laid Off

If you've been fired or laid off, you're not the first and won't be the last to go through this traumatic experience. In today's changing economy, thousands of professionals lose their jobs every year. Even if you were terminated with just cause, don't lose heart.

Severance and Unemployment Compensation

A thorough job search could take months, so be sure to negotiate a reasonable severance package, if possible, and determine what benefits, such as health insurance, you are still legally entitled. Also, register for unemployment compensation immediately. Don't be surprised to find other professionals collecting unemployment compensation—it's for everyone who has lost his or her job.

Follow a Plan

Don't start your job search with a flurry of unplanned activity. Start by choosing a strategy and working out a plan. Now is not the time for major changes in your life. If possible, remain in the same career and in the same geographical location, at least until you've been working again for a while. On the other hand, if the only industry for which you're trained is leaving or is severely depressed in your area, give prompt consideration to moving or switching careers.

Expect the Inevitable Question

Avoid mentioning you were fired when arranging interviews, but be prepared for the question "Why were you fired?" during an interview. Be honest, but try to detail the reason as favorably as possible and portray what you've learned from your mistakes. If you're confident one of your past managers will give you a good reference, tell the interviewer to contact that person. Don't speak negatively of your past employer, and try not to sound particularly worried about being unemployed. If you were laid off as a result of downsizing, briefly explain, being sure to reinforce that your job loss was not due to performance.

Finally, don't spend too much time reflecting on why you were let go or how you might have avoided it. Think positively, look to the future, and be sure to follow a careful plan during your job search.

In addition to being stressful, looking for a new job can be costly. Expenses relating to your job search, in addition to everyday living expenses, can mount to a formidable sum in the face of a reduced income. Following are some guidelines to help you make this aspect of your job search somewhat smoother.

- If you're laid off, you should know that most companies offer one week's to one month's severance pay for every year of service. Get a written copy of your company's policy. Immediately file for unemployment benefits and, if you can afford it, extend your health insurance. Some larger companies will also offer outplacement services to help employees in their transition to another job. Find out if your company offers any such assistance.

- Assess your financial fitness. Make a detailed list of your expenses, separating them into three categories: priority one, priority two, and priority three. Priority one expenses should include the essentials, like rent/mortgage, utilities, groceries, and car payment. Be sure to figure job-search expenses in your priority one list. Priority two and three expenses should include items that can be sacrificed temporarily. Total your estimated expenses in each category.

- Make a detailed list of your income and assets. This should include any income from part-time, temporary, and freelance work, unemployment insurance, severance pay, savings, investments, spouse's income, and alimony.

- Estimate it will take you six months to find a new job (not a bad measure for today's market), multiply the total of your priority one expenses by six and subtract it from your current income and/or savings for that same period of time. You may find that some budgeting is in order. Perhaps you can cut down or eliminate some of those priority expenses. Determine what is essential and what can be sacrificed for the time being.

- You may also decide to write your creditors to request a reduced payment schedule in light of your employment situation. This may not always be possible, and it can affect your credit rating. But many creditors, when given a choice between receiving partial payment or no payment at all, will agree to work out an acceptable plan. Be sure to ask your creditors to help preserve your good credit rating.

Once you've determined how much money you have and how much you'll need, establish a realistic budget. It should be detailed and laid out on paper. Monitor your budget on a regular basis, so you don't suddenly find yourself overwhelmed by a financial predicament that could otherwise have been avoided.

Getting Organized

Planning and keeping track of your efforts will pay off in the long run. A few hours of organizing can save you countless days of unnecessary footwork and can make or break your quest for a rewarding position. Make a to-do list at the beginning of each day and try to accomplish each of your goals by the end of that day. Try to keep your desk or work area free of clutter. A large date book will house all your appointments, names, and phone numbers. Next to each entry, write down all the pertinent information that space permits. Then take the book with you to each appointment.

Record of Activity

Create a chart or similar system that shows where and to whom you've sent your resume. Use it to track whether or not companies have responded and when and if you need to follow up with a phone call.

Oversized index cards or pages in a looseleaf notebook are another useful way to organize your job search. Keep each contact's name, position, company, address, telephone number, contact method, follow-up date, status, and other important details on individual cards for quick reference. Notes detailing when you called, with whom you spoke, and what responses you received should be stashed on this card. If you are responding to an advertisement in a newspaper, clip the ad and paste it onto the card, along with the name of the newspaper and the date. If an employer or networking contact gives you his or her business card, you can staple it to an index card and jot down any other pertinent information. Keep your cards in an index-card box in alphabetical order.

Archive File

The information you collect along the way and any relevant documents, like cover letters and articles, will have to be stored. You never can tell when the phone will ring. While you may have forgotten all about your application a month back, your credentials may have been making the rounds at the office. Even if you land a prestigious position, don't destroy your painstakingly compiled research. You may not want to admit it so soon after your coup,

but the future remains uncertain; another job hunt may be just around the bend.

Planning Your Job-Search Campaign

No matter how terrific they may be, your resume and cover letter alone will not land you a job. You need a comprehensive and well-defined plan to go job seeking effectively. A plan will help you keep up the vigorous pace of the job-search process and keep you from becoming frustrated or unmotivated. It will also enable you pace yourself and monitor your progress against predetermined goals. If your plan is not effective, you'll be able to see problems more clearly and tackle them head-on by changing direction or using different techniques.

Your job-search plan should incorporate a number of different job-finding methods, described later in this chapter. Predict how much time you are going to spend pursuing these different avenues and set up a specific weekly schedule for yourself. It's important not to overlook this step; it will help you be more productive and will make it more difficult to fall behind.

Do Your Homework

If you're trying to enter a new field, your first order of business is to do a little background research. Find out the current trends in the industry and become familiar with names of the major and up-and-coming players. Your industry's trade journal and informational interviews are two terrific ways to find this kind of "insider" information. Check your local library for the *Encyclopedia of Business Information Sources* or *Predicasts F&S Index* to identify publications in your field of interest. Your library will also have the *Occupational Outlook Handbook,* published by the U.S. Department of Labor. This publication lists information on most jobs, including significant points about the job, responsibilities, the outlook for jobs in that field, salaries, related occupations, and sources of additional information.

Fastest-Growing Occupations

Certain professionals will be consistently in higher demand than others. Here are some of the fastest-growing jobs/careers for the coming years:

- Childcare Center Director
- Engineer
- Geneticist
- Industrial Designer
- Intellectual Property Lawyer
- Landscape Architect
- Molecular Biologist
- On-line Sales Manager
- Technical Education Teacher
- Technical Support Manager
- Web Advertising Specialist
- Web Site Developer
- Webmaster

If you're a veteran of the field in which you're looking, make sure you keep up with industry trends by talking with your associates, attending your professional association's functions, and reading your industry's trade journals.

Informational Interviews

Particularly if you're an entry-level job seeker or a career changer, consider conducting at least one informational interview. An informational interview is simply a meeting that you arrange to talk to someone in a field, industry, or company that interests you. With the help of this kind of interview, you can prepare for a real job interview in several ways, including:

- examining your compatibility with the company by comparing the realities of the field (skills required, working conditions, schedules, and common traits of people you meet) to your own personal interests
- finding out how people in a particular business, industry, or job view their roles and the growth opportunities in their business
- conducting primary research on companies and industries
- gaining insight into the kinds of topics your potential interviewers will be concerned about and the methods for interviewing
- getting feedback on your relative strengths and weaknesses as a potential job candidate
- becoming comfortable talking to people in the industry and learning the industry jargon
- building your network, which can lead to further valuable information and opportunities

Set Up the Interview

To set up an informational appointment, request a meeting, either by phone or by letter, with someone who has at least several years' experience working in your field of interest. Your goal is to learn how that person got into the business, what he or she likes about it, and what kind of advice someone with experience might pass on to someone interested in entering the field.

Tell your contact right away that you'd like to learn more about the industry or company and that you'll be the one asking all the questions. Most people won't feel threatened (especially if you assure them you're not asking them for a job) and will usually be inclined to help you.

If you tell a contact that all you want is advice, though, make sure you mean it. Never approach an informational interview as though it were a job interview—stick to gathering information and leads and see what happens. Also, unless specifically requested to do so, sending your resume to someone you'd like to meet for an informational interview will probably give the wrong impression.

Take the Lead

Now that you've scheduled an informational interview, make sure you're prepared to take the lead. After all, you're the one doing the interviewing. Prepare a list of ten to twenty questions, such as:

How did you get started in this business?

- What experience helped you to be prepared and qualified for this job? (How did you get to this point in your career?)
- What do you believe is the ideal education and background?
- What are your primary responsibilities in your current job?
- What do you like most about your job, your company, and your industry?
- What do you dislike most about them? What's been your greatest challenge?
- If you could work with anybody in this field, whom would you want to work with?
- Five years out, what are your career goals?
- What are typical career path options from here?
- If you could change something about your career path, what would you change?
- What are the most valuable skills to have in this field?
- What specific experiences helped you build these skills?
- What opportunities do you see in this business?

- Why did you want this job?
- What would you say are the current career opportunities for someone with my qualifications in the industry?
- If you were in the job market tomorrow, how would you get started? What would you do?
- What are the basic requirements for an entry-level position in the industry?
- What would be on a must-read list in your field?
- Where do you see the industry heading in the near future?
- Is there a trade association that might aid me in my job search?
- What things impress you when you interview candidates for positions in this field?
- What would be turn-offs when you interview candidates?
- What critical questions should I expect to be asked in a job interview?
- What advice would you give to someone looking for a job in the industry?
- Is there anything else I should know about the industry?
- Do you know of anyone who might be looking for someone with my qualifications?
- Is there anything you think I should have brought up (but didn't) that I should consider? (What have I missed in this line of questioning?)

. . . And Thanks Again

Always end by thanking the person, promising to follow up on any important leads he or she has provided and to let the person know how things turn out. You should also send a thank-you note within one or two days of the informational interview.

Follow up periodically with everyone in your network—even after you get a job. Once you develop a network, it's important not to lose those contacts. You want to translate your informational network into a support network and maintain it throughout your career.

Following the Pack

Don't let yourself get caught up in what everyone else is doing! If you know that a large number of people are trying to interview with just a few highly sought-after companies, don't spend all of your time doing the same. Instead, try to interview at the companies others may have overlooked. Try something different, and you'll be likely to come across several job openings before your competition does.

Setting Your Schedule

The most important detail of your job search is setting up a schedule. Of course, since job searches aren't something most people do regularly, it may be hard to estimate how long each step will take. Nonetheless, it's important to have a plan so you can monitor your progress.

When outlining your job-search schedule, have a realistic time frame in mind. If you are searching full-time, it could take two months or more. If you can devote only part time, it will probably take at least four months.

If you're unemployed, remember that job-seeking is tough work, both physically and emotionally. It's also intellectually demanding work that requires you to be at your best. So don't tire yourself out by working on your job campaign around the clock. At the same time, be sure to keep at it. The most logical way to manage your time while looking for a job is to keep your regular work hours.

If you're searching full-time using several different contact methods, try dividing up each week, designating some time for each method. By trying several approaches at once, you can evaluate how promising each seems and alter your schedule accordingly. Keep in mind that the *majority of openings are filled without being advertised.*

The Best and Worst Ways to Find Jobs

You may be surprised to learn that some of the most popular job-search methods are unsuccessful for most of the people who use them. Ideally, you want to use a variety of methods to contact employers. Among the most popular resources and methods are:

- Contacting employers directly
- Classified ads
- Networking (see Chapter 3)
- Internet job search (see Chapter 10)
- CD-ROM job search (see Chapter 11)
- Employment services (see Chapter 12)

The first two are discussed below; the last four are covered in separate chapters.

Contacting Employers Directly

The most effective way to get a job is to contact employers directly, regardless of whether you know of an opening. Step number one is to make up a checklist for categorizing the types of firms for which you'd like to work. You might categorize them by product line, size, customer type (like industrial or consumer), growth prospects, or geographical location. Your list of criteria might be short. If so, good! The shorter it is, the easier it'll be to locate the company that's right for you.

Sources of Company Information

How do you find out which companies you should contact? One of the obvious sources is the *JobBank* series, a group of employment directories that profile companies in each of the 35 largest cities and metropolitan areas in the United States. Each *JobBank* book is a complete research tool for job seekers, providing up-to-date information including contact names and company Web sites.

Many directories, like *Dun & Bradstreet's Million Dollar Directory* and *Standard & Poor's* investment guide, list basic information about companies, including the name of the president and a brief description of the company's products and/or services. These directories, as well as many state manufacturer listings, can be found in your local library. The advantage the *JobBank* books have over these directories is that they list typical job titles at each firm and include the name of the person you should contact where possible.

JobBank books include the following information:

- Full name, address, and telephone number of firm
- Web sites and e-mail addresses
- Contact name for professional hiring
- Listings of common positions, educational backgrounds sought, and fringe benefits offered
- Addresses of professional associations and executive search and job placement agencies

Each book covers every industry, from Accounting to Utilities. The number of employers listed in each book ranges from a few thousand for smaller cities to almost eight thousand for metro New York and Los Angeles.

These books are available for the following cities/regions:

Atlanta	Las Vegas	Pittsburgh
Austin/San Antonio	Los Angeles	Portland
Boston	Minneapolis-St. Paul	Salt Lake City
The Carolinas	Missouri	San Francisco
Chicago	Northern New England	Seattle
Connecticut	New Jersey	Tennessee
Dallas-Fort Worth	New Mexico	Virginia
Denver	New York City	Washington, DC
Detroit	Upstate New York	Wisconsin
Florida	Ohio	
Houston	Philadelphia	
Indiana	Phoenix	

Remember, your aim is to learn a little about many companies. You do not need a tremendous amount of information before you contact a firm, particularly if you're up to speed with what's going on in the industry.

What Kinds of Companies Should You Contact?

Aren't the largest, most successful companies the best places to look for a job? Don't they offer the most security?

Contrary to what many believe, this is not always the case. In recent years, some of the largest and most successful companies in America have been dramatically downsizing their work forces. These companies are *not* necessarily secure places to work. Furthermore, these giants are the very companies that are deluged with resumes and job applications. For example, some of the largest banking corporations receive as many as three thousand resumes every day!

A better plan is to contact the many moderate-size companies that are not necessarily as well known. These companies are a much better source of jobs: they're large enough to have a number of job openings at any given time but small enough that they're often overlooked by other job seekers.

Next, try to decide at which of these firms you're most likely to find a job. Try matching your skills with those that a specific job demands. Consider where your skills might be in demand, the degree of competition for employment, and the employment outlook at each firm.

Likely Prospects

Now you'll want to assemble your list of potential employers. Build up your list to at least one hundred prospects. Then separate your prospect list into three groups. The first tier of around twenty-five firms will be your primary target group, the second tier of another twenty-five firms will be your secondary group, and the remaining names you can keep in reserve.

After you form your prospect list, begin working on your resume. Once your resume is done, start researching your first batch of twenty-five prospective employers. Can you see yourself on the job? Would you be happy working at each of the firms you're researching? You also need to find out enough about each company to sound like you've done your homework. Far too few job seekers—especially recent college graduates—take the time to find out details about the companies to which they apply. Find out what products the company makes, with whom they compete, what their annual revenues are, and any other meaningful information. Use this information during phone conversations and in correspondence with recruiters at the company.

But don't go all out on your research yet! You won't get interviews at every company you contact, so save your big research effort for when you start to arrange interviews. Use one resource at a time and find out what you can about each of the twenty-five firms in the batch, keeping a folder on each firm. If you know anyone at a company on your list, add to your research by contacting that person. See if you can arrange an informational interview.

If you find out something that might disqualify a company from staying on your list—they're about to close their only local office, they've just begun a hiring freeze, or they're being investigated for wrongdoing—cross that firm off your prospect list.

The First Step

The first step in contacting a company directly is to send out your resume with a personalized cover letter. The letter should be addressed to a specific person; avoid mass mailings of identical letters that say "To whom it may concern" or "To the Personnel Office."

After sending your letter and allowing sufficient time for the person to receive it, call. The idea is to call that person one or two days after your resume arrives, so you are likely to be remembered.

Can you call the company to see if there are any job openings *before* you make the effort of sending your resume? If you're unusually confident and articulate on the phone, you may have success with this approach. Such calls are especially effective if you're contacting smaller companies, since you're more likely to reach a key decision-maker directly rather than being blocked by a secretary. However, at larger companies, you'll find that simply sending a resume and cover letter is much more effective. Many companies have recorded joblines to announce their job openings.

Follow-Up Call Tip

When you make a follow-up phone call after sending a resume, you'll customarily find yourself speaking with someone from Human Resources. This is common, and often unavoidable. If at all possible, however, try to speak directly with the hiring manager. If you responded to an ad for a job opening and addressed your resume to a particular contact person, you should try to speak with that person. Remember, the Human Resources Department weeds out applicants, but the specific hiring manager is the one doing the hiring!

Follow Up with a Phone Call

After you've sent your resume and cover letter, always follow up with a phone call. What you say on the phone is important, but so is *how* you say it. You need to speak with an air of confidence. Even though a company may not have a particular job opening, you need not be apologetic for calling. All companies hire at some point, and each has, at least in theory, a responsibility to be courteous when an outsider makes a call inquiring about potential job openings.

Will all your calls be answered courteously? No. Some will be answered brusquely—often you'll be calling someone who is busy. But you must project confidence on the phone.

It's important to be succinct on the phone. One good way to do this is by writing out a short script for yourself. Be sure not to sound as if you're reading this script, but do become familiar with it, so you won't forget what you want to say even if you're nervous.

You need to make three points:

- why you're calling
- why you'd be a strong candidate for hiring
- what kind of position you're interested in

You should do this briefly—in twenty seconds or less. At the same time, be sure to speak clearly and slowly enough to be understood.

Classified Advertisements

Are newspaper ads a good source of opportunities for those entering the job market? Unfortunately, not always. Department of Labor statistics show that most people do not get their jobs through newspaper ads.

One of the reasons newspapers are not a good source for job opportunities is that once a company advertises a job opening in a newspaper, it is deluged with hundreds of applications. This is often quite disruptive; a company will typically try anything and everything to fill a job opening before resorting to listing it in the classified section. This means that few job openings are listed in the newspaper relative to the number of jobs available at any given time.

There's more bad news. By the time a job is listed in the classified ads, there's a good chance the position has already been filled or is close to being filled. Even if the position is still available by the time the company receives your resume, the competition will be so fierce that your chances of getting an interview are small.

For all these reasons, relying solely on newspaper ads is usually a tough way to get a job. This is not to say that you should ignore promising opportunities you see advertised, but you certainly shouldn't make scanning the want ads your only research activity.

Think of your job search as a military campaign—you have to follow every avenue possible to win, but some avenues are likely to be more productive than others. It's hard to say which approach is going to pan out, so you shouldn't rule out any possibilities. At the same time, you can't afford to spend too much time in any one area that's less likely to be productive.

Old Newspaper Ads

Instead of responding only to current newspaper ads, try responding to the old ones too. If you respond to a newspaper ad that's many months old, it's possible the person who was hired to fill the position didn't work out. In a situation like this, there won't be hundreds of other people responding to that ad when you call. Also, a company that had a job opening seven months ago is likely to have a different position opening up now that hasn't been advertised yet. Old help-wanted ads can help you to find companies you'd like to work for, and you can send a resume and cover letter inquiring about possible openings. You should not, of course, mention that you are applying for the specific position listed in the newspaper months earlier.

There is often a fairly long interval between the time a manager first starts thinking about filling a position and the time an opening is publicized. You may find old newspapers almost as useful as newer newspapers for unearthing potential job opportunities.

How to Get That Extra Edge Over the Competition

The difference between finding a terrific job in a relatively short time and suffering through a prolonged job-seeking campaign can be a little extra effort. Following are some of the ways you can get that "extra edge" and outshine the competition:

Read the Trade Literature

Make a habit of reading the trade literature of the industry you're focusing on; you should also read some background books about the field. Remember, your aim is to sound like an industry insider; you'll need to be familiar with industry-related topics while you're networking and interviewing.

Re-evaluate Your Plan If Necessary

Another key to job searching is staying with the plan you made, even if it doesn't seem to be working at first. Of course, you'll need to re-evaluate every once in a while to make sure your chances of getting the job you want are realistic. If everyone you speak to tells you the industry is in bad shape, that there are lay-offs at companies of all sizes, that the outlook for newcomers is bleak—maybe you should look into a different field. If everyone you speak to tells you you're underqualified, perhaps you need to look into firms where the competition for positions is not as fierce—or consider a position where your qualifications are more suitable. You may decide to try another city or even another field.

Get Tips from Other Job Seekers

Meet and talk with other job hunters from time to time. Seek out job hunters who, like you, are creative and innovative in their search; share leads, insights, and techniques. Doing this on a regular basis will yield fresh ideas and help keep up your morale.

Keep Networking

Go back and call once again those people you already contacted for leads several months ago. Such a conversation might sound like this:

You: You know, I'm still interested in a career in banking. I know that we talked a few months ago, but I wondered if any other people might have possibly come to mind with a background in banking.

You may be pleasantly surprised. It's not uncommon to catch a contact in a different frame of mind and learn of someone new. Or perhaps, since the last time you spoke with your contact, new leads have arisen, but you haven't heard about them due to a hectic schedule.

Long-Distance Job Hunting

As if finding a job isn't tough enough, long-distance job hunting can be even more difficult. The ideal way to apply for a job in another city is to move there first, although this is not a viable option for everyone. Job searching long-distance is possible, but you should explain immediately that you're willing to relocate to that particular area.

If you're going to move, you can take several steps to make the transition as smooth as possible. First, call or write your new city's chamber of commerce or purchase the appropriate *JobBank* book from any major bookstore to get information on the city's major employers. Subscribe to a local newspaper, check for job postings on-line (see Chapter 10), and sign up with local employment agencies. Inform your networking contacts of your plans and ask them for any leads or suggestions they can give you in this new location. Do they know of anyone who works in that area who can give you suggestions? Also, be sure to check with your national trade or professional association. Most large associations offer members access to a national network. Contact the national office for a list of chapters in your new city.

Relocating

If you're looking for work and need to relocate to a different part of the country, check out this Web site: *http://homes.wsj.com*

This site offers resources for moving to a new city and buying a new home. The one hundred largest cities in the U.S. are profiled. Another option of this site is the "Best Places to Live," which allows you to choose from different criteria and then tells you which metro areas are your best match.

If you're relocating to a new city because your spouse has been transferred, be sure to ask your spouse's company about spouse relocation assistance. Some larger companies may offer free career counseling and other job-search services to you. If your spouse's employer does not offer this service, consider contacting a career counseling center for guidance. You may be able to negotiate with your future employer to pay the center's fees.

How Long Should Your Job Search Take?

It is very hard to determine how long a typical job search will take because there are so many factors involved in what is usually a very important life decision. One school of thought suggests that the average job search lasts approximately one week for every $2,000 of income sought. For example, if your goal is a position that pays in the $30,000 range, your search will take approximately fifteen weeks. This is only a rule of thumb; keep in mind that a lot of it is chance, depending on the job market, your personal preferences, and your qualifications and presentation.

If you're like many job seekers, you'll have to contact several hundred companies before you find the right job. If you put tremendous effort into your job search and contact many companies each week, you'll probably get a job much sooner than someone who is only searching casually and sending out one or two resumes a week.

Again and again during your job search, you'll face rejection. You'll be rejected when you apply for interviews. You'll be rejected after interviews. For every job offer you finally receive, you'll probably have been rejected many times. Don't let rejections slow you down. Keep reminding yourself that the sooner you apply to companies and get those rejections flowing in, the closer you'll be to obtaining the job you want.

Avoid the trap of letting yourself believe that job searching is easier for everyone else than it is for you. It's all too easy to become frustrated when you aren't seeing immediate results from your hard work. At this stage in the job-search process, it's normal to have self-doubts. Don't let your doubts overwhelm you. Job searching is tough, whether you're a recent college graduate or someone who's been in the workplace for years. Stay with it, work hard, have confidence, and you will get the right job!

For Students and Recent Graduates

As a rule, the best jobs do *not* go to the best-qualified individuals—they go to the best job seekers. This is a vitally important point, especially if you are competing for an entry-level position. Even though you may compete with people who have stronger credentials, you can still get the job you want if you're willing to put in the extra effort and energy necessary to outshine the competition.

Standing Out from the Pack

You can increase your chances of landing a great job by standing out from the pack. Most college students, regardless of their grades, have all the basic requirements for the typical entry-level job. You must demonstrate that in addition to fulfilling the basic requirements, you stand out from the competition and deserve that extra consideration.

Gaining Experience

Perhaps the biggest problem college students face is lack of experience. Many schools have internship programs designed to give students exposure to the field of their choice as well as the opportunity to make valuable contacts. Check out your school's career services department to see what internships are available. If your school does not have a formal internship program or if no available internships appeal to you, try contacting local businesses and offering your services. Often, businesses are more than willing to have an extra pair of hands (especially if those hands are unpaid!) for a day or two each week. Or try contacting school alumni to see if you can "shadow" them for a few days and see what their daily duties are like.

What do you do if, for whatever reason, you weren't able to get experience directly related to your desired career? First, look at

Cost-of-Living Salary Calculations

If you're offered a job in a new city and you're contemplating relocation, you'll have to consider the city's cost of living. The easiest way to make comparisons and calculate your real earning potential in the new city is by checking out a Web site that offers a "salary comparator." Simply type in the city and country you're moving from, the city and country you're moving to, the salary you currently make, and the salary you would make in the new city. The Web site's salary comparator uses a cost-of-living database to make earnings calculations for you in minutes. Following are two Web sites that offer this service: Homefair.com at *www.home-fair.com/calc/salcalc.html.* and money.com (*MONEY* magazine on-line) at *http://cgi.pathfinder.com/ cgi-bin/Money/col.cgi*

your previous jobs and see if you can highlight anything. Did you supervise or train other employees? Did you reorganize the accounting system or boost productivity in some way? Accomplishments like these demonstrate leadership, responsibility, and innovation—qualities that most companies look for in employees. And don't forget volunteer activities and school clubs, which can also showcase these traits.

Start Early

One important way to get that "extra edge" in your job hunting campaign is to start as soon as you can. It bears repeating that the beginning of your senior year is an ideal time to begin; by the time graduation comes along, you'll be well into your search and will have several possibilities in mind that you're prepared to take action on.

On-Campus Recruiting

Companies often send recruiters to interview at various colleges. The on-campus interview is generally a screening interview, to see if it's worth the company's time to invite you for a second interview. So do everything possible to make yourself stand out from the crowd.

The first step is to check out any and all information your school's career center has on the company. If the information seems out of date, check out the company on the Internet or call the company's headquarters and ask for any printed information.

Make that Meeting

Many companies will host an informational meeting for interviewees, often the evening before interviews are scheduled to take place. *Do not miss this meeting.* The recruiter will almost certainly ask if you attended. Make an effort to stay after the meeting and talk with the company's representatives. Not only does this give you an opportunity to find out more information about both the company and the position, it also makes you stand out in the recruiter's mind. If you had your heart set on a particular company but weren't able to interview with them, attend the information session anyway. You may be able to persuade the recruiter to squeeze you into the schedule. (Or you may discover that the company really isn't the right fit for you after all.)

Interviewing

Try to check out the interview site beforehand. Some colleges may conduct "mock" interviews in one of the standard interview rooms, or you may be able to convince a career counselor (or even a custodian) to let you sneak a peek during off hours. Either way, having an idea of the room's setup will help you prepare mentally.

Arrive at least fifteen minutes early. The recruiter may be ahead of schedule and might meet you early. But don't be surprised if previous interviews have run over, resulting in your thirty-minute slot being reduced to twenty minutes (or less). Don't complain or appear anxious; just use the time you do have as efficiently as possible to showcase the reasons *you* are the ideal candidate. Staying calm and composed in these situations will work to your advantage.

How Many Students Land a Job Before They Graduate?

Most students won't have jobs by the time they graduate. So if you fall into this category, don't panic—you can still take plenty of other steps to distinguish yourself.

What to Expect

Many graduating students enter the job market thinking that getting a job will be like applying to college. Applying to companies isn't like that at all. Success will not go to the job searcher who invests little effort, becomes discouraged, and takes the first job possibility that comes around. Remember, the time you put into your job search will be time well spent if you make sure all of that effort and energy is going in the right direction.

Conducting Your First Job Search

Ideally, for the first few months after graduation, try to look for a job full-time. If you're able to do this, be sure to work from a vigorous, intense job-search plan that allows you to invest about forty hours a week.

Steve

I was big on the classifieds for a while. I loved to mark up the paper with bright red slashes and circles. It was more fun than the crossword puzzle. Unfortunately, this pastime was nowhere near as rewarding as it was entertaining. I wrote what seemed to be hundreds of cover letters and altered my resume to suit the criteria in the ads on a daily basis. I would get a nibble here and there, but nothing ever panned out. Someone later told me that many of the jobs advertised aren't even legitimate positions. Then I got a call and was invited to interview at a small catering company looking for a general assistant. I did get the job, but I wouldn't count on just the classifieds to get a job in the future.

—STEVE,
MICHIGAN STATE
UNIVERSITY

Vary your activities a little bit from day to day—otherwise it will quickly become tedious. For example, every Sunday you can look through the classified ads. On Monday, follow up on these ads by sending out your resume and cover letter and making some phone calls. On Tuesday, you might decide to focus on contacting companies directly. On Wednesday, you can do more research to find listings of other companies to contact. Thursday and Friday might be spent networking as you try to set up appointments to meet with people and develop more contacts.

Internships

You should have been busy completing internships during the school year or your summer vacations. Now that you're out of school, you may wonder how a person can live on an intern's salary. It'll be tough, but there are ways. Most graduates in your position intern on a part-time basis, taking a second job at night or on their days off. It's manageable, and, if you're planning on getting into some of the more competitive fields, practically unavoidable. Advertising, public relations, entertainment, and publishing companies have a history of hiring former interns. Even if your temp job doesn't turn into a full-time situation, you'll be well on your way in the field. You'll have made contacts, learned important skills, and added another credential to your resume.

Half a Loaf

You might also consider finding a part-time position, even if it's not in your field. (Financially, it may be something of a necessity at this point.) With a part-time job, you'll earn some money and gain a valuable sense of personal accomplishment. After several months of tedious searching, you'll probably have dealt with your share of stress; a part-time job will break up your routine and keep you motivated and enthusiastic about your job search. Working part-time also displays initiative and a good work ethic, which is something recruiters like to see.

Speech Therapy

You know how, like, when you're talking to your friends, and you say "um" a lot and use that hip slang like *cool, fat, fly*, and maybe even *dope*? That won't cut it when you're talking to potential employers. Good communication skills are a must in every field. If you want to be taken seriously, you've got to talk the talk. Practice talking into a tape recorder or request that your friends emit a loud BUZZ! whenever you're caught in the act of slanging it up. If you're still having trouble mastering your native tongue, invest in a speech therapy/elocution session or two—it'll be money well spent.

The GPA Question

You're interviewing for the job of your dreams. Everything is going well: You've established a good rapport, the interviewer seems impressed with your qualifications, and you're almost positive the job is yours. Then you're asked about your GPA, which is pitifully low. Do you tell the truth and watch your dream job fly out the window?

Never lie about your GPA. They may request your transcript, and no company will hire a liar. You can, however, explain if there is a reason you don't feel your grades reflect your abilities, and mention any other impressive statistics. For example, if you have a high GPA in your major or in the last few semesters (as opposed to your cumulative college career), you can use that fact to your advantage.

Computer Literacy

If you're not computer literate, consider yourself substantially disadvantaged. To be adequately prepared for today's work force, take an introductory computer course. For a nominal fee, community colleges in your area can help you master most commonly used programs, like WordPerfect and Microsoft Word. If you're low on funds, ask your friends for help. There's a PC-owner in every bunch, and you're bound to run into one who'll agree to show you the ropes.

Find A Computer

If you don't have access to a computer that can be used for job-hunting purposes, fear not! Places such as Kinko's Copies are open twenty-four hours and let you sign in to use a computer for about $12 per hour. This can be well worth the cost if you're typing up a quick cover letter, for example. However, if you're planning on spending a significant amount of time on the computer, you may opt to sign up to use a computer at a public library. Many libraries have a number of computers set aside for public use (including some that have Internet access). Call ahead of time to find out the library's policies.

CALL HEAD HUNTER

FAX RESUMES

LL HEAD HUNTER

PICK UP SUIT AT Dry Clean
SEND THANK Y
Note

9 A.M.
INTERVIEW WITH THOM TAN
AT NARD INC.

WEDNESDAY Mercredi/Mittwoch/Me

THURSDAY Jeudi/Donnerstag/Giove

FORMATIO
RNS RES
UR OF

RVIE
URN

8 A.M.
MEET WITH BILL MACNEILL
DIRECTOR OF CAREER PLANNING
AT BIG RED UNIVERSITY

FRIDAY Vendredi/Freitag/Venerdi/Vie

SATURDAY Samedi/Samstag/Sabato/Sáb

TO DO

ACTION LIST

DATE:

Get Sunday Newspaper WANT-ADS MAIL/FAX RESUMES	✓
Call Head Hunter	✓
Pick up Suit at Dry Cleaners	☐
Send Thank You Notes	✓

ACTION LIST

One Page Per Day (Undated)

HEAD HUNTER

11	INFORMATIONAL MEETING A BURNS RESEARCH AGENCY TOUR OF FACILITY
12	
1	INTERVIEW WITH KARA FORRE AT BURNS RESEARCH AGENC
2	
3	Commute Home ★ SEND THANK YOU NOT GO TO CAREER FAIR
4	
5	
6	

TUESDAY Ma

TOUR, IN
EARCH AGE

NESDAY Mercredi/Mittwoch/Me

ITH THOM TAN
NC.

THURSDAY Jeudi/Donnerstag/Giove

11 INFORMATIONAL M
BURNS RESEARCH A
12 TOUR OF FACILITY
1 INTERVIEW WITH KARA H
AT BURNS RESEARCH AGEN
2
3 Commute Home
* SEND THANK YOU NOTE
4 GO TO CAREER FAIR
5
6

SEND R

www.careercity.com
*

9
INFORMATIONAL MEE
BURNS RESEARCH AGE
R OF FACILITY
EW WITH KARA
RESEARCH

CALL HEAD HUNTE

11 A.M. - 3 p.m.   T
INFO. MEETING, TO
AT BURNS RESEARC

9 A.M.   WEDNESDAY
INTERVIEW WITH
AT NARD INC.

THURSDA

8 A.M.   FRIDAY
MEET WITH BILL
DIRECTOR OF CAREER
AT BIG RED UNIV
SATURDAY

TO DO	ACTION LIST	DATE:	☐

CHAPTER 3

Networking

N etworking is the process of exchanging information, contacts, and experience for professional purposes. One reason so many people use networking is that it's a great method for finding a new or better job.

Developing Your Contacts

Some career counselors feel that the best route to a better job is through somebody you already know or to whom you can be introduced. These counselors recommend that you build your contact base beyond your current acquaintances by asking each one to introduce you, or refer you, to additional people in your field of interest.

The theory goes like this: You might start with fifteen personal contacts, each of whom introduces you to three additional people, for a total of forty-five additional contacts. Then each of these people introduces you to three other people, which adds one hundred thirty-five contacts. Theoretically, you'll soon know every person in the industry.

Of course, developing your personal contacts doesn't work quite as smoothly as the theory suggests, because some people won't be able to introduce you to anyone. The further you stray from your initial contact base, the weaker your references may be. So if you do try developing your own contacts, begin with as many people whom you know personally as you can. Dig into your personal phone book and your holiday greeting card list and locate old classmates from school. Be sure to approach people who perform your personal business, like your doctor or insurance agent. By the nature of their professions, these people develop a broad contact base.

By Mail

It's essential to achieve the right tone in your networking letters. Unless you're familiar with a contact, word your correspondence in a businesslike manner. In other words, don't use your addressee's first name or an overly casual writing style. Likewise, if you've been in contact with this person recently, it could be useful to remind him or her, "It was great seeing you at the Chicago Writers' Convention last month" or "It's been several months since we bumped into each other on that flight to London. How are you?"

Many networking letters are written to an addressee to whom the candidate has been referred by a mutual acquaintance. In this case, immediately state the name of the person who referred you, such as "Jean Rawlins suggested I contact you." It is generally more effective to ask a contact with whom you are unfamiliar for assistance and names of people to contact than to ask for a job. Chances are, if your letter is politely persuasive, people will be interested in talking with you.

By Phone

A good self-introduction is a tremendous asset to your networking agenda. Aim for a balance of brevity and completeness. Don't simply call someone and say, "Hi, Mr. Pitt. This is George. Elaine told me you do quite a business in the stock market. Do you mind telling me about it?" Write out a short statement, including not only what you want but also who you are and how you're qualified. If you waste people's time, their opinion of you will take a nosedive. So practice your delivery before giving the pitch, and make sure to tailor each one to the situation at hand.

Many people are, at first, a little uncomfortable calling people they don't know and asking for contact names and interviews. You'll be nervous the first few times, but with practice you'll feel much more comfortable and confident making calls. The key is to think about what you're going to say in advance, pick up that phone, and just do it. No one else can network for you. Once you gain some confidence, you'll find that your calls will make a big difference in your job-search campaign.

Hot Networking Zones

Some places are optimally suited for carrying out your networking schemes. Here are some you may want to check out:

- Business seminars
- Community events
- Conferences
- Fund-raisers
- Health clubs
- Industry trade shows
- Professional organizations

Networking Letter
(Administrative Assistant)

1701 Burk Street
Durango, CO 81301
November 16, 1999

Nikita Wilson
Attorney at Law
Baldini, Limbert & Lock
1140 Main Street
Pueblo, CO 81001

Dear Ms. Wilson:

Recently, Luke Gokey suggested I contact you concerning any assistance you might be able to provide with my job search. I am interested in joining an organization in a position that would utilize my legal, administrative, and managerial knowledge and experience. The enclosed resume will provide you with information concerning my background and abilities.

As indicated, my law-related background is extensive and varied. For twelve years, I have supervised records and staff activities within the North County Registry of Deeds. Unfortunately, I have reached the plateau of responsibility level within the structure of this position, and am now seeking to continue in my career progression.

I am especially interested in a legal administrative position, preferably with a private firm or corporation. I am willing to relocate and/or travel and am not restrictive on starting salary.

Should you know of any related openings or contacts to whom I should pass my resume, please do not hesitate to call me at (303) 555-5555. Thank you for your time. I look forward to hearing from you in the near future.

Sincerely,

Michael Picard

Michael Picard

In Person

If you're serious about networking, you can't afford to bypass the business card. Buy yourself a set, and give one to anyone who'll have it. Have plenty on you at all times, because the more you get into circulation, the greater your chance of pinning down another connection. If someone seems less than enthused about accepting it, don't press it on him or her. A vigorous shake of the head or a backing away and a frown all mean the same thing—keep your card in your pocket. If you're really bent on scoring the reluctant connection, you could always request the other person's card and call when he or she is in better cheer.

On-line

Networking on-line is discussed in Chapter 10 **[Internet Job Search]**.

Whenever and Wherever

Networking is a commitment. Always be on the lookout for new opportunities. You never know when or where you'll meet your new employer or an industry expert. Being prepared to network in even the oddest settings will have you interviewing for more positions than you ever thought possible.

Send a Thank-You Letter

If a networking contact has been particularly helpful to you, by all means send a thank-you note. Not only is this courteous, it keeps your contacts current. That person may be an important business contact for years to come—especially if the individual is active in your industry.

For Students and Recent Graduates

Traditionally, networking is used by people with a great deal of work experience. But you can use it even if you have no experience whatsoever.

Perry

We were at my friend's bachelor party and sitting next to these middle-aged men in suits. One of my buddies struck up a conversation, and the next thing you know, we're one big party.

I'm talking to one of the guys, telling him about how hard it is to get a break in television production in Chicago. I couldn't believe it when the guy told me he worked for NBC. I asked him a ton of questions, completely ignoring the exotic dancers and the guest of honor. By the end of our talk, he said he might be able to help me. We exchanged cards, and a couple of days later I was being interviewed for the position of production assistant on a popular daytime talk show. I was given an offer the next day.

—PERRY, OBERLIN COLLEGE

Name Dropping

Be sure to drop names; it's one of the most important ways to get ahead in the business world. ("Ally Kendreck suggested I call you.")

As you continue networking, you'll find yourself dropping names of people you've met only by phone. Don't be uncomfortable with this; this is the way it's done.

Someday you may be in a position to help other job seekers networking, but right now you need to do everything you can to increase *your* chances of finding a job.

Perhaps you're asking yourself, "Don't I have to know people who are in a position to hire to be able to network? Don't I have to know a lot of people in general, or in a specific geographic area, to get a job through networking?" The answer to both questions is no. You don't have to know anybody at all—you just have to *get to know* people.

The Key to Networking

One of the secrets of networking is knowing what you want—or at least appearing to know what you want. If, when you are making networking calls, you tell your contacts you're interested in the industry they work in and if you sound even somewhat knowledgeable about that industry, that makes you more or less an industry insider.

How do you start? Keep up to date with the industry. Read the trade publications. These are specialized journals and magazines that address the concerns of professionals in a given industry. Virtually every type of business has at least one.

Who You Know

Your friends may not have any close relations with professionals, but their parents might. Asking close pals to contact their relatives on your behalf is a most effective way of building a network—as long as you have no problem reciprocating the favor. Teachers come into contact with experts from various fields on a daily basis. Asking them about their associates may secure you several informational interviews with leaders in each industry.

Alumni Placement Offices

These services are now part of many universities and colleges. They function basically as clearinghouses for companies interested in matching job-seeking alumni to their needs. If your school doesn't offer placement services, try to take advantage of the membership listings many alumni associations make available, which can serve as a valuable source for contacts.

Career fairs are another great, often overlooked job-hunting resource. These organized gatherings of representatives and hiring managers from various companies afford you the opportunity to introduce yourself and often interview on-the-spot. Since putting a face and personality to a resume is a crucial part of decision-making in the hiring process, going to a career fair is a proactive way to make a good impression and get your foot in the door.

- At career fairs you are given the chance to exhibit your skills, enthusiasm, and experience to many companies all in one day at one location, some of which have specific openings to fill. In addition, this can save you time and money that would have been spent sending out multiple resumes by mail or waiting for advertised openings.

- Be sure to dress just as you would for a formal interview and have lots of resumes on hand to pass out to potential employers.

- Many career fairs are industry-specific. For instance, you can find fairs that specialize in high-tech, sales and marketing, or health care fields. Others are simply labeled "professional," and consist of representatives from a wide variety of industries.

- Information on upcoming career fairs is often advertised in newspapers, and can also be obtained on-line through job-hunting Web sites as well as Web sites solely dedicated to providing career fair information.

- Some sponsors hold career fairs nationwide and year-round—such as Kaplan Career Services—and have information listed on their Web site including dates, times, locations, and which companies will attend. This type of information can also be obtained by calling the sponsor.

For more information on career fairs, contact: Kaplan Career Services at 800-288-2890 *www.lendman.com*; or American Job Fairs at 800-77-EXPOS *www.americanjobfairs.com*

What Does a Networking Conversation Sound Like?

Here's a sample of what your networking conversations should sound like:

You: Hi, Uncle Ted! It's Emily. As you might have heard, I just graduated from college, and I want to pursue a career in banking. Is there anyone you can think of who might be willing to talk to me about the banking industry, to fill me in on some background information?

Relative: I really can't think of anyone in the banking industry—but why don't you call up my attorney, Don Silva. He's not a real close friend, but I deal with him every month or so. He knows a lot of business people, not necessarily in the banking industry, but you never know. Why don't you call him and see if he can be of any help. His number is 555-1234.

You: Thanks, Uncle Ted!

You then call the attorney, immediately identifying who referred you:

You: Mr. Silva, my name is Emily Sampson. My uncle, Ted Giemza, suggested I call you. I'm interested in a career in banking, and I wondered if you might know anyone in that field who might be able to talk to me briefly about the industry.

Attorney: Well, I'm not really sure. Let me think about it a little and I'll get back to you.

Keep the momentum on your side by offering to follow up yourself.

You: That's fine. If you want I can call you back. If there's someone in the industry you can refer me to or someone who might know somebody else in the industry, I'd really appreciate it.

If a networking contact seems reluctant, you could redirect the conversation in this way:

Attorney: Gee, I do know a few people in the industry, but they're probably not hiring now. . . .

You: That's fine. I just want to talk to someone briefly to find out what's going on in the industry. If you'd like, I can stop by for a few minutes at your convenience so we can meet, and in the meantime maybe you could think of some other names you'd feel comfortable referring me to.

That way, if your contact is hesitant to give any names out without seeing in person that you're a polished, professional individual, you may be able to overcome some of that reluctance by setting up a face-to-face meeting. This technique also gives your contact the opportunity to think of some more names of people he can refer you to.

The attorney example is a good one; you should consider meeting with people who service others in your chosen industry. If the contact is still unwilling to meet with you, don't be overly insistent. Instead, ask the contact to recommend someone else for you to call. Eventually, you should network your way to someone who works within your chosen industry.

Don't Ask for a Job

Remember, you don't want to scare your contacts off. If for some reason you suspect a particular contact is in a position to hire, you should *not* specifically ask about a job. Ask about the industry, relay that you are interested in pursuing a career in that field, and try to set up a time to meet briefly so you can get some background information.

Suppose you know for a fact that a certain contact has an opening available for which you'd be suitable. Perhaps you saw the ad in the classifieds. Should you mention it in your conversation with this person? Absolutely not. Remember, you earned this contact through networking, not by reading a classified ad. (Of course, if the person asks whether you saw the ad, don't lie, but point out that you're calling as a result of speaking to so-and-so.) You want to position yourself as an industry insider who is networking around, not as just another person responding to an ad.

CALL HEAD HUNTER

ADS
FAX RESUMES

LL HEAD HUNTER

PICK UP SUIT AT
DRY CLEAN
SEND THANK Y
NOTE

9 A.M.
INTERVIEW WITH THOM TAN
AT NARD INC.

WEDNESDAY Mercredi/Mittwoch/M

THURSDAY Jeudi/Donnerstag/Glo

INFORMATIO
RNS RES
UR OF

RVIE
URN

8 A.M.
MEET WITH BILL MacNEILL
DIRECTOR OF CAREER PLANNING
AT BIG RED UNIVERSITY

FRIDAY Vendredi/Freitag/Venerdi/V

SATURDAY Samedi/Samstag/Sabato/Sab

TO DO

ACTION LIST   DATE:

GET SUNDAY NEWSPAPER ✓
WANT-ADS
MAIL/FAX RESUMES ✓

CALL HEAD HUNTER ✓

PICK UP SUIT AT
DRY CLEANERS ✓
SEND THANK YOU
NOTES

ACTION LIST

HEAD HUNTER

11 INFORMATIONAL MEETING
    BURNS RESEARCH AGENCY
12 TOUR OF FACILITY

1   INTERVIEW WITH KARA FORRE
    AT BURNS RESEARCH AGENC

2

3   COMMUTE HOME
    * SEND THANK YOU NOT
4   GO TO CAREER FAIR

5

6

TUESDAY Ma

OUR, IN
ARCH AGE.

NESDAY Mercredi/Mittwoch/M

WITH THOM TAN
NC.

THURSDAY Jeudi/Donnerstag/G

NW.CAREERCITY.COM

TO DO   ACTION LIST   DATE:

11 INFORMATIONAL M.
BURNS RESEARCH A
12 TOUR OF FACILITY
1 INTERVIEW WITH KARA H
AT BURNS RESEARCH AGE
2
3 Commute Home
* SEND THANK YOU NOTE
4 GO TO CAREER FAIR
5
6

SEND

WWW.CAREERCITY.COM

CALL HEAD HUNTE
9

INFORMATIONAL MEE
RNS RESEARCH AGE
R OF FACILITY

EW WITH KARA F
RESEARCH G

11 A.M. - 3 p.m.
INFO. MEETING, TO
AT BURNS RESEARC

9 A.M.   WEDNESDAY
INTERVIEW WITH
AT NARD INC.

THURSDA

8 A.M.   FRIDAY
MEET WITH BILL
DIRECTOR OF CAREER
AT BIG RED UNIV
SATURDAY

When filling a position, an employer will often have a hundred-plus applicants but time to interview only a handful of the most promising ones. As a result, a recruiter will reject most applicants after only briefly skimming their resumes.

Unless you've phoned and talked to the employer—which you should do whenever you can—you'll be chosen or rejected entirely on the basis of your resume and cover letter. *Your cover letter must catch the employer's attention, and your resume must hold it.* (But remember—a resume is no substitute for a job-search campaign. *You* must seek a job. Your resume is only one tool, albeit a critical one.)

Both the appearance, or format, of your resume and the content are important. These are discussed in separate sections below.

Format

First impressions matter, so make sure the recruiter's first impression of your resume is a good one.

Types

The most common resume formats are the chronological resume and the functional resume. You may also see references to a "chrono-functional," or "combination," resume, but this is usually a variant on one of the other two—a chronological type with an expanded skills summary or a functional type with an expanded work-history section.

Chronological

The chronological format is the most common. Choose a chronological format if you're currently working or were working recently and if your most recent experiences relate to your desired field. Use reverse chronological order and include dates. To a recruiter, your last job and your latest schooling are the most important, so put the last first and list the rest going back in time. Remember: There is no need to capitalize "present" in "1999–present."

Functional

A functional resume focuses on skills and strengths that your most recent jobs don't necessarily reflect, while de-emphasizing job titles, employers, etc. A functional resume may be useful if you have no work experience, have been out of the work force for a long time, or are changing careers. But some recruiters may wonder if you're trying to hide something, so be ready for questions of that nature. In some cases, a skills summary section at the top of a chronological resume may be useful.

Typing

A word processing or desktop publishing program is the most common way to generate your resume. This allows you the flexibility to make changes instantly and store different drafts. These programs also offer many different fonts, each taking up different amounts of space. (It's best to stay between 10-point and 12-point type size.) Many other options are also available, like boldface or italics for emphasis and the ability to manipulate spacing. Leave the right-hand margin unjustified to keep the spacing between the letters even and easier to read.

Organization

Your name, phone number, e-mail address (if you have one), and mailing address should be at the top of the resume. Make your name stand out by using a slightly larger font size and boldface. Be sure to spell out everything—don't abbreviate "St." for "Street" or "Rd." for "Road." The word "present" (as in "1997–present") should be lowercase.

Next, list your experience, then your education. If you're a recent graduate, list your education first, unless your experience is more important than your education. (For example, if you've just graduated from a teaching school, have some business experience, and are applying for a job in business, list your business experience first.)

The important thing is to break up the text in some logical way that makes your resume visually attractive and easy to scan, so experiment to see which layout works best. However you set it up,

Typeface

Typefaces come in two general categories: *serif* and *sans serif*.

This is a serif face.
This is a sans serif face.

Serif faces are generally easier to read—the serifs and variable thicknesses of the strokes help the eye perceive the letters. They also tend to convey a more upscale image than sans serif. This doesn't mean choosing a fancy, designer typeface—something standard and conservative is best.

stay consistent. Inconsistencies in fonts, spacing, or tenses make your resume look sloppy. Use tabs rather than the less precise space bar to keep information aligned vertically.

Length

Employers dislike long resumes, so keep it to one page if possible. If you must squeeze in more information than would otherwise fit, try using a slightly smaller typeface or changing the margins. Watch also for "widows" (a word or two on a separate line at the end of a paragraph). You can often free up some space if you can edit the information enough to get rid of those single words taking up an entire line. Another tactic that works with some word processing programs is to decrease the size of your paragraph returns and change the spacing between lines.

Paper Color and Quality

Use quality paper that is standard 8½-by-11-inches and has weight and texture, in a conservative color like white or ivory. Good resume paper is easy to find at stores that sell stationery or office products and is even available at some drug stores. Use *matching* paper and envelopes for both your resume and cover letter. One hiring manager at a major magazine throws out all resumes that arrive on paper that differs in color from the envelope!

Do not buy paper with images of clouds and rainbows in the background or anything that looks like casual stationery you would send your favorite aunt. Do not spray perfume or cologne on your resume. Also, never use the stationery of your current employer.

Printing

For a resume on paper, the result will depend on the quality of the printer you use. Laser printers are best. Do not use a dot matrix printer. If you don't print out each copy individually, use a high-quality photocopier, such as in a professional copy shop.

Household typewriters and office typewriters with nylon or other cloth ribbons are *not* good enough for typing your resume. If you don't have access to a quality word processing program, hire a professional with the resources to prepare your resume for you. Keep in mind that businesses like Kinko's (open twenty-four hours) provide access to computers with quality printers.

Many companies now use scanning equipment to screen the resumes they receive, and certain paper, fonts, and other features are more compatible with this technology. Formatting a resume for scanning is discussed in Chapter 6 **[Electronic Resumes]**.

Watermark

When you print your resume (and cover letter), hold it up to a light to make sure the watermark reads correctly—that it's not upside down or backward. As trivial as this may sound, it's the accepted style in formal correspondence, and some recruiters check for it. One recruiter at a law firm in New Hampshire sheepishly admitted this is the first thing he checks: "I open each envelope and check the watermarks on the resume and cover letter. Those candidates that have it wrong go into a different pile."

Proof with Care

Mistakes on resumes are not only embarrassing, they will often remove you from consideration (particularly if something obvious, like your name, is misspelled). No matter how much you paid someone else to type, write, or typeset your resume, *you* lose if there is a mistake. So proofread it as carefully as possible. Get a friend to help you. Read your draft aloud as your friend checks the proof copy. Then have your friend read aloud while you check. Next, read it letter by letter to check spelling and punctuation.

If you're having it typed or typeset by a resume service or a printer and you don't have time to proof it, pay for it and take it home. Proof it there and bring it back later to get it corrected and printed.

If you wrote your resume with a word processing program, use the built-in spell checker to double-check for spelling errors. Keep in mind that a spell checker will not find errors like "to" for "two" or "wok" for "work." Many spell-check programs don't recognize missing or misused punctuation, nor are they set to check the spelling of capitalized words. It's important to still proofread your resume for grammatical mistakes and other problems, even after it's been spell-checked.

If you find mistakes, do not fix them with pen, pencil, or white-out! Make the changes on the computer and print out the resume again.

Content

Sell Yourself . . .

You're selling your skills and accomplishments in your resume, so it's important to take inventory and know yourself. If you've achieved something, say so. Put it in the best possible light. But avoid subjective statements, like "I am a hard worker" or "I get along well with my coworkers." Stick to the facts.

While you shouldn't hold back or be modest, don't exaggerate your achievements to the point of misrepresentation. Be honest. Many companies will immediately drop an applicant from consideration (or fire a current employee) upon discovering inaccurate or untrue information on a resume or other application material.

. . . But Be Concise

Write down the important (and pertinent) things you've done, but do it in as few words as possible. Short, concise phrases are more effective than long-winded sentences. Avoid the use of "I" when emphasizing your accomplishments. Instead, use phrases beginning with action verbs. Use present tense for your current job and past tense for previous jobs.

Also, try to hold your paragraphs to six lines or less. If you have more than six lines of information about one job or school, put it in two or more paragraphs. A short resume will be examined more carefully. Remember: your resume usually has between eight and forty-five seconds to catch an employer's eye, so make every second count.

Give 'Em What They Want

Employers favor certain skills. Here are the top contenders:
* *Supervising/managing skills* mean you can take responsibility for the work of others.

- *Coordinating/organizing skills* allow you to plan events or see projects to completion.
- *Negotiating skills* allow you to bring about compromise and resolve differences.
- *Customer service/public relations skills* enable you to be a spokesperson for your organization.
- *Training/instructing skills* allow you to show newcomers the ropes.
- *Interviewing skills* enable you to ask tough questions, then listen to get insight from the answers.
- *Speaking skills* involve presenting your ideas verbally in a coherent fashion.
- *Writing skills* enable you to express your ideas convincingly on paper.
- *Deadline-meeting skills* enable you to work under pressure.
- *Budgeting skills* involve the ability to save your employer money.

Avoid Catch Phrases

In the course of a job search, it's tempting to use catch phrases you've picked up from advertisements or reference materials, phrases that sound as though they *should* go in a resume or cover letter. Many people are tempted to reach for expressions like "self-starter," "excellent interpersonal skills," and "work well independently or as part of a team."

Improve on these descriptions by listing actual projects and goals. For example, rephrase "Determined achiever with proven leadership skills" as follows: "Supervised staff of fifteen and increased the number of projects completed before deadline by X percent." Once you begin working, employers will discover your personal attributes for themselves. While you're under consideration, concrete experiences are more valuable than vague phrases or obscure promises.

Job Objective

Objectives tend to sound generic, and the information they contain should be clear from your cover letter. Also, an overly specific

The Kitchen-Sink Sentence

Being concise doesn't mean trying to cram every facet of your job into a single sentence. Break up long, unwieldy sentences:

Example (wrong way): "Responsible for editing, writing, and production coordination of bid proposals for government, industrial, and utility engineering and construction contracts."

Example (right way): "Prepare bid proposals for government, industrial, and utility contracts, including engineering and construction. Write and edit proposals; coordinate production."

Remember that seemingly efficient strings of nouns can become hard to understand and are often better off broken up for purposes of grammar AND common sense.

The Appropriate Apostrophe

A common mistake on resumes, especially in describing your work experience, is to refer to " . . . over five years experience in. . . ."

"Years" here is a type of possessive and must have an apostrophe: ". . . over five years' experience in. . . ."

objective may eliminate you from consideration for other positions that a recruiter feels are a better match for your qualifications.

In certain instances, an objective may be suitable—for example, if your previous work experience is unrelated to the position for which you're applying, or if you're a recent graduate with no work experience. Sometimes an objective can give a functional resume focus. One or two sentences describing the job you're seeking may clarify the capacity in which your skills can best be put to use. Be sure your objective is in line with the position for which you're applying, and don't state that you're looking for a position that will allow you to grow or to develop certain capacities. Employers are interested in what you can do for them, not what they can do for you. This is something to keep in mind throughout the job-search and interview process.

Experience

Emphasize continued experience in a particular job area or continued interest in a particular industry. De-emphasize irrelevant positions. Delete positions you held for less than four months (unless you're a recent college graduate or still in school). It's okay to include one opening line providing a general description of each company at which you've worked.

Stress your results and achievements, elaborating on how you contributed in your previous jobs. Did you increase sales, reduce costs, improve a product, implement a new program? Were you promoted? Use specific numbers (quantities, percentages, dollar amounts) whenever possible. Always avoid "etc." when presenting your experiences. Don't expect a potential employer to imagine what else you mean.

Gaps in Your Employment History

You may be asked about gaps in your employment history. Although you'll need to be prepared to explain them, gaps aren't the stigma they used to be. Many people now have some kind of irregularity in their work histories—they were laid off, went back to school, took off for personal reasons, changed careers, had a baby—you name it. Because this is now so prevalent, recruiters

Action Verbs

Action verbs make your resume more interesting to read. These are some you may want to use. (This list is not all-inclusive.)

achieved	developed	integrated	purchased
administered	devised	interpreted	reduced
advised	directed	interviewed	regulated
analyzed	discovered	invented	reorganized
arranged	distributed	launched	represented
assembled	eliminated	maintained	researched
assisted	established	managed	resolved
attained	evaluated	marketed	restored
budgeted	examined	mediated	restructured
built	executed	monitored	revised
calculated	expanded	negotiated	scheduled
collaborated	expedited	obtained	selected
collected	facilitated	operated	served
compiled	formulated	ordered	sold
completed	founded	organized	solved
computed	generated	participated	streamlined
conducted	headed	performed	studied
consolidated	identified	planned	supervised
constructed	implemented	prepared	supplied
consulted	improved	presented	supported
controlled	increased	processed	tested
coordinated	initiated	produced	trained
created	installed	proposed	updated
designed	instituted	provided	upgraded
determined	instructed	published	wrote

Instead of creating a long list of uncategorized bullet points, you may want to group responsibilities and accomplishments conceptually. In the following example, a resume entry is done both ways:

Director of Student Services (1993–present)
- Plan, administer, and evaluate a comprehensive freshman academic support program.
- Coordinate activities, including academic advising and placement and academic, personal, and career counseling; administer placement tests, new student orientation, parent/student workshops, cultural activities, academic tracking, and early warning system for "at risk" freshmen.
- Chair meetings of faculty/administration committee for student services. Propose new programs and changes to existing programs.
- Analyze administration data on student services to determine benefits of programs.
- Distribute evaluations to students and collate data to determine student satisfaction with programs.
- Initiated a newsletter and a recognition dinner for student achievements in academics, activities and sports.
- Instituted cultural awareness activities, including a guest lecture series, field trips to the Boston Art Museum and the Ryder Early American Collection, and a tour to retrace the stops in Paul Revere's ride.

Grouping the bullet points conceptually makes them easier to read and understand, as do arranging the categories in logical order (planning, administration, and evaluation) and the bullets in order of importance within each category:

Director of Student Services (1993–present)
Responsibilities include planning, administering, and evaluating a comprehensive freshman academic support program.

- *Planning*
  Chair meetings of faculty/administration committee for student services. Propose new programs and changes to existing programs.

- *Administration*
  Coordinate activities, including academic advising and placement and academic, personal, and career counseling.

  Administer placement tests, new student orientation, parent/student workshops, cultural activities, academic tracking, and early warning system for "at risk" freshmen.

  Instituted cultural awareness activities, including a guest lecture series, field trips to the Boston Art Museum and the Ryder Early American Collection, and a tour to retrace the stops on Paul Revere's ride.

  Initiated a newsletter and a recognition dinner for student achievements in academics, activities, and sports.

- *Evaluation*
  Analyze administration data on student services to determine benefits of programs.

  Distribute evaluations to students and collate data to determine student satisfaction with programs.

can't very well hold it against you, as long as you have a plausible explanation and the skills for the job.

Action Verbs

In describing previous work experiences, the strongest resumes use short phrases beginning with action verbs. Remember, however, that if you upload your resume to an on-line job hunting site like CareerCity, the keywords or key nouns a computer would search for become as important as action verbs. For more on keywords in electronic resumes, see Chapter 6 **[Electronic Resumes]**.

Bullets

Bullets are useful for drawing attention to significant points, but make sure that your resume is not too bullety. A long column of bullet points in random order can lack cohesion. An alternative is to group them conceptually—in relevant categories, with a few bullets under each one—to make them easier to grasp. This may also permit you to combine several bullets into one or, conversely, to break up long paragraphs. Do remember, however, that bulleted blocks, capitals, or italics are hard to read and are best avoided. Also, periods following elements of bulleted lists are optional. The general rule is to use periods for statements that are full sentences; otherwise don't.

Avoid Excessive Jargon and Excessive Words

Some technical terms may be necessary, but try to avoid excessive "technicalese." Keep in mind that the first person to see your resume may be a human resources person, who won't necessarily know all the jargon—and can't be impressed by something he or she doesn't understand. Also strive to use the fewest number necessary to convey your message. Example: "Responsible for directing" can be "Directed" (if a past experience) or "Direct" (if current).

Temporary Work

If you do your temporary work through an agency, list the company name and job description for any longer-term assignments (perhaps a month or longer) you held. For shorter assignments, use

Volunteer Work

If you would like to include your volunteer work with your paid work experiences to give your resume a more continuous work history, make sure to title this section "Experience" rather than "Employment Background" or "Professional Experience."

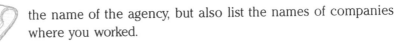

the name of the agency, but also list the names of companies where you worked.

ProTemps Employment, Houston, TX
Short-term clerk/typist assignments at the following companies:
Acme Products
Bonding Devices
Development Partners
Morrison Manufacturing
Terragard Fabrics

Skills

Most jobs now require computer knowledge. Therefore, it's usually advisable to include a section titled "Computer Skills," in which you list software programs you know. If the list is long, subdivide them by category.

Example:
Operating systems	DOS, Windows, Macintosh
Writing/publishing tools	Word, WordPerfect, QuarkXPress, PageMaker, Photoshop, Illustrator
Business [or *Financial*]	Excel, Lotus 1-2-3, Access
Languages	C++, BASIC

It isn't usually necessary to include the version number of an application. Nor do you need to be perfectly fluent with a program to list it. As long as you've used it in the past and could pick it up again with a little practice, it's legitimate to include it.

The skills section is also an ideal place to mention fluency in a foreign language. If you're listing skills other than computer knowledge, subdivide them by category under the "Skills" heading: "Computer," "Foreign Languages," etc.

Education

Keep the education section brief if you have more than two years of career experience. Elaborate more if you have less experience. If you're a recent college graduate, you may choose to include high school activities that are *directly* relevant to your career.

Mention degrees received and any honors or special awards. Note individual courses that might be relevant to employers. (These should be at least a semester long. Shorter courses of a day or two, even a week or two, should not generally be mentioned unless they're important in your field. It's also unnecessary to list courses taken in pursuit of a degree.)

Certifications

Mention any applicable certifications or licenses you hold, such as teaching or social work.

Personal Information

Do not include your age, health, physical characteristics, marital status, race, religion, political/moral beliefs, or any other personal information. List your personal interests and hobbies only if they're directly relevant to the type of job you're seeking. If you're applying to a company that greatly values teamwork, for instance, citing that you organized a community fundraiser or played on a basketball team may be advantageous. When in doubt, however, leave it out.

Do not include your picture with your resume unless you have a specific and appropriate reason to do so—for example, if you're applying for a job as an actor or model.

Professional Affiliations

These are worth noting if you're a member of a professional organization in your industry.

References

"References available upon request" is unnecessary on a resume. It's understood that if you're considered for the position, you'll be asked for references and will provide them. Don't send references with your resume and cover letter unless they're specifically requested.

It's Illegal

"Those things [marital status, church affiliations, etc.] have no place on a resume. Those are illegal questions, so why even put that information on your resume?"

—BECKY HAYES
CAREER COUNSELOR,
CAREER SERVICES,
RICE UNIVERSITY

When to Get Help

If you write reasonably well, it's to your advantage to write your own resume. This forces you to review your experiences and figure out how to explain your accomplishments in clear, brief phrases. This will help you when you explain your work to interviewers. It's also easier to tailor your resume to each position you're applying for when you've put it together yourself.

If you have difficulty writing in resume style (which is quite unlike normal written language), if you're unsure which parts of your background to emphasize, or if you think your resume would make your case better if it didn't follow one of the standard forms outlined either here or in a book on resumes, consider having it professionally written.

The best way to choose a resume writer is by reputation: the recommendation of a friend, a personnel director, your school placement officer, or someone else knowledgeable in the field.

> *Important questions:*
> "How long have you been writing resumes?"
> "If I'm not satisfied with what you write, will you go over it with me and change it?"
> "Do you charge by the hour or a flat rate?"

For more information on resume services, contact the Professional Association of Resume Writers at 3637 Fourth Street, Suite 330, St. Petersburg, FL 33704, USA. Correspondence can be addressed to the attention of Mr. Frank Fox, Executive Director.

Price and Quality

There is no guaranteed relation between price and quality, except that you're unlikely to get a good writer for less than $50 for an uncomplicated resume, and you shouldn't have to pay more than $300 unless your experience is extensive or complicated. Printing charges will be extra. Assume nothing, no matter how much you pay. It's your career at stake if your resume has mistakes!

Few resume services will give you a firm price over the phone, simply because some resumes are too complicated and take too long to do for a predetermined price. Some services will quote you a price that applies to almost all of their customers. Once you decide to use a specific writer, you should insist on a firm price quote *before* engaging his or her services. Also, find out how expensive minor changes will be.

For Students and Recent Graduates

Which Type of Resume Is Right for You?

The type of resume you use depends on your job experience. If you don't have any work history, use a functional resume format, emphasizing your strong points:

Education. This should be your primary focus.
Special achievements. This could be almost anything from having an article published to graduating with honors.
Awards and competitive scholarships
Classes, internships, theses, or special projects that relate to your job objective
Computer knowledge. Are you familiar with a Mac or PC? What software programs do you know?
Language skills. Are you fluent in a foreign language? Be sure to indicate both written and verbal skills.
Volunteer work
Committees and organizations
Extracurricular activities

Recruiters like to see some kind of work history, even if it doesn't relate to your job objective, because it demonstrates that you have a good work ethic. However, it's also important to emphasize special skills or qualifications, including the above information.

Work History

When describing your work history, avoid simply listing your job duties. Focus on accomplishments and achievements, even if they're small. Consider the difference:

Show It to People

"The one piece of advice I give to everyone about their resume is: Show it to people, show it to people, show it to people. Before you ever send out a resume, show it to at least a dozen people."

—Cate Talbot Ashton
Associate Director,
Career Services, Colby
College

Weak: "Lifeguard at busy public beach. Responsible for safety of bathers and cleanliness of the beach and parking areas."
Strong: "Lifeguard at busy public beach. Rescued eight people during summer. Established recycling program for bottles and cans."

If you've held many jobs, you may choose to emphasize only two or three of the most relevant and list the rest under the heading "Other Experience" without individual job descriptions:

Other Experience: Floor and stockroom clerk at university bookstore, server, lifeguard, and courier.

When Functional Is Appropriate

As indicated earlier, under some circumstances, a functional resume may be more appropriate. These may include the following:

- You haven't worked for over a year.
- You want to highlight specific skills by category that would not stand out as easily with a chronological format.
- You've held a variety of jobs.
- Your career goal has taken a dramatic turn.

In this case, a functional resume may be more suitable. It focuses not so much on what positions you've held and when but on what you've learned from your experiences that would be of use in the job. The functions you served in your old jobs are the crux of this format. The actual titles and dates don't come until the very end. An example of each type is shown in Chapter 5.

GPA

Never include a grade point average (GPA) under 3.0 on your resume. If your GPA in your major is higher than your overall GPA, include it either in addition to or instead of your overall GPA.

In certain fields, it is requested that you send a Curriculum Vitae, or "CV," instead of a resume. Sometimes this is referred to as an "International Resume," since all European countries use some form of the Vitae. A CV is mainly used when applying for jobs in the education and health care industries.

A CV differs from a resume in that it is tailored toward these industries by providing specific, more comprehensive information. It is usually longer in length, depending on the applicant's degree of experience. Typically, a CV is anywhere from two to eight pages (with those who have a master's degree or more experience at the higher end of the scale). A CV contains information such as:

- Details on educational background including degrees and certificates accrued, master's thesis and/or doctoral dissertation, honors and awards, and GPA.
- A summary of relevant work experience.
- A list of publications authored.
- A list of papers presented at conferences.
- Professional association membership(s).

An example of a Curriculum Vitae appears on page 77, Chapter 5, *Resume Samples*. For more extensive information on how to write a CV, check out a Web site called *Curriculum Vitae Tips* at *www.cvtips.com*

High School Information

Including high school information is optional for college graduates, but such information should be used sparingly. If you have exceptional achievements in college and in summer or part-time jobs, omit your high school information. High school information should really only be used if the experience is directly related to the types of jobs or industry for which you are applying. If you decide to include high school achievements, describe them more briefly than your college achievements.

Keep in Touch

Put your home address and phone number at the top of the resume. Change the message on your answering machine if necessary—the Beastie Boys blaring in the background or your sorority sisters screaming may not come across well to all recruiters. If you think you may be moving within six months, include a second address and phone number of a trusted friend or relative who can reach you no matter where you are.

Remember that employers may keep your resume on file and contact you months later if a position opens that fits your qualifications. All too often, candidates are unreachable because they moved and didn't provide enough contact options on their resumes.

11 INFORMATIONAL M.
BURNS RESEARCH A
12 TOUR OF FACILITY
1 INTERVIEW WITH KARA H
AT BURNS RESEARCH AGE
2
3 Commute Home
* SEND THANK YOU NOTE
4 GO TO CAREER FAIR
5
6

SEND N

www.careercity.com
*

9

ALL HEAD HUNTE

INFORMATIONAL MEE
BURNS RESEARCH AGE
R OF FACILITY
EW WITH KARA
RESEARCH A

11 A.M. - 3 p.m.
INFO. MEETING, TO
AT BURNS RESEARCH

9 A.M.   WEDNESDAY
INTERVIEW WITH
AT NARD INC.

THURSDA

8 A.M.   FRIDAY
MEET WITH BILL M
DIRECTOR OF CAREER P
AT BIG RED UNIV
SATURDAY

DATE:

TO DO   ACTION LIST

Jeffrey Shaefer
178 Green Street
Baltimore, MD 21202
(301) 555-5555

EXPERIENCE

1999-present
BANK OF BALTIMORE,   Baltimore, MD
Teller
- Process account transactions, reconcile and deposit daily funds.
- Inform customers of bank products, refer public to designated personnel, provide account status data, and handle busy phone.
- Orient, train, supervise, and delegate tasks for new hires.
- Serve as team leader for Christmas Clothing Campaign for homeless.

1998-99
MEYER, GREEN AND FAZIO, Office Assistant   Princess Anne, MD
- Collected, sorted and distributed incoming mail. Processed outgoing mail.

1997-98
TANNENBAUM SOCIETY, Sales Associate   Washington, DC
- Serviced customers, reconciled cash drawer.
- Created effective product displays.

1995-96
KENT AND LANE ASSOCIATES, Office Assistant   Richmond, VA
- Produced correspondence, responded to public inquiries, monitored and maintained confidential records.

EDUCATION
GENEVA COLLEGE, Annapolis, MD
Associate in Business/Travel

COMPUTERS
WordPerfect, Lotus 1-2-3, SABRE

Jake Colquitte

178 Southport Road
Calgary, Alberta, Canada T2W 3X6
(403) 258-5555
jcolquitte@coldmail.com

EMPLOYMENT

Nessman Radio Systems, Oakville, Ontario   1993–present
Copywriter/Service Director
Compose copy for advertisements and promotions. Edit client copy, client newsletter, and executive correspondence. Communicate with clients and listeners by phone. Produce commercials. Organize and oversee copy and taped spots. Assign on-air personalities for recording. Coordinate technical aspects of on-air programming.

Temieux Mutual Inc., Vancouver, B.C.   1992–93
Claims Coder
Processed claims reports and encoded data to computer system. Reviewed and revised reinsurance files. Conducted inventory. Balanced daily accounts for each computer system.

University of Calgary, Calgary, Alberta   1991–92
Mathematics Tutor
Tutored college students.

EDUCATION

University of Calgary, Calgary, Alberta
BS in Education, *summa cum laude*, 1992; minor in English
Member of Kappa Kappa Gamma Honor Society

SPECIAL INTERESTS

Volunteer at Ma Maison, a battered women's shelter

Judd Meisterson
15 Forge Lane, Suite 10
Lukeville, LA 70719
(504) 555-5555
e-mail: judd.meister@rols.com

SUMMARY OF QUALIFICATIONS
- More than six years' writing/editing experience
- Adept at managing multiple responsibilities simultaneously
- Experienced at delegating authority and motivating others, to ensure efficiency and productivity

COMPUTER SKILLS
Operating Systems: DOS, Windows 97
Writing/publishing: Word, WordPerfect, PageMaker
Business: Lotus 1-2-3

WORK EXPERIENCE
Editor-in-Chief, *Muldar of Fortune* magazine, Star, SC   1998–present
Selected submissions, edited and wrote headlines for submissions and columns, laid out pages, recruited columnists, trained associates. Frequently performed copy-editing and research.

Associate Editor, *Modern Sabre,* New York, NY   1996–98
Wrote articles for both the magazine and its associated newsletter, Royce's Voices. Edited features and department articles. Read and critiqued assigned articles from contributing editors.

Copy Editor, *Lack of Culture* magazine, Boston, MA   1994–95
Edited news stories, wrote headlines, assisted with layout of pages, occasionally solicited advertising and helped with distribution.

OTHER EXPERIENCE
Writer, professional musician

MILITARY
Army Corporal (honorable discharge)

EDUCATION
University of Richmond, Richmond, VA—Bachelor of Arts in English, 1992
Le Student Roma, Rome, Italy
Intensive study of Italian language and culture, 1991

Marcie Keegan
26 Maman-Lobster Road
Seattle, WA 98060
(206) 555-5555
e-mail: fancypants@slicklink.com

EXPERIENCE
Freelance Writer   1998–present
Projects include:
- *Teaching the Gifted Child* (7–12), Ben Curtis and Company
- *Writing* (handbooks, 7–9), Tallvia Kincaide, Inc.
- *Ancient Civilizations* (textbook, 12), Jean K. Simmons Press
- *Studies in Literature* (9–12), Jean K. Simmons Press

- Create original manuscripts for student textbooks; annotate teacher's editions. Materials include teaching apparatus; questions for responding, analyzing, and interpreting; thinking, writing, language, and vocabulary exercises and worksheets; multipage writing workshops; end-of-unit features for writing and language skills; and collaborative learning activities. Design prototypes for textbook and ancillary features. Conduct multicultural literature searches.

Jean K. Simmons Press, Washburn, NH
Senior Editor, Secondary English   1997–98
- Acted as project supervisor for teacher's editions of a composition and grammar program, levels 6–9. Edited manuscript for Writing Is Fun, levels 7 and 8. Wrote manuscript for *Writing Is Fun*, levels 9–12, including instruction, model paragraphs, and assignments. Developed content and approach for units on critical thinking and word processor use.

Educational Press, Orangeville, MA
Editor, Secondary English   1996–97
- Acted as project supervisor for teacher's editions and teacher's resource masters of vocabulary program, levels 9-12. Edited manuscript for four levels of pupil books for vocabulary program. Wrote exercises, reading comprehension passages, and activities to support instruction. Conducted writing workshops for teachers as follow-up to sales.

EDUCATION
Stonehill College, Easton, MA
Bachelor of Arts in English, 1996

Melissa Singer

12 Wah Circle, Apt. 9C
Buffalo, NY 14201
(716) 555-5555
msinger@coldmail.com

PROFESSIONAL EXPERIENCE

1996–present   **Research Assistant**
City Hospital Pathology Unit   Amherst, NY
- Establish protocols and procedures on cell culture and freezing methods. Maintain and establish transgenic, oscular meloma cell lines, and in vitro studies.
- Perform chemotherapy toxicity studies, cytospins, dot blots, DNA extractions.
- Maintain and breed transgenic SV40, CDI Nude, NIH III, Bg-NU-Xid and blood sampling. Maintain mouse colonies; supervise dissections, autopsy reports, in vitro injections, and recordkeeping.
- Perform various other laboratory and maintenance processes.

1993–96   **Skin Bank Technician**
Arlington Hospital Burn Institute   Arlington, VA
- Harvested and processed postmortem (cadaver) allographs under sterile technique. Processed human/artificial tissue for freezing (auto-grafts, pig skin biobrane).
- Researched in vitro culture cells, auto- and all-graft cells in mice.
- Maintained all laboratory equipment.

1991–92   **Research Clinical Technician**
Langly & Byers Research Associates   Alexandria, VA
- Performed FDA and IRB pharmacokinetic research studies, including statistical analyses of safety; human tolerance studies in bioavailability, bioequivalence, cardiology, alpha and beta blockers, hypertension, neurology, and ulcer endoscopy.
- Administered protocols and case report forms.
- Performed various clinical nursing and laboratory duties.

EDUCATION

Gallaudet College for the Deaf, Washington, DC
B.S. in Biology, 1991

Ann Aikenson
25 Alderam Avenue
Empire, LA 70050
(504) 555-5555
aaikenson@coldmail.com

EXPERIENCE
KASS AND SON, INC., Empire, LA
Operations and Process Clerk   1997–present
- Open, log, reconcile, and verify new accounts. Reconcile daily customer service/new accounts input against computer printouts. Research and correct problems. Maintain and update files.
- Handle high-volume mailings to welcome new clients; handle initial mailing of electronic funds transfer forms and letters.
- Recommend procedural changes to facilitate workflow. Interact with branch representatives. Assist with special projects as required, including bookkeeping, handling president's incoming calls, and responding directly to customer inquiries. Converted manual check processing to electronic function. Eliminated major filing backlog.

OTHER EXPERIENCE
Camp Teutonahwa, Butte, MT   Administrative assistant (part-time)
Billings Middle School, Billings, MT   Administrative assistant (part-time)

VOLUNTEER WORK
Max F. Enigs' Soup Kitchen, Empire, LA   Shelter Coordinator

EDUCATION
Widener University, Chester, PA   B.A. in Management, 1996

HONORS AND AFFILIATIONS
President of class, 1994–96
Formed Widener Chapter of Young Business People of America

Kara Forrend
178 Green Street
Laramie, WY 82071
(307) 555-5555

EMPLOYMENT
MARSTON CONVENT, Laramie, WY, 1998-present
Receptionist
Answer phone, greet visitors and provide information, tours, and literature. Record and monitor thank-you notes for all received donations. Perform light typing, filing, and word processing.

RINALDO RANCH, Laramie, WY, 1993-98
Secretary
Provided word processing, customer relations, some accounts payable processing. Implemented new system for check processing; increased prompt payment of client bills.

WOMANPOWER INC., Laramie, WY, 1985-93
Secretary
Acted as liaison between public and CEO.

SKILLS
Computer
Word, WordPerfect, Excel, Lotus 1-2-3

Other
Typing (65 wpm), statistical typing, shorthand, dictaphone, multi-line phones/switchboard, bookkeeping, credit checks

EDUCATION
TRAINING, INC., Boston, MA, 1984
Office careers training program in bookkeeping, typing, reception, word processing, and office procedures

ST. JOSEPH'S ACADEMY, Portland, ME—Diploma, 1983

Jenn Bezos

260 Allan Road
Hometown, PA 18252
(215) 555-5304
bezelbub@coldmail.com

SUMMARY

Over five years' experience recruiting high-technology personnel, support staff, and marketing professionals. Expertise in recruiting and marketing engineers, programmers, and other professionals for management information systems, software development, and related support positions in the electronics and software industries.

EXPERIENCE

1996–99
Professional Recruiter
Elworth Associates, Philadelphia, PA

- Recruited degreed engineers of all types, physicists, administrators, controllers, accountants, EDP, sales, and marketing personnel. Initiated recruiting program in search for critically needed electronic technicians.
- Traveled 15-20 percent of the time on recruiting trips to universities, career centers, conferences, and major U.S. cities. Participated in field trips to local technical, business, and secretarial schools.
- Established and maintained agency contacts with professional, administrative, and technical personnel.

1995–96
Independent Consultant/Contract Recruiter
Clients: Any Corporation; Kerrigan Inc.; MPB

- Recruited top MBAs for major corporations.

1994–95
Technical Recruiter
Phoenix Foundation, Reading, PA

- Recruited engineers, programmer/analysts, and technicians for satellite and telecommunications, signal processing, C3, electronic warfare, alien military technology, and database development.

EDUCATION

Bachelor of Arts, Duke University, 1994
Major in Psychology, minor in Business Administration

Tim Rafferty

178 Green Street
Lancaster, PA 17064
(717) 555-5555

EDUCATION
LESLEY COLLEGE, Cambridge, MA
B.A., Politics and History, 1997
Minor: English

SALES EXPERIENCE

PETIE'S PET LAND, Pittsburgh, PA   1997-99
Salesperson
Sold merchandise, increasing sales volume by 6% in first 3 months. Developed ongoing customer relationships, enhancing future sales. Developed special seasonal sales. Handled cash transactions and kennel care.

THE TIRE BARON, INC., Beaver Falls, PA   Summer 1994
Upper Bay/Lower Bay Technician
Sold merchandise. Provided customers with technical advice. Trained new employees. Received Employee of the Month award in July 1997 for highest sales volume in 7 stores.

THE SUBVERSIVE PAGES BOOKSTORE, Erie, PA   Summer 1993
Salesperson
Sold merchandise. Provided customer service. Purchased materials and monitored books.

OTHER EXPERIENCE
UNITED PACKAGERS, Boston, MA   Summer 1996
Material Handler

LESLEY COLLEGE, Cambridge, MA   Summer 1995
Maintenance Technician, Buildings and Grounds

ACCOMPLISHMENTS
Fluent in French
Student Government Representative, 1995-96
Founder, Debate Team, 1996

MARCIE JONES
178 Green Street
Washington, DC 20057
(202) 555-5555

EXPERIENCE

JENNINGS HOSPITAL, Washington, D.C.
Secretary, Radiation Therapy Department 1998-present
- Answer phones, schedule appointments, greet patients and visitors, prepare and file charts.
- Type and print invoices and requisitions.
- Supervise inventory and general office organization.
- Serve as liaison between physicians, staff, and patients.

Senior Birth Registrar 1994-98
- Recorded live births. Prepared and processed birth certificates, infant data, and associated documentation.
- Served as liaison between physicians, staff, and patients regarding legal documentation.
- Inaugurated a pilot program to facilitate networking between hospital and Registry of Vital Statistics.

Purchasing Assistant 1992-94
Assisted in purchasing chemical and equipment requisitions. Controlled inventories and distribution. Implemented procedure enhancements.

EDUCATION
TRIBORO JUNIOR COLLEGE, Denver, CO
A.S., Business, Major in Executive Secretarial Sciences (1988)

COMPUTERS
Word, Excel, WordPerfect, Lotus 1-2-3

Scott E. Ville
44 Biggles Road, #2
Austin, TX 78701
(512) 555-5306
seville@aol.com

EXPERIENCE

Web Site Manager, BusinessVillage.com LLC, Fort Bliss, Texas
November 1998–present
- Direct the development, design, programming, and day-to-day operation of small business assistance Web site. Coordinate strategic relationships, marketing, and advertising campaigns to maximize traffic and revenue.
- Oversee daily operations and management of BusinessVillage.com.
- Research and select editorial materials for site content.
- Optimize page design for search engine ranking.
- Appraise effectiveness of site features to increase repeat users.
- Develop strategic alliances with complementing sites.
- Manage the production of non-Web promotional materials.
- Supervise and assist HTML, ASP, and PERL coding.

Manager, Grove Creek LLC, Freedom, Texas
November 1996–August 1998

Information Systems
- Developed a PC base LAN for Financial and Purchasing departments.
- Instituted Kronos automated time clock for labor tracking.
- Provided technical support for PC, MAC, and AS400 users.

Marketing
- Designed Web pages to target new customers.
- Identified and located potential new retail outlets.
- Conducted market research on new product concepts.

EDUCATION

Master of Business Administration, May 1997
Powerson University, Sharp, Texas

Bachelor of Arts, Psychology, May 1992
Swinett College, Flower Hill, Texas

Ernest Lapagis
37 Island Grove Street
Newtown, PA 18940
(215) 555-5888
elap@logicworks.com

QUALIFICATIONS

Web Design & Development
- Multimedia Production
- Graphics Production

Intranet Design & Development
- Visual Basic Script
- Java Script

HTML
- Project Management
- Internet Information Server (IIS)

EXPERIENCE

Webmaster (April 1997–present)
Logical Works Inc., Princeton, NJ
Marketing Department
- Maintain and update Logical Works Internet and Intranet sites.
- Designed and developed new customer-oriented sections of Internet site including programming in Visual Basic script, Java script, and HTML.
- Interacted with various departments to design and develop departmental Intranet sites to provide access of information to company employees.
- Generated Web site reports to track customer usage and usability of Web site to increase productivity of the Internet as a communications tool.

Associate Producer (September 1996–April 1997)
Cognet Corporation, Princeton Junction, NJ
Intern
- Designed and scripted a kiosk application for the United States Post Office.
- Developed programming specifications and programmed prototypes using Visual Basic 4.0.
- Coordinated production of graphics and interfaced with third-party software developers.
- Served as project manager for Spender Inc. Intranet Web site.

Web Designer & HTML Programmer (January 1996–August 1996)
University Relations, Bloomsburg University of Pennsylvania
Graduate Assistant
- Designed and programmed Bloomsburg University's Athletic Department Web pages.

Production Assistant (June 1994–November 1994)
WSST-TV 12 (ABC affiliate), Moosic, PA
- Wrote, directed, photographed, and edited PSAs ready for air in the local programming department, as well as audio assistant for special events.
- Operated camera and tape during live newscasts in the news department.
- Coordinated and produced *Good Morning America* greetings.

EDUCATION

Master of Science in Instructional Technology (December 1996)
Bloomsburg University of Pennsylvania, Bloomsburg, PA
Graduated *cum laude* 3.73/4.00

Bachelor of Arts in Mass Communications (August 1994)
Bloomsburg University of Pennsylvania, Bloomsburg, PA
Graduated *cum laude* 3.52/4.00

Adelle Weiss, Ph.D.
17 Leisl Street
Suite 16
Montpelier, VT 05601
(802) 555-5555
e-mail: aweiss@coldmail.com

EMPLOYMENT EXPERIENCE

Brown University, Providence, RI
Director of Women's Studies (1998–present)
- Plan, administer, and evaluate a comprehensive freshman academic support program.

Planning
- Chair meetings of faculty/administration committee for student services. Propose new programs and changes to existing programs.

Administration
- Coordinate activities, including academic advising and placement, and academic, personal, and career counseling.
- Administer placement tests, new student orientation, parent/student workshops, cultural activities, academic tracking, and early warning system for "at risk" freshmen.
- Instituted cultural awareness activities, including a guest lecture series, field trips to the Boston Art Museum and the Ryder Early American Collection, and a tour to retrace the stops on Paul Revere's ride.
- Initiated a newsletter and a recognition dinner for student achievements in academics, activities, and sports.

Evaluation
- Analyze administration data on student services to determine benefits of programs.
- Distribute evaluations to students and collate data to determine student satisfaction with programs.

Admissions Director (1996–98)
Supervision
- Managed the admissions and recruitment program; create and design strategies to enhance the total program, concept, and mission.
- Supervised professional and clerical staff; provided and encouraged in-service training and professional growth.

Recruitment
- Developed a marketing plan for recruitment; wrote recruitment brochures for the Office of Admissions and academic departments of the university.
- Maintained a positive working relationship between high school and community college counselors and the Office of Admissions.

Liaison
- Served as representative to the Academic Council.
- Acted as liaison between the Office of Admissions, faculty, the administration, and the alumni.
- Compiled data for statistical reporting to various state and federal agencies.

Assistant to the Admissions Director (1993–96)
- Developed high school recruitment programs; visited high school and local two-year college for recruitment.
- Served as foreign student advisor.
- Evaluated transcripts of transfer students for transferable credits.
- Substituted for director in her absence.

Teaching (1992–present)
Women's Orientation, a two-hour required course for all students. Units include eating disorders, value clarification, relationships, substance abuse, domestic violence.

EDUCATION

Brown University, Providence, RI
   Ph.D. in Sociology, 1997
Carnegie Mellon University, Pittsburgh, PA
   Master of Education, Counseling major, 1993
Middlebury College, Middlebury, VT
   Bachelor of Arts in Elementary Education, Art minor, 1991

Marika Covarubis
178 Mean Street
Dillon, MT 59725
(406) 555-5555
e-mail: mcovarubis@coldmail.com

EDUCATION

Burdan Junior College, Missoula, MT
Major: Criminal Justice   BA candidate, 1999

WORK HISTORY

THOMPSON'S STORE, Dillon, MT   1997–present
Cashier
Provide customer and personnel assistance. Handle cash intake, inventory control, and perform light maintenance. Train and schedule new employees. Instituted store recycling program to benefit the Dillon Homeless Shelter.

RONDELL IMAGE, HELENA, MT   1996–97
Data/File Clerk
Assisted sales staff. General office responsibilities included data entry, typing, and filing invoices.

TARPY PERSONNEL SERVICES, Bozeman, MT   1994–96
General Clerk
Duties included shipping/receiving and filing invoices.

Jeremiah Smyth

School Address:
178 Shift Street
Skidell, LA 70458
(504) 555-5555

Permanent Address:
23 Blue Street
New Orleans, LA 70128
(504) 555-5555

e-mail: jsmyth@tulane.edu

OBJECTIVE
A summer internship in the book publishing industry.

SKILLS
Copyediting: Two years' experience copyediting monthly church newsletter using *Chicago Manual of Style*
Proofreading: Familiar with proofreading symbols
Computer: Windows 97, Microsoft Word
Languages: Intermediate-level French, American Sign Language
Prolific writer; voracious reader

EDUCATION
Tulane University, New Orleans, LA
Bachelor of Arts in English and American Literature, with a concentration in film.
Degree to be awarded May 1999. Dean's list.

University of Manitoba, Winnipeg, Manitoba. Semester abroad,
fall 1996. Studied photography, literature, Canadian drama/theater.

EMPLOYMENT
The New Orleans People First Program, Skidell, LA
2/97–present   **Adult Literacy Tutor**
Travel to various prisons, nursing homes, boardinghouses, and learning centers. Tutor residents in elements of spelling, grammar, and parts of speech. Issue progress reports, bestow awards.

Tulane University, New Orleans, LA
10/96–present   **Manager, film series**
Booked and publicized weekly films, arranged for projectionist and ticket taker, maintained accounts, paid bills.

Tulane Mailroom, New Orleans, LA
Fall 1995   **Mail sorter**
Routed mail to appropriate departments and individual mailboxes (incoming); sorted mail by zip code (outgoing).

John E. Bravo
One Suitfits Lane
Grooverville, GA 31626
912-555-1212
e-mail: jeb@slicklink.com

EDUCATION
University of Minnesota B.S. in Psychology, 1998, *summa cum laude*
3.8 GPA on 4.0 scale

WORK EXPERIENCE
7/98–present **Troubled Kids Network**, Arnot, MN
Youth Counselor
Oversaw the academic progress of emotionally disturbed children. Taught study skills to underachieving teens. Designed new program agendas that received positive feedback from the participants. Brought about a great improvement in student academic performance.

10/97–6/98 **University of Minnesota**, Minneapolis, MN
Research Assistant
Psychology Department
Administered psychological evaluations to college students. Codified test results to obtain desired statistical data. Coordinated group meetings to compile research. Promoted to first assistant after producing highly favorable results.

ACTIVITIES AND HONORS
Phi Beta Kappa
Psychology Honor Society
Multiple Dean's list appearances
Intramural soccer team
Fraternity social chairman

SKILLS
Computer: Windows, Word, WordPerfect, Lotus 1-2-3
Languages: Fluent Spanish; competent French

Janice Plumb

25 Clinton Avenue
American House, CA 95981
(530) 555-5555
e-mail: fruitloop@coldmail.com

EDUCATIONAL BACKGROUND

Whitworth College, Spokane, WA
Master of Science in Mass Communications, 1999
Walla Walla College, College Place, WA
Bachelor of Arts in Communications and Theater, 1995

PROFESSIONAL BACKGROUND

Lockwood Engineering, Ravensdale, CA   1995–present
Editor/Writer, Worldwide Business Development Division
- Prepare bid proposals for government, industrial, and utility contracts, including engineering and construction.
- Interpret client RFP requirements; determine applicability of proposal response to RFP.
- Write and edit proposals; coordinate production, organize and maintain up-to-date dummy book through several revision cycles.
- Act as liaison between proposal/marketing engineer and graphic arts, word processing, and production departments.

Glacier Peak, Inc., Nahcotta, WA   Summers, 1993–95
Assistant to the Director, Publications Department
- Researched, wrote, and supervised production of employee orientation brochures. Edited and proofread published materials. Established corporate slide library and prepared quarterly budget forecasts/analyses.

TECHNICAL EXPERIENCE

Operating systems	DOS, Windows, UNIX, Macintosh
Writing/publishing	Quark, Word, WordPerfect
Business	Excel, Lotus 1-2-3, INFORMIX

Cal Esianberg
20 Banta Street
Chewelah, WA 99109
(206) 555-5555

OBJECTIVE
An entry-level position in customer service

COMPUTER SKILLS
Windows 97, Word, Lotus 1-2-3

EXPERIENCE
Wukey National Bank, Seattle, WA
Customer Service Representative (6/98–present)
- Open new accounts, take applications and process loans, handle customer transactions, cross-sell bank products, purchase supplies, resolve customer problems and complaints.
- Collect overdrawn accounts, answer telephones, perform clerical duties.
- Won Premier Performance award.

My Special Place, Seattle, WA
Sales Associate, Children's Department (9/97–6/98)
- Provided sales and customer service, resolved customer problems, received merchandise, arranged displays, set up sales and operational paperwork, including price markdowns and transfers. Ranked among top five salespeople in the store (Fall 1997). Received award for opening most store credit cards (December 1997).

Damon and Blaine, Seattle, WA (11/95–6/97)
Sales Associate, Linens
- Waited on customers, handled register transactions.

Windsor Sporting Goods, Seattle, WA (1/95–9/95)
Sales Associate
- Waited on customers, handled register transactions. Promoted to Lead Sales Associate.

EDUCATION
M.F. Luder High School, Seattle, WA
- Activities: Editor-in-chief, school newspaper; Literary editor, yearbook; Captain, drill team, 1997

Wally S. Kinnar
431 Oak Street
Goodwell, OK 73939
(405) 555-5555
e-mail: wisk@slicklink.com

EDUCATION
University of Miami, Coral Gables, FL
   MBA with concentration in Finance, 1998
College of the Holy Cross, Worcester, MA
   Bachelor of Science in Economics/Finance, 1993

EMPLOYMENT

Naot, Inc., Goodwell, OK   1997–present
Accountant
- Prepare payroll, general ledger, daily cash, accounts payable and receivable, monthly financial statements, and general ledger reconciliations.
- Act as project manager for ongoing upgrade to accounting database.
- Provide cost proposals on government and commercial accounts.
- Bill Timberline Software System for company projects and maintaining Timberline system.

O'Connor, Raisty & Ross, Oklahoma City, OK   1993–95
Contract Billing Administrator
- Worked for BBN Systems & Technologies. Interpreted billing provisions of government and commercial contracts, maintained interactive billing systems, prepared accounts receivable and sales adjustments. Maintained MIS database and reconciled mailing list to invoice register.

The Mutual Corp., Shawnee, OK   1992–93
ABI-Boston Coordinator
- Designed procedures for implementation of new Automated Brokerage Interface. Supervised transformation from manual to computerized operation, trained personnel. Maintained system software and daily records. Researched and reconciled complex international transactions.

COMPUTERS
DOS, Windows 98, Excel, Lotus 1-2-3, Timberline, dBase II, WordPerfect

Alexandria Cryor
1440 Armor Street
Rocky Bluff, IA 50318
712-555-1212
e-mail: acryor@aon.com

OBJECTIVE
To pursue a career in the tourism industry that utilizes my organizational, communication, and interpersonal skills

EDUCATION
Private University, College Town, KS
Gabriel College study abroad in Tokyo

B.S. in Business, 1998

RELEVANT SKILLS
Organization
- Planned and budgeted social events for 200 residents of a university dormitory.
- Updated and implemented new filing system at a busy corporate office.
- Developed personal itinerary for 3-month tour of the Far East.
- Expedited delivery of as many as 40 simultaneous dinner orders.
- Computerized accounts of a large restaurant and caterer with Quicken software.

Communication
- Coordinated itineraries through effectively communicating with tourism businesses like airlines, train companies, bus lines, travel agents, hotels, and hostels in various foreign countries.
- Presented explanations of meals to large parties of customers to help them select those best suited to their individual tastes and dietary needs.
- Exhibited strong persuasive abilities to achieve highest sales in telemarketing division.
- Wrote promotional flyers for residence-hall activities.

Interpersonal
- Interacted with people from diverse cultures and backgrounds through extensive foreign travel and advising dormitory residents.
- Mediated multiple dormitory disputes to arrive at outcomes favorable to all parties.
- Established amiable rapport with restaurant patrons.

EMPLOYMENT HISTORY
8/97–5/98	Resident advisor: freshman dorm, Blevins University, College Town, IA
Summer 1997	Food server: Smorgazborg, Decatur, IA
Summer 1996	Telemarketer: Unsuspecting Homes Co., Newtown, IA
Summer 1995	Secretary: The Tire Shop, Wheeling, IA

Vick E. Tombs

56 Yellow Oak Street
Rochester, NY 14623
(716) 555-5555
e-mail: vick.sue@coldmail.com

EDUCATION

Cornell University, Ithaca, NY   *B.S. in Earth Science,* 1999
Massachusetts Institute of Technology, Cambridge, MA, 1997
  Coursework in biology, chemistry, and environmental science

WORK EXPERIENCE

Cornell University, Ithaca, NY
Intern, Biobased Materials Center, Forest Products Department, 1998–99
- Researched the materials science aspects of polysaccharide (cellulose, hemicellulose, chitin) regeneration in the form of hydrogen beads by examining relationships between the nature of the polysaccharide (chemistry, molecular weight, viscosity) and important hydrogen parameters (gel structure, morphology, bead pore size, flow characteristics, mechanical strength, reactivity).

Assistant, Wood Chemistry Laboratory, Forest Products Department, 1997
- Assisted professor on chemical modification of lignin with propylene oxide for the synthesis of urethanes and thermoplastic elastomers.
- Developed methods for the synthesis of telechelic oligomers from lignin with controlled number and length of arms. Performed the synthesis and full characterization (chemical, thermal, mechanical, and morphological) of multiphase block copolymers containing lignin and either polycaprolactone, cellulose propionate, or polystyrene as the hard segments.
- Produced blends of thermoplastic formulations of multiphase block copolymers containing lignin as compatibilizers in polymer blends with commercial polymers like PVC, polystyrene, and cellulose propionate.

American Center of Technology (ACT), Boston, MA, 1996
Assistant
- Developed projects on alternative energy from biomass residues, mainly sugar cane bagasse. Worked on projects for ethanol production.

SKILLS

Languages: Fluent in English and German, proficient in Spanish.

INFORMATIONAL N...
BURNS RESEARCH A
12 TOUR OF FACILITY
1 INTERVIEW WITH KARA H...
AT BURNS RESEARCH AGEN
2
3 Commute Home
* SEND THANK YOU NOTE
4 GO TO CAREER FAIR
5

SEND

9

WWW.CAREERCITY.COM
*

INFORMATIONAL MEE
...RNS RESEARCH AGE
...R OF FACILITY
...EW WITH KARA F...
...RESEARCH A...

CALL HEAD HUNTE

1 A.M. - 3 P.M.
NFO. MEETING, TO...
T BURNS RESEARC...

9 A.M.   WEDNESDAY
NTERVIEW WITH
AT NARD INC.

THURSDA...

8 A.M.   FRIDAY
MEET WITH BILL...
DIRECTOR OF CAREER...
AT BIG RED UNIV...
SATURDAY

DATE:

TO DO   ACTION LIST

CHAPTER 6

Electronic Resumes

Many companies use automated applicant tracking systems to process and sort employment applications. Others use the services of electronic employment database companies to fill specific openings. This means that your resume will be read by more computers and fewer people. Whether you're applying to a company that uses automated tracking systems or paying to have your resume loaded onto an electronic employment database or online database, your resume must be in a format that's easy for a computer to recognize. Otherwise, your application may quickly begin collecting dust.

The good news about this technology is that it enables you to market your resume to thousands of employers quite easily. The bad news is that you must create an electronic resume in order to take advantage of the technology. An electronic resume is simply a modified version of your conventional resume.

Before you go ahead and throw out your old paper resume, be advised that not all companies stay up to speed on the latest technology. Many companies simply don't have the equipment to directly receive e-mailed resumes and search on-line databases for job candidates. Having a paper copy of your resume is still a necessity, especially since you'll need it to bring with you to all those job interviews!

Format

Keep your resume simple. The same elaborate formatting that makes your resume beautiful for the human eye to behold makes it impossible for a computer to understand.

Length

Your resume should be no longer than one page, except in unusual circumstances.

Abbreviations

Most resume scanning systems recognize a few common abbreviations, like BS, MBA, and state names, with or without periods.

Widely used acronyms for industry jargon, like A/R and A/P on an accounting resume, are also generally accepted, although it's advisable to spell out most abbreviations. If there's any question about whether an abbreviation is standard, play it safe and spell it out.

Paper

Don't bother with expensive paper. Use standard, twenty-pound, 8½- by 11-inch paper. Because your resume needs to be as sharp and legible as possible, your best bet is to use black ink on white paper.

Font

Stick to the basics; this is no time to express your creativity. Choose a nondecorative font with clear, distinct characters, like Times or Helvetica. It's more difficult for a scanner to accurately pick up decorative fonts like script. Usually the results are unintelligible letters and words.

Size

A size of 12 points is ideal. Don't go below 10 points, as type that's too small may not scan well.

Style

Most scanners will accept boldface, but if a potential employer specifically tells you to avoid it, you can substitute all capital letters. Boldface and capitals are best used only for major section headings, like "Experience" and "Education." Avoid boldface for your name, address, and telephone number. It's also best to avoid italics or underlining, since this can make the words unintelligible.

Graphics, Lines, and Shading

Avoid the temptation to use lines and graphics to liven up what is an otherwise visually uninteresting resume. A resume scanner will try to "read" graphics, lines, and shading as text, resulting in computer chaos. Also avoid nontraditional layouts, like two-column formats.

Should You Include a Cover Letter with Your Resume?

Yes. While your cover letter won't help in the initial selection process, it can distinguish you from the competition in the final rounds. If you've taken the time to craft a letter that summarizes your strongest qualifications, you'll have the edge over other contenders who skip this important step.

If you're responding to a classified ad, try to use some of the same keywords the ad mentions. And if you're sending your resume to a new networking contact, be sure to mention who referred you. Even in this anonymous electronic age, the old adage "It's not what you know but who you know" still holds true.

White Space

Don't try to compress space between letters, words, or lines to fit everything on one page—this makes it more difficult for the computer to read. Leave plenty of space between sections.

Printing

Make sure the result is letter quality. Avoid typewriters and dot matrix printers, since the quality of type they produce is inadequate for most scanners. Because your resume needs to be as sharp and legible as possible, always send an original, not a photocopy, and mail your resume rather than faxing it. For the same reason, in the unlikely event your resume is longer than one page, don't staple the pages together.

Content

The information you include in your electronic resume doesn't really differ from a traditional resume—it's simply the manner in which you present it that changes. Traditionally, resumes include action verbs, like "managed," "coordinated," or "developed." Now, employers are more likely to do keyword searches filled with nouns, like degree held or software you're familiar with. Personal traits are rarely used in keyword searches by employers, but when they are, traits like team player, creative, and problem-solving are among the most common.

Keywords

Using the right keywords or key phrases in your resume is critical. Keyword searches tend to focus on nouns. Let's say an employer searches an employment database for a sales representative with the following keyword criteria: sales representative, BS/BA, exceeded quota, cold calls, high energy, willing to travel. Even if you have the right qualifications, if you don't use these keywords on your resume, the computer will pass over your application. To complicate matters further, different employers search for different keywords. These are usually buzzwords common to your field or industry that describe your experience, education, skills, and abilities.

Although there is no way to know for sure which keywords employers are most likely to search for, you can make educated guesses. Check help-wanted advertisements for job openings in your field. What terms do employers commonly use to describe their requirements? Job seekers in your field are another source, as are executive recruiters who specialize in your field. You'll want to use as many keywords in your resume as possible, but keep in mind that using the same keyword five times won't increase your chances of getting matched with an employer. Note, however, that if you're posting your resume to a job hunting Web site, a small number of such sites rank resumes by the number of keywords and their frequency of occurrence. Your best bet is to find out ahead of time by reading the information on the site.

Name

Your name should appear at the top of the resume, with your address, telephone number, and e-mail address immediately underneath.

Keyword Summary

This is a compendium of your qualifications, usually written in a series of succinct keyword phrases that immediately follow your name and address. Place the most important words first on the list, since the computer may be limited in the number of words it will read.

Objective

As with traditional resumes, including a job objective is advisable only in certain circumstances. (See Chapter 4 [**Resumes**].) If you choose to use a job objective, try to keep it general, so as not to limit your opportunities. After all, while the computer does the initial screening, your resume will eventually be seen by a human hiring manager. Your objective should express a general interest in a particular field or industry ("an entry-level position in advertising") but should not designate a specific job title ("a position as a senior

What Is HTML?

HTML (hypertext markup language) is the text formatting language used to publish information on the World Wide Web. With HTML, you can format your resume on the Web the way you did on paper, using different fonts, sizes, boldface, italics, and so on. Otherwise it would appear just as lines of unformatted text.

agency recruitment specialist"). Include a few keywords in the objective, to increase your chances of getting matched ("a position as a financial analyst where I can utilize my on-the-job experience and MBA").

Experience and Achievements

Your professional experience should immediately follow the keyword summary, beginning with your most recent position. (If you're a recent college graduate, list your education before your experience.) Be sure your job title, employer, location, and dates of employment are all clearly displayed. Highlight your accomplishments and key responsibilities with dashes (in place of bullets on an electronic resume). Again, try to incorporate as many buzzwords as possible into these phrases.

Education

This section immediately follows the experience section. List your degrees, licenses, permits, certifications, relevant course work, and academic awards or honors. Be sure to clearly display the names of the schools, locations, and years of graduation. List any professional organizations or associations you're a member of; many recruiters will include such organizations when doing a keyword search.

References

Don't waste valuable space with statements like "References available upon request." Although this was standard fare for resumes of old, it won't win you any points on an electronic resume.

Personal Data

Don't include personal data, like your birthdate, marital status, or information regarding your hobbies and interests. Since it's unlikely these sections would include any keywords, they're only taking up space, and the computer will pass right over them.

An Electronic Cover Letter

69 Pageant Drive
Cambridge, MA 02138
(617) 555-5555
mrepass@coldmail.com

January 5, 1999

Mr. Steven Peepers
Controller
Section One Inc.
1140 Bones Street
Boston, MA 02215

Dear Mr. Peepers:

This letter is in response to your advertisement in the *Boston Globe* for the position of Assistant Controller. I am very interested in the position and believe I have the qualifications you are looking for. Please consider the following:

- I have over twenty years' experience in accounting and systems management, budgeting, forecasting, cost containment, financial reporting, and international accounting.
- I implemented a team-oriented cross-training program within my accounting group, resulting in timely month-end closings and increased productivity of key accounting staff.
- I have an MBA in Management from Northeastern University.
- I am a results-oriented professional and proven team leader.

These are only a few of my credentials that may be of interest to you. I look forward to discussing them with you further in a personal interview.

Thank you for your consideration.

Sincerely,

Madeline Repass

Madeline Repass

Your Cover Letter

Omit a cover letter only if the ad to which you are responding says to. Send your cover letter in the same e-mail as your resume (preceding it, of course), and be as attentive to your grammar and spelling as with a paper cover letter. Because this way of sending information is so quick, more and more jobseekers are forgetting that the same rules apply. Sloppy cover letters via e-mail will be viewed just as poorly as sloppy work sent by regular mail.

Circulating Your Electronic Resume

Once you've designed a computer-friendly resume, you can circulate it in three ways. The first is to send it to a company with an in-house resume database or applicant tracking system. Whenever there's an opening, the hiring manager submits a search request, which generally includes a job description and a list of keywords. An operator searches the database to come up with viable candidates.

The second way is to send your resume to an electronic employment database service. When outside companies need candidates for a job opening, they contact the service and provide a list of qualifications (or keywords) the position requires. The service then searches the database (using a keyword search) to find suitable candidates.

The third way is to post your resume via the Internet, either by e-mail, to an on-line database service (this is the same as an electronic employment database service, except that you send your resume electronically rather than by mail), a site on the World Wide Web, a commercial on-line service (like America Online or CompuServe), or a newsgroup. Another option is to create a resume in HTML and post it to special sites on the Web that accept HTML resumes. You can even design your own home page for potential employers to visit. (For more information on using the Internet as a job search tool, see Chapter 10 [**Internet Job Search**].)

An Electronic Resume for Scanning

On page 95 and 96 is an example of an electronic resume for scanning contains no bullets, italics, or underlining. All text begins flush left, with spaces between paragraphs and sections. Boldface is usually acceptable, but if not, capital letters may be substituted.

An Electronic Request for E-mail

On page 97 is the same resume prepared for e-mail. Remember that each line must be **sixty-five characters or less.**

An Electronic Resume for Scanning

Michael S. Dipenstein
27 Pageant Drive, Apartment 7
Cambridge, MA 02138
(617) 555-5555

KEYWORD SUMMARY
Accounting manager with seven years' experience in general ledger, accounts payable, and financial reporting. MBA in Management. Proficient in Windows, Lotus 1-2-3, and Excel.

PROFESSIONAL EXPERIENCE
COLWELL CORPORATION, Wellesley, MA
$100-million division of Bancroft Corporation

Accounting Manager   1996 - present

Manage a staff of six in general ledger and accounts payable. Responsible for the design and refinement of financial reporting package. Assist in month-end closings.

Established guidelines for month-end closing procedures, speeding up closing by five business days.

Implemented team-oriented cross-training program within accounting group, increasing productivity of key accounting staff.

FRANKLIN AND DELANY COMPANY, Melrose, MA

Senior Accountant   1994–96

Managed accounts payable, general ledger, transaction processing, and financial reporting. Supervised staff of two.

Developed management reporting package, including variance reports and cash flow reporting.

Staff Accountant   1993–94

Managed accounts payable, including vouchering, cash disbursements, and bank reconciliation. Wrote and issued policies. Maintained supporting schedules used during year-end audits. Trained new employees.

EDUCATION
MBA in Management, Northeastern University, Boston, MA, 1995
BS in Accounting, Boston College, Boston, MA, 1993

ASSOCIATIONS
National Association of Accountants

An Electronic Resume for E-mail

Michael S. Dipenstein
27 Pageant Drive, Apartment 7
Cambridge, MA 02138
(617) 555-5555

KEYWORD SUMMARY
Accounting manager with seven years' experience in general ledger, accounts payable, and financial reporting. MBA in Management. Proficient in Windows, Lotus 1-2-3, and Excel.

PROFESSIONAL EXPERIENCE
COLWELL CORPORATION, Wellesley, MA
$100-million division of Bancroft Corporation

Accounting Manager   1996 - present

Manage a staff of six in general ledger and accounts payable. Responsible for the design and refinement of financial reporting package. Assist in month-end closings.

Established guidelines for month-end closing procedures, speeding up closing by five business days.

Implemented team-oriented cross-training program within accounting group, increasing productivity of key accounting staff.

FRANKLIN AND DELANY COMPANY, Melrose, MA

Senior Accountant   1994 - 96

Managed accounts payable, general ledger, transaction processing, and financial reporting. Supervised staff of two.

Developed management reporting package, including variance reports and cash flow reporting.

Staff Accountant   1993 - 94

Managed accounts payable, including vouchering, cash disbursements, and bank reconciliation. Wrote and issued policies. Maintained supporting schedules used during year-end audits. Trained new employees.

EDUCATION
MBA in Management, Northeastern University, Boston, MA, 1995
BS in Accounting, Boston College, Boston, MA, 1993

ASSOCIATIONS
National Association of Accountants

Applicant Tracking Systems

As the name implies, applicant tracking systems, or in-house resume databases, are used by companies to keep track of the hordes of resumes they receive. Many companies, especially large, well-known companies, can receive two hundred resumes per week. Where once these unsolicited resumes may have headed straight for a filing cabinet or even the trash, never to be looked at again, electronic applicant tracking systems now allow employers to keep resumes in an active file.

Basically, here's how it works: a company receives your resume, either unsolicited, through a career fair, or in response to a classified advertisement. Your resume is scanned into the computer, dated, coded, and placed into the appropriate file (like administrative, financial, or technical). Other systems may simply sort resumes according to date received.

When there's a job opening, the hiring manager submits a search request to the database operator, who is usually someone in human resources or information systems. The database operator performs a keyword search to find resumes that match the criteria.

Electronic Employment Databases

An electronic employment database is simply an applicant tracking system operated by an independent commercial firm. The procedure for submitting resumes to these services varies, and most charge a nominal fee, usually $30–50. But what you get for your money is fabulous: nationwide exposure to hundreds of companies of all sizes, from *Fortune* 500 to smaller, rapidly expanding companies.

In many ways, an electronic resume database is similar to a traditional employment agency: you send in your resume to a service, and the service begins working to find a job for you. However, with an electronic employment "agency," you are, theoretically, in the running for every job request that comes in. While each resume database service is different, it generally works as follows:

You submit your resume to an electronic employment database service. Some services also send you a "professional profile" sheet

Applicant Tracking Systems

Advantages to job seekers include the following:

- A computer is completely impartial.
- You don't have to worry about your resume getting misplaced accidentally.
- Even if you don't get the job, your resume is kept in the database, so you can be considered for later openings.
- You don't need to send in multiple resumes to different department managers at the same company. (If you do send in multiple resumes, the system usually deletes the old one and keeps the most recent one.)
- Companies prefer this new technology because it's more efficient, in terms of both time and money. The automated system cuts down on paperwork for many human resources managers and lowers administrative and advertising costs.

Applicant tracking systems have some major disadvantages:

- A computer will look for only those resumes that exactly meet the strict criteria of the search. This tends to put recent college graduates, borderline candidates, or those switching careers at a disadvantage, since these job seekers are less likely to have as many key-words included in their resumes.
- No automated system is infallible. If the computer rejects your resume because the scanner is unable to read it or turns it into an unintelligible

mess, you're out of luck. Therefore, it's essential to send a clean, computer-friendly resume.

Electronic Employment Databases

- Job seekers benefit because they can easily be exposed to hundreds of companies with only one resume and minimal cost. In the past, it would take hours of research to come up with the company names, addresses, and contact names of potential employers, not to mention the cost of stationery, printing, and postage to mail out those hundreds of resumes. Job seekers are exposed to employers nationwide, not just in their own town or region. So if you're willing to relocate, you can find your dream job, even if it's thousands of miles away.
- Electronic employment database services can potentially save companies the cost of advertising and, by prescreening candidates, hours of work. Also, employers have easy exposure to thousands of candidates.
- Companies generally don't rely on this method. Some database searches only turn up a few qualified candidates.
- These databases serve hundreds of employers, but they don't serve all employers. Job seekers should use these databases as a part of their overall job hunt.

to fill out. Essentially an employment application, these forms ask you to indicate your work experience, skills, and other information, like geographical preferences or whether you're willing to relocate. This form is used either in addition to or instead of your resume. Your resume and/or professional profile are scanned or entered into the computer.

Client companies call the service with job openings and give the service a list of keywords and desired qualifications. Some services allow employers on-line access to the database, so they can do the search themselves. The database is searched for candidates who match the keywords.

How the candidates are presented to the client varies. Some services provide candidate summaries; others provide the actual resume; still others include information from the professional profile. Some services call you before forwarding your resume or any information to the client company.

The following is some information on selected electronic employment databases. One word of caution: Be sure to check with each service before sending your resume or any registration fees. With today's ever-changing technology, procedures or fees can change quickly. You should also call a prospective service to obtain more detailed information on how the service works and whether the employer will see your actual resume or just a candidate profile or summary.

Spelled with a lower-case "c," cors can be reached at 800-323-1352, or by fax at 630-250-7362. This service boasts almost 1.5 million resumes in their database. With over 6,000 clients, the service matches about 200 jobs each month. The firm attracts clients in all fields—computers, health care, finance, engineering, and communications. You can join this service for a one-time fee of $25; simply mail your resume to the address indicated. Once the service receives your resume, you'll receive a confirmation letter in the mail that includes an identification number, which you can use to check on the status of your resume or make free updates to it.

Another electronic employment database service is DORS. This service can be contacted at 800-727-3677 or by fax at 831-583-2475. This service is for military personnel and workers in select civil service organizations who are leaving the military or civil service to work in the private sector. The goal is to help military personnel make a successful transition to civilian life by giving them exposure to a wide range of companies in diverse fields and locations. Military personnel receive information on this service as part of their transition training. This service is also available for the spouses of military personnel. There are no fees for job seekers; employers assume all fees. According to information supplied by DORS, more than 20,000 employers have registered to use the service. This service is offered to the job seeker at no cost.

Electronic Job Matching is a database that is free to all job seekers and contains over 30,000 resumes. This service can be e-mailed at ejm@hrmc.com, or called at 813-879-4200. More than 700 employers actively search the database, including private-sector companies in all fields and industries, from communications and law to manufacturing and health care. To enter the database, mail your resume to the address indicated. Your resume will be scanned into the system, and the computer will create a personalized "electronic portfolio." Job seekers can specify certain search criteria, such as location, salary, or industry. Resumes that are e-mailed to HRMC can be in a variety of formats, while resumes that are either faxed or sent through postal mail to HRMC should use a simple, plain format easily read by a scanner.

University ProNet is yet another good service to know about. This service, at *www.universitypronet.com*, is a resume database serving more than 100,000 alumni, and is sponsored by many of the country's leading universities: California Institute of Technology, Carnegie-Mellon, Columbia, Cornell, Massachusetts Institute of Technology, Ohio State, Stanford, University of California at Berkeley, UCLA, University of Chicago, University of Illinois, University of Michigan, University of Pennsylvania, University of Texas at Austin, University of Wisconsin, and Yale. The service is open only to alumni of these universities but is accessible to over 400 companies. One-time fees run about $50; the fee varies slightly, depending on the school. If you hold a degree from one of these universities, contact your alumni association for more information on how to join this service.

Posting Your Resume Via the Internet

To remain truly competitive, your resume needs to be in a plain-text format you can send to employers and on-line databases electronically through cyberspace.

Converting Your Resume to a Plain-Text File

An electronic resume is sparsely formatted but is filled with key-words and important facts. If you've already prepared a resume that's computer-friendly, you don't have far to go to be able to post your resume on the Internet. A plain-text resume is the next step.

Instead of a Microsoft Word, WordPerfect, or other word processing document, save your resume as a plain text, DOS, or ASCII file. These three terms are basically interchangeable; different software will use different terms. These words describe text at its simplest, most basic level, without formatting like boldface or italics. Furthermore, an ASCII document appears on the recipient's screen as left-aligned. If you have e-mail, your messages are written and received in this format. By converting your resume to a plain-text file, you can be assured it will be readable, regardless of where you send it.

Before you attempt to create your own plain-text resume, study the resumes on the on-line databases. This will give you a good idea of what a plain text resume looks like and will help you create your own.

Following are the basic steps for creating a plain-text resume. The particulars of the process will differ, depending on what type of computer system and software you're using:

1. Remove all formatting from your resume. This includes bold-face, italics, underlining, bullets, different font sizes, lines,

and any and all graphics. To highlight certain parts of your resume, like education or experience, you may use capital letters. You can also use dashes (-) or asterisks (*) to emphasize certain accomplishments or experiences. Leave a blank line or two between sections.

2. Save your resume as a plain-text file. Most word processing programs, like Word and WordPerfect, have a "Save As" feature that allows you to save files in different formats. Some of your options in Word for Windows, for instance, are saving a document as a Word document, a text-only document, or a WordPerfect document. Many programs, like Word, don't specifically give you an "ASCII" option; in these programs, choose "Text Only" or "Plain Text." In Word, plain text files have the extension ".txt."

3. After saving your resume as a plain-text file, check the document with the text editor that most computers have. In Windows, use Notepad. Open the file to be sure your margins look right and that you don't have extra spaces between lines or letters. If parts of the text are garbled, with a group of strange characters, it most likely means you forgot to take out some formatting. A resume with a lot of formatting is likely to end up looking like hieroglyphics if it's read as a plain-text file. If this happens, go back to your original document and repeat the process.

4. Be sure all the lines contain sixty-five characters or fewer. This includes all spacing, letters, and punctuation. Often you will need to go through your entire resume line by line, counting each space, letter, punctuation, asterisk, and so forth. You may need to manually insert hard returns where the lines are longer than sixty-five characters. This may seem trivial, but it's actually extremely important. While some computers may recognize as many as seventy-five characters per line, the majority cannot recognize more than sixty-five characters.

5. Finally, e-mail your resume to yourself or a friend to test the file. Be sure it stays intact, that no extra spaces or returns are inserted during transmission, and that all text appears readable. If something doesn't look right, go back to your

What Is ASCII?

ASCII stands for American Standard Code for Information Interchange and is pronounced "*Ask-ee.*" ASCII is a code that virtually all computers can understand. It was invented to allow different types of computers to exchange information easily.

text editor, fix the problem, and test the resume again before e-mailing it to any companies or posting it to on-line databases.

E-mail

E-mailing your resume to potential employers is generally done in response to a help-wanted advertisement or simply as a method of direct contact. In fact, many companies now request that resumes be submitted through e-mail, rather than the U.S. mail or by fax machine. Some job listings that you find on the Internet, particularly for technical positions, include only an e-mail address for contact information; no street address or telephone number is provided. And with many companies, you can e-mail your resume directly into their in-house resume database. This eliminates the concern that it will be found unreadable by a computerized resume scanner. When e-mailing, paste your resume into the body of the message; many companies won't open an attachment because of the possibility that it may contain a computer virus.

After e-mailing your resume, wait a few days to be sure the recipient has read it. Call or e-mail the company to confirm that your resume was received intact. As with a paper resume, an e-mailed resume may do you little good unless you follow up to express your genuine interest. If you sent your resume to an individual, ask if he or she would like you to elaborate on any sections of your resume. If you sent it to a general e-mail address, call the human resources department to check the status of your application.

On-line Resume Databases

On-line resume databases are similar to electronic employment databases. Cyberspace offers three main areas for resume posting: the World Wide Web, commercial on-line services, and Usenet newsgroups. These sites range from the general *www.hotresume.com* to the specific *www.medsearch.com*. Of the three areas, you'll find the

E-mail

- E-mailing your resume is quick and efficient. Instead of spending time printing out a copy of your resume, addressing an envelope, and mailing it, you can send your resume with a few clicks of your mouse. This allows you to respond almost instantly to job listings on-line as well as ads you see in the newspaper.
- Employers like e-mailed resumes because they cut down on paperwork and lower administrative costs.

The disadvantages are:

- Some job seekers work very hard at developing a professional looking hard-copy of their resume, laser-printed on high-quality resume paper. An e-mailed resume, while still capable of sounding professional, cannot always offer the same presentation or look as its hard-copy cousin. Spacing and formatting can sometimes be thrown off.
- There can be problems with sending or receiving, and also the possibility that e-mail sent to a general e-mail address may not be delivered to the appropriate person.
- Sometimes recruiters just don't check their e-mail all that often.

As with faxed resumes, it is good to follow-up your e-mailed resume with a hard copy in the mail.

On-line Databases

- Recent reports indicate that over twenty million people worldwide have access to the Internet, including thousands of human resources professionals and recruiters. Why *wouldn't* you want your skills to have that breadth of exposure? Since these services pre-screen candidates, they may be a more efficient method of searching for employers.
- Another reason to use an on-line database is its reach. If you're considering relocating, posting your resume on-line is a good way to get it circulating in another city before you move. Most job-search sites on the Web are searched by recruiters nationwide, even worldwide.
- You can also post your resume to a number of regional databases (mostly newsgroups).

The disadvantages are:

- While on-line databases have lots of benefits, they will not open the door to employers not using the Web, or those who are looking to the employment database to do the candidate "screening" for them.

Confidentiality

Many job seekers are wary of on-line resume database services because of issues of confidentiality. When your resume is on-line, it's accessible to virtually anyone with a computer and an Internet connection. This includes personal information like your name, address, telephone number, and other details. This lack of control over who sees their resume worries many job seekers. You may receive phone calls or e-mail messages from companies, organizations, and individuals you have absolutely no interest in.

However, the biggest concern to most job seekers is, what if one of those twenty million people cruising the Internet happens to be your boss? Many services offer safeguards to ensure that this doesn't happen.

(continued)

most options on the Web. Virtually all the major job-search sites on the Web, like Monster.com and E-Span, offer resume databases. One major database service, the Worldwide Resume/Talent Bank, is accessible through both the Internet and America Online. The Web also contains dozens of other sites for resume posting, including the only sites where you can post HTML resumes.

Bulletin Board Systems (BBSs), Gopher, and Telnet aren't generally considered destinations for resume posting and are best used to find job listings or gather information on specific industries and employers. While you may post resumes to most Bulletin Board Systems, they're not an efficient way to circulate your resume. For this reason, you're better off sticking to sites on the Web and Usenet newsgroups.

How to Decide

Given all the choices available, you may be wondering where to post your resume. Nothing says you can't post to more than one database. Since most on-line resume databases don't charge job seekers, you could, theoretically, post to every site. However, since that's not necessarily practical, the best approach is to visit a database of potential interest to see what types of resumes it has.

For instance, if you visit a site where most resumes showcase technical backgrounds, it's a safe bet that most of the companies that search that database are interested in filling technical positions. Similarly, if you notice that most resumes show little experience, you may have stumbled on a posting site for new graduates. Finally, if you're thinking of posting your resume to a general job posting site, like Monster.com, check out the companies that advertise in the site's job listings sections. Generally, those sponsors will be the primary companies to scan the database for candidates.

Fees

Most on-line sites don't charge for posting your resume; charges, if any, are usually incurred by client employers and recruiters. Some, especially those run by independent recruiters or career placement services, do charge a small fee, which may include resume preparation and advice. These databases are smaller

and may not have the wide exposure of some of the larger, free databases, but if you feel you need help composing your resume, the fee might be worth it.

How to Post

Most sites have instructions for entering a resume into their database. These instructions should tell you how long resumes remain in the database, how to update and remove your resume, who has access to the database, and the fee (if any). If a database doesn't have instructions, e-mail or call the site administrators for more information.

Some sites may require you to fill out personal information on-line, like your name, e-mail address, and resume title, but most allow you to attach your own resume or paste it in a specific area.

When e-mailing your resume to a database, don't overlook one important part of your e-mail: the subject line. This generally becomes your resume title, so it's important for it to give an indication of your field and job title. Many people mistakenly type "resume" or even their name on the subject line. The subject line is typically the first information seen by employers scanning the database and is often the only information a recruiter will look at. For this reason, it's important to be fairly specific on your subject line. Mention your profession, experience, and—since many resumes are seen by recruiters nationwide—your location. For instance, "Financial Analyst-3 yrs. exp.-CFA-IL." You could also mention if you're willing to relocate: "Financial Analyst-3 yrs. exp.-CFA-will relocate."

After e-mailing your resume to a database, try to download it. Once your resume is downloaded, make sure all the information is there and presented clearly. This serves a dual purpose. In addition to ensuring that your resume survived electronic transmission, you can then conduct a keyword search to check that your resume turns up when appropriate. Be sure that downloading your resume is free before attempting this.

Major Resume Sites on the Web

Following are just some of the major job-search sites on the Web. These listings discuss only these sites' resume posting capabil-

(continued from previous page)

The resume posting site *Monster.com,* for example, hides your personal information from employers until after they've purchased access to your resume. Some allow you to submit names of companies you'd prefer not receive your resume. Others will contact you to get your permission before forwarding your resume or employment profile to a company. Still others allow you to join the database anonymously—that is, your name, company names, education, and other identifying characteristics won't be shown to prospective employers. There are also a number of Web sites that don't offer these safeguards, so you'll want to check with your service to determine its particular policy.

A Word of Caution

Before writing a check or giving your credit card number to a company over the Internet, it's a good idea to check its reputation with the Better Business Bureau or a similar agency. While the majority of companies selling services over the Internet are reputable, remember that simply because a company has a presence on the Internet doesn't mean it's legitimate.

ities; their job listings are discussed in Chapter 10 [**Internet Job Search**].

Unlike Usenet newsgroup databases, resume posting sites on the Web typically contain resumes from job seekers everywhere, which means that thousands of employers search the databases for potential candidates. For this reason, it's a good idea to add a line to your resume stating whether you're willing to relocate.

CareerCity *www.careercity.com* is "The Web's Big Career Site" giving job hunters access to tens of thousands of jobs via three search engines: its own CareerCity jobs database; a newsgroup job-search engine covering hundreds of newsgroups; and addresses, phone numbers, descriptions, and hot links to 27,000 major U.S. employers. You'll find access to thousands of executive search firms and employment agencies, comprehensive salary surveys for all fields, and directories of associations and other industry resources. CareerCity's easy-to-use resume database gives job seekers the opportunity to market their qualifications free to employers subscribing to the database. The site is filled with hundreds of articles on getting started, changing careers, job interviews, resumes and cover letters, and more.

CareerMart *www.careermart.com* features its "Resume Bank" which offers free resume postings to job seekers, and its "E-mail Agent" which automatically notifies you when new positions crop up. Run by BSA Advertising, the site offers links to more than four hundred major employers and some seven hundred colleges and universities. Resumes should be submitted as text files.

CareerMosaic *www.careermosaic.com* has a database called ResumeCM, which contains resumes from job seekers in all geographic areas and occupations. Besides the database on the Web, it also indexes the most popular Usenet newsgroups and automatically adds your resume to their databases. Unlike most databases, ResumeCM also allows employers to conduct a full-text search of your resume instead of searching only subject lines.

Career Shop *www.careershop.com* has a site produced by TenKey Interactive which enables you to post your resume and also e-mail it directly to employers, free. Career Shop also offers a jobs database and allows employers who register with them to search the resume database free.

CareerSite *www.careersite.com* is a free service of Virtual Resources Corporation. CareerSite's resume database allows you to submit your resume as a fully formatted document. You simply fill in some fields online to summarize your credentials. Information is presented to participating employers without your name and address, and your resume isn't released to a company without your consent—a great relief to job seekers concerned with confidentiality.

E-Span's JobOptions *www.joboptions.com/esp/plsql/espan_enter. espan_home* is available to thousands of employers. E-Span's JobOptions Resume Database allows you to enter your resume data into a section that formats the information for you, or you may paste in your resume as a plain text file.

Monster.com *www.monster.com* has its Resume On-Line Database that allows you to paste either plain text or HTML resumes. Monster.com protects applicants by keeping their personal information, including name and address, separated from the resume. Employers can access that information only after they've purchased the resume.

Targeted Sites on the Web

Many resume sites on the Web are regional or geared toward a specific field or experience level. Some accept only ASCII or HTML resumes; others accept both. Some of the lesser-known sites in the following list charge fees.

This list is only a sample of additional sites you'll find on the Web; new ones pop up all the time. To find more databases, use a search engine like Yahoo or Alta Vista and enter the keywords "resumes" or "resume posting."

Resume Web Sites

A+ ONLINE RESUMES: *www.ol-resume.com*

AAAA: JOB RESUME SERVICES: *www.aaaa-job.com*

ACORN CAREER COUNSELING AND RESUME WRITING:
http://acornresume.com

CANDIDATEPOOL: *www.candidatepool.com*

EMPLOYNET: *www.employnet-inc.com*

1ST IMPRESSIONS RESUME & CAREER STRATEGIES:
www.1st-imp.com

HOTRESUME: *www.hotresume.com*

#1 RESUME WRITING SERVICES: *www.free-resume-tips.com/index.html*

OMICRONET PERSONAL CAREER CENTER:
www.omicronet.com/career/resume.htm

PURSUITNET ONLINE: *www.tiac.net/users/jobs/index.html*

RESUMEBLASTER: *www.resumeblaster.com*

RESUME'NET: *www.resumenet.com*

THE RESUME PLACE: *www.resume-place.com*

RESUMEXPRESS: *www.resumexpress.com*

SHAWN'S INTERNET RESUME CENTER:
www.inpursuit.com/sirc

SKILLBANK: *www.lapis.com/skillbank*

US RESUME: *www.usresume.com*

Commercial On-line Services

In comparison to the Web and newsgroups, commercial on-line services, like America Online, CompuServe, Microsoft Network, and Prodigy, offer only limited resume posting services. However, they provide easy access to both the Web and newsgroups, so you can use those resume posting resources.

One exception is the Worldwide Resume/Talent Bank Service on America Online. This service is available through both America Online (keyword: Career Center) and the Internet, at the Internet Career Connection *www.icweb.com/resume* Besides full- or part-time help, many members have found consulting and volunteer work as well as positions on advisory boards. The service costs around $25 for a six-month subscription and accepts only plain-text resumes. To access the site through AOL, type in the keyword "Career Center," select the Gonyea On-line Career Center, then select Resume Bank.

Usenet newsgroups tend to be more focused in scope, in terms of both region and subject matter. Posting your resume to a newsgroup makes it more likely to be seen by a local employer or one that really matches your interests than posting it to a large national database. What's the point of having twenty employers call to request interviews if they're all in one part of the country and you prefer to remain in another?

Usenet newsgroups tend to follow strict protocol. Most newsgroups contain postings with advice that outlines the protocol for that particular newsgroup. Be sure to read these *before* posting your resume. Finally, be careful not to post your resume to just any newsgroup with the word "job" in the address, since not every job-related newsgroup accepts resume postings. Following is a brief list of some newsgroups that do: alt.medical.sales.jobs.resumes—for medical sales positions; misc.jobs.resumes—for all types of jobs; and us.jobs.resume—for jobs within the United States.

Creating an HTML Resume

HTML allows you to format your resume so it appears on-line the way it would on paper. The real usefulness of HTML resumes is still being explored. Most of the major on-line databases don't

Learning HTML

HTML is relatively easy to learn. You can find dozens of books in your local bookstore on the subject, and the Web contains a number of sites where you can learn the code. Many Web browsers have such sites, including Netscape Navigator. From Netscape's home page *http://home.netscape.com* choose "Creating Net Sites" from the Assistance menu. Select "A Beginner's Guide to HTML," which will teach you the basics of the language, then move on to "Composing Good HTML," a style guide on how to use the code properly. You can also take lessons on adding frames, graphics, sound, and so forth. Or, using a search engine like Yahoo!, try the keyword "HTML" to find other sites for learning the code. If you don't feel up to learning a new computer language, many of the listed resume posting sites will, for a fee, convert your resume to HTML.

accept HTML resumes, and the vast majority of companies accept only plain-text resumes by e-mail. But new sites that accept HTML resumes are constantly cropping up on the Web.

Creating Your Own Home Page

You may be wondering whether it's worthwhile for you to have your own home page or HTML resume. The answer is, it depends. First, remember that you can have an HTML resume without creating your own home page. In most cases, a plain-text resume is really all you need. Unless you're looking for a job as a Web page designer or another technical position, most companies don't care whether applicants know HTML or can create a home page. However, if you have the time and inclination, learning HTML and creating your own home page can be a valuable skill. Many Internet providers and commercial on-line services provide subscribers with the server hard-disk space to create a personal home page. You can alert employers to your home page by including your URL (Uniform Resource Locator) in your traditional paper or electronic resume. A typical job seeker's home page will include a resume, graphics, perhaps some audio or video, and samples of your work, like drawings or writing clips.

When creating your own home page, be sure your employment background is emphasized over all else. It's easy to get carried away with creating a home page full of elaborate graphics or other links, but your resume should still be the core. Remember also that the home page strategy can backfire. If your design skills are weak and employers aren't impressed, you'll be worse off than before.

Multimedia and Video Resumes

Multimedia and video resumes are suitable for certain specialized applications. If you're in a creative field where knowledge of cutting-edge technology is valued, a multimedia or video resume may be effective or even essential.

A multimedia resume takes full advantage of the Web's capabilities by incorporating computer technology like graphics, scanned photographs, sound, and links to other sites. The applicant's information is virtually the same as in a regular resume but in an interactive format. For instance, clicking on an icon may present examples of an applicant's work. This type of resume is usually sent directly to an employer on disk or posted on an on-line resume database. Check out resumes posted on-line for ideas regarding design and content. (You can do a search on Yahoo! for "multimedia resumes.")

Video resumes are generally in the form of dialogues or "question and answer" formats, in which an off-camera participant asks the candidate questions regarding his or her background. The video itself is short; usually no longer than five minutes, or the equivalent of a three-to-five-page resume.

The simplest advice to give someone considering using a multimedia or video resume is to know your audience. Send it only to companies on the leading edge, where your technological know-how and creativity will be appreciated. Before sending such a resume, call to find out if the company will accept it and if they have the equipment to view it.

For more information on multimedia and video resumes, see *The Adams Electronic Job Search Almanac,* published by Adams Media Corporation, *www.careercity.com/booksoftware/ealmanac.asp*

CALL HEAD HUNTER

NFORMATIO
RNS RES
UR OF

RVIE
URN

ACTION LIST

ADS
FAX RESUMES

LL HEAD HUNTER

PICK UP SUIT AT
DRY CLEAN

SEND THANK Y
NOTE

9 A.M.
INTERVIEW WITH THOM TAN
AT NARD INC.

RESEARCH AGE

WEDNESDAY · Mercredi/Mittwoch/M

THURSDAY · Jeudi/Donnerstag/G

8 A.M.
MEET WITH BILL MacNEILL
DIRECTOR OF CAREER PLANNING
AT BIG RED UNIVERSITY

FRIDAY · Vendredi/Freitag/Venerdi/

SATURDAY · Samedi/Samstag/Sabato/Sö

TO DO

ACTION LIST   DATE:

GET SUNDAY NEWSPAPER
WANT-ADS
MAIL/FAX RESUMES ✓

CALL HEAD HUNTER ✓

PICK UP SUIT AT
DRY CLEANERS ✓

SEND THANK YOU
NOTES

ACTION LIST

HEAD HUNTER

11 INFORMATIONAL MEETING
    BURNS RESEARCH AGENCY
    TOUR OF FACILITY

12 INTERVIEW WITH KARA FORR
    AT BURNS RESEARCH AGEN

1

2

3   COMMUTE HOME
    * SEND THANK YOU NO
4   GO TO CAREER FAIR

5

6

TOUR, IN
ARCH AGE

NESDAY · Mercredi/Mittwoch/M

WITH THOM TAN
NC.

WW.CAREERCITY.COM

THURSDAY · Jeudi/Donnerst

11
INFORMATIONAL M...
BURNS RESEARCH A...

12 TOUR OF FACILITY

1 INTERVIEW WITH KARA H...
AT BURNS RESEARCH AGE...

2

3 Commute Home
* SEND THANK YOU NOTE

4 GO TO CAREER FAIR

5

SEND...

9

WWW.CAREERCITY.COM

CALL HEAD HUNTE...

9

INFORMATIONAL MEE...
URNS RESEARCH AGE...
OF FACILITY
...EW WITH KARA F...
RESEARCH A...

1 A.M. – 3 P.M.
NFO. MEETING, TO...
T BURNS RESEAR...

9 A.M.   WEDNESDAY
NTERVIEW WITH
AT NARD INC.

THURSDA...

8 A.M.   FRIDAY
MEET WITH BILL...
DIRECTOR OF CAREER...
AT BIG RED UNIV...

SATURDAY

DATE:

TO DO   ACTION LIST

CHAPTER 7
Cover Letters

Your cover letter, like your resume, is a marketing tool. Too many cover letters are merely an additional piece of paper accompanying a resume, saying "Enclosed please find my resume." Like effective advertisements, effective cover letters attract an employer's attention by highlighting the most attractive features of the product. Begin by learning how to create an effective sales pitch. As with resumes, both the format and the content of your cover letter are important.

Format

Before reading a word of your cover letter, a potential employer has already made an assessment of your organizational skills and attention to detail simply by observing its appearance. How your correspondence looks to a reader can mean the difference between serious consideration and dismissal. You can't afford to settle for a less than perfect presentation of your credentials. This chapter outlines the basic format you should follow when writing a cover letter and shows you how to put the finishing touches on a top-notch product.

The Parts of a Letter

Your cover letter may be printed on the highest-quality paper and typed on a state-of-the-art computer, but if it isn't arranged according to the proper format, you won't come across as a credible candidate. Certain guidelines apply when composing any letter.

Either of two styles may be used for cover letters: business style (sometimes called block style) or personal style. The only difference between them is that in business style, all the elements of the letter—the return address, salutation, body, and complimentary close—begin at the left margin. In personal style, the return address and complimentary close begin at the centerline of the page, and paragraphs are indented.

Return Address

Your return address should appear at the top margin, without your name, either flush left or beginning at the centerline, depending on whether you're using business style or personal style. As a rule, avoid abbreviations in the addresses of your cover letter,

although abbreviating the state is acceptable. Include your phone number if you're not using letterhead that contains it or it doesn't appear in the last paragraph of the letter. The idea is to make sure contact information is on both the letter and the resume, in case they get separated in the hiring manager's office (this happens more often than you would expect)!

Date

The date appears on the line below your return address, either flush left or centered, depending on which style you're using. Write out the date; don't abbreviate. *Example:* October 12, 1999.

Inside Address

Four lines beneath the date, give the addressee's full name. On subsequent lines, give the person's title, the company's name, and the company's address. Occasionally, the person's full title or the company's name and address will be very long and can appear awkward on the usual number of lines. In this case, you can use an extra line.

The text of the letter below the date should be centered approximately vertically on the page, so if your letter is short, you can begin the inside address six or even eight lines down. If the letter is long, two lines is acceptable.

Salutation

The salutation should be typed two lines beneath the company's address. It should begin "Dear Mr." or "Dear Ms.," followed by the individual's last name and a colon. Even if you've previously spoken with an addressee who has asked to be called by his or her first name, never use a first name in the salutation. In some cases, as when responding to "blind" advertisements, a general salutation may be necessary. In such circumstances, "Dear Sir or Madam" is appropriate, followed by a colon.

Enclosure

An enclosure line is used primarily in formal or official correspondence. It's not wrong to include it in a cover letter, but it's unnecessary.

Design a Letterhead

If you have a computer, you can design a letterhead for yourself and save it in a file to use for cover letters and other correspondence. Include your name, address, telephone, and e-mail, if you have it. Experiment to find an attractive design that's different from the way this information looks on your resume. If you want typefaces other than the default fonts that come with the computer, a CD-ROM containing several thousand fonts is available in software stores for about $15. However, avoid anything too flashy for business correspondence.

Length

Three or four short paragraphs on one page is ideal. A longer letter may not be read.

Paper Size

As with your resume, use standard 8½-by-11-inch paper. A smaller size will appear more personal than professional and is easily lost in an employer's files; a larger size will look awkward and may be discarded for not fitting with other documents.

Paper Color and Quality

The same suggestions in Chapter 4 [**Resumes**] about paper for resumes also apply to cover letters. Remember to use matching paper for both your resume, cover letter, and envelope.

Typing and Printing

Your best bet is to use a word processing program on a computer with a letter-quality printer. Handwritten letters are not acceptable. You will generally want to use the same typeface and size that you used on your resume. As discussed in Chapter 4 [**Resumes**], remember that serif typefaces are generally easier to read.

Don't try the cheap and easy ways, like photocopying the body of your letter and typing in the inside address and salutation. Such letters will not be taken seriously.

Envelope

Mail your cover letter and resume in a standard, business-sized envelope that matches your stationery. Unless your handwriting is *extremely* neat and easy to read, type your envelopes. Address your envelope, by full name and title, specifically to the contact person you identified in your cover letter.

Content
Personalize Each Letter

If you are *not* responding to a job posting that specifies a contact name, try to determine the appropriate person to whom you should address your cover letter. (In general, the more influential the person, the better.) Try to contact the head of the department in which you're interested. This will be easiest in mid-sized and small companies, where the head of the department is likely to have an active role in the initial screening. If you're applying to a larger corporation, your application will probably be screened by the human resources department. If you're instructed to direct your inquiry to this division, try to find out the name of the senior human resources manager. This may cut down on the number of hands through which your resume passes on its way to the final decision-maker. At any rate, be sure to include your contact's name and title on both your letter and the envelope. This way, even if a new person occupies the position, your letter should get through.

Mapping It Out

A cover letter need not be longer than three or four paragraphs. Two of them, the first and last, can be as short as one sentence. The idea of the cover letter is not to repeat what's in the resume. The idea is to give an overview of your capabilities and show why you're a good candidate for the job. The best way to distinguish yourself is to highlight one or two of your accomplishments or abilities. Stressing only one or two increases your chances of being remembered.

Be sure it's clear from your letter why you have an interest in the company—*so many candidates apply for jobs with no apparent knowledge of what the company does!* This conveys the message that they just want any job. Indicating an interest doesn't mean you should tell every employer you have a burning desire to work at that company, because these statements are easy to make and invariably sound insincere. Indicating how your qualifications or experience meet their requirements may be sufficient to show why you're applying.

Don't Philosophize

Don't:

*"Dear Ms. Sampson:
Finding the right person for the job is often difficult, costly, and at times disappointing. However, if you are in need of a reliable individual for your management staff, I have the qualifications and dedication for the position . . ."*

Do:

*"Dear Ms. Sampson:
I would like to apply for the position of marketing manager advertised in the Sunday Planet."*

The Comedian and the Chemist

Tone may vary somewhat according to profession: a comedian and a chemist would choose dissimilar tones. While it would be perfectly fitting for a comedian to adopt a lighthearted, familiar tone, the chemist would be best served by a more formal voice. Err on the side of caution, for there may be a lot of comedians out there, but there aren't many applying to be one.

First paragraph. State the position for which you're applying. If you're responding to an ad or listing, mention the source. *Example:* "I would like to apply for the position of research assistant advertised in the *Sunday Planet*" (or "listed on the Internet").

Second paragraph. Indicate what you could contribute to this company and show how your qualifications will benefit them. If you're responding to an ad or listing, discuss how your skills relate to the job's requirements. Don't talk about what you can't do. Remember, keep it brief! *Example:* "In addition to my strong background in mathematics, I offer significant business experience, having worked in a data processing firm, a bookstore, and a restaurant. I am sure that my courses in statistics and computer programming would prove particularly useful in the position of trainee."

Third paragraph. If possible, show how you not only meet but exceed their requirements—why you're not just an average candidate but a superior one. Mention any noteworthy accomplishments, high-profile projects, instances where you went above and beyond the call of duty, or awards you've received for your work. If you have testimonials, commendations, or evaluations that are particularly complimentary, you may want to quote a sentence from one or two of them. *Example:* "In a letter to me, Dewayne Berry, president of NICAP Inc., said, 'Your ideas were instrumental to our success with this project.' "

Fourth paragraph. Close by saying you look forward to hearing from them. If you wish, you can also thank them for their consideration. Don't ask for an interview. If they're interested, they'll call. If not, asking won't help. Don't tell them you'll call them—many ads say "No phone calls." If you haven't heard anything in one or two weeks, a call is acceptable.

Complimentary Close. The complimentary close should be two lines beneath the body of the letter, aligned with your return address and the date. Keep it simple—"Sincerely," followed by a comma, suffices. Three lines under this, type your full name as it appears on your resume. Sign above your typed name in black ink.

Don't forget to sign the letter! As silly as it sounds, people often forget this seemingly obvious detail. An oversight like this suggests you don't take care with your work. To avoid this implication if

you're faxing the letter and resume directly from your computer, you can type your name directly below the complimentary close, without any intervening space. Then follow up with a hard copy of the resume and the signed letter, with your name typed in the traditional place under the signature.

Tips for Successful Cover Letters

What Writing Style Is Appropriate?

Adopt a polite, formal style that balances your confidence in yourself with respect for the employer. Keep the style clear, objective, and persuasive rather than narrative. Don't waste space boasting instead of presenting relevant qualifications.

Example: "In addition to a Bachelor of Arts degree in Business Administration, I recently received a Master's degree, *cum laude*, in International Marketing from Brown University. This educational experience is supported by two years' part-time experience with J&D Products, where my marketing efforts resulted in increased annual product sales of 25 percent."

Tone: Reserved Confidence Is Always in Style

Think of how you'd sell your qualifications in a job interview. You'd probably think harder about what to say and how to say it than in an informal conversation. Above all, you'd want to sound polite, confident, and professional. Adopt a similar tone in your cover letter. It should immediately communicate confidence in your abilities. The trick is to sound enthusiastic without becoming melodramatic. Take, for example, the candidate who expressed his desire to enter the advertising field as "the single most important thing I have ever wanted in my entire twenty-three years of existence." The candidate who was actually offered the position began her letter as follows: "My extensive research into the industry, coupled with my internship and education, have confirmed my interest in pursuing an entry-level position in advertising."

Don't Be Longwinded

Don't:

"*Please accept the enclosed resume as an expressed interest in contributing relevant experience to the position of Sales Representative, as advertised in the* Pittsburgh Post-Gazette, *on Wednesday, April 11.*"

Do:

"*I would like to apply for the position of sales representative advertised in the* Pittsburgh Post-Gazette.*"

Emphasize Concrete Examples

Your resume details the duties you've performed in your jobs. In contrast, your cover letter should highlight your most significant accomplishments. Instead of stating something like "My career is highlighted by several major achievements," use concrete examples:

"While Sales Manager at Shayko Chicken, I supervised a team that increased revenues by 35 percent in 18 months."

"I published four articles in the *The Magical Bullet Newsletter*."

"At MUFON Corporation, I advanced from telephone fundraiser to field manager to canvassing director within two years."

List tangible, relevant skills rather than personal attributes. A sentence like "I am fluent in C+, Pascal, and COBOL" is a good substitute for a vague statement like "I am a goal-oriented, highly skilled computer programmer." Avoid using "etc."—don't expect a potential employer to imagine what else you mean. Either describe it or leave it out.

Use Powerful Language

Your language should be hard-hitting and easy to understand. Your message should be expressed using the fewest words possible. As with your resume, make your letters interesting by using action verbs like "designed," "implemented," and "increased," rather than passive verbs like "was" and "did." Use simple, common language and avoid abbreviations and slang. Change "Responsible for directing" to "Directed" if appropriate. Also steer clear of language that's too technical or jargon-heavy. The first person who reads your cover letter may not possess the same breadth of knowledge as your future boss.

Avoid Catchphrases

The same suggestions in Chapter 4 [**Resumes**] about avoiding catch phrases in resumes also apply to cover letters.

Mention Personal Preferences?

Candidates often worry if, and how, they should include salary requirements and availability to travel or relocate. Refrain from offering salary information unless the advertisement you are responding to requires it. If you must include salary requirements, give a salary range rather than a number. Another option is to simply indicate that salary concerns are negotiable.

If you're applying to an out-of-state firm, indicate a willingness to relocate; otherwise, a hiring manager may question your purpose in writing and may not take the initiative to inquire.

Proof with Care

Mistakes can be embarrassing, so proofread carefully, following the suggestions in Chapter 4 [**Resumes**] for proofreading your resume.

Cover Letter Blunders to Avoid

The following discussion focuses on examples that have been adapted from real-life cover letters. Although some of these blunders may seem obvious, they occur far more often than one might think. Needless to say, none of the inquiries that included these mistakes met with positive results.

Unrelated Career Goals

Tailor your cover letter to the position you're applying for. A hiring manager is only interested in what you can do for the company, not what you hope to accomplish for yourself. Convey a genuine interest in the position and a long-term pledge to fulfilling its duties.

Example A (wrong way): "While my true goal is to become a professional dancer, I am exploring the option of taking on proofreading work while continuing to train for the Boston Ballet's next audition."

Example B (right way): "I am very interested in this proofreading position, and I am confident of my ability to make a long-term contribution to your capable staff."

Cover Letter Do's and Don'ts

Do be sure your phone number and address are on the letter, just in case it gets separated from your resume (this happens!).

Do keep the letter brief and to the point.

Do accentuate what you can offer the company, not what you hope to gain from them.

Do make sure the watermark reads correctly.

Do be sure your letter is error free.

Do sign your letter with blue or black ink (or type your name if you're sending it electronically).

Don't just repeat information verbatim from your resume.

Don't overuse the personal pronoun "I."

Don't send a generic cover letter.

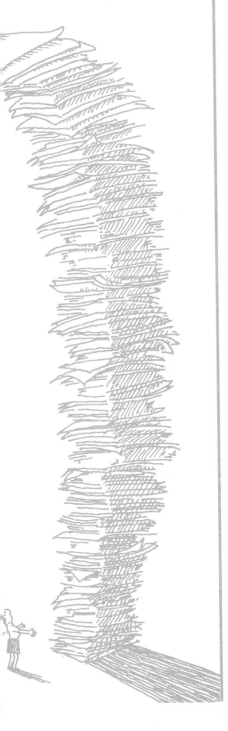

Comparisons and Clichés

Avoid clichés and obvious comparisons. These expressions detract from your letter's purpose: to highlight your most impressive skills and accomplishments.

Examples of what not to do:

"My word processor runs like the wind."

"I am a people person."

"Teamwork is my middle name."

"Your company is known as the crème de la crème of accounting firms."

"I am as smart as a whip."

"Among the responses you receive for this position, I hope my qualifications make me leader of the pack."

Wasted Space

Since cover letters are generally four paragraphs long, every word of every sentence should be directly related to your purpose for writing. In other words, if you are applying for a position as a chemist, include only those skills and experiences most applicable to that field. Any other information weakens your application.

Examples of what not to do:

"As my enclosed resume reveals, I possess the technical experience and educational background to succeed as your newest civil engineer. In addition, I am a certified gymnastics instructor who has won several local competitions."

"I am writing in response to your advertisement for an accounting clerk. Currently, I am finishing an associate degree at Peacock Junior College. My courses have included medieval architecture, film theory, basic home surgery, and nutrition."

Form Letters

Mass mailings, in which you send a form letter to a large number of employers, are not recommended. This approach doesn't allow you to personalize each application. Every cover letter you write should be tailored to the position you're seeking and should demonstrate your commitment to a specific industry and familiarity with each employer. Mass mailings may indicate to a hiring manager that you're not truly interested in joining that organization.

Inappropriate Stationery

White and ivory are the only acceptable paper colors for a cover letter. Also, don't rely on graphics to "improve" your cover letter; let your qualifications speak for themselves. If you're a cat enthusiast, don't use stationery with images of favorite felines. If you're a musician, don't send a letter decorated with a border of musical notes and instruments.

"Amusing" Anecdotes

Imagine yourself in an interview setting. Since you don't know your interviewer, you wouldn't joke with him or her until you determined what demeanor was appropriate. Similarly, when writing, remain polite and professional.

Erroneous Company Information

If you were the employer, would you want to hire a candidate who confuses your company's products and services or misquotes recent activities? To avoid such errors, verify the accuracy of any company information you mention in your cover letter. On the other hand, if you haven't researched the company, don't bluff. Statements like "I know something about your company" or "I am familiar with your products" signal to an employer that you haven't done your homework.

Desperation

In your cover letter, sound determined, not desperate. While an employer appreciates enthusiasm, he or she may be turned off by a desperate plea for employment. However, a fine line often separates the two.

Examples of what not to do:

"I am desperately eager to start, as I have been out of work for six months."

Next Candidate, Please

Certain formats and phrases signal an employer that you're using a form letter. Some job candidates turn this blunder into an art. In one real-life example, a candidate created a form letter with blank spaces where he penned in the employer's name and position applied for.

Another applicant who was indecisive about her field of interest created a list of possible positions in her letter. She then circled the most appropriate job description, depending on the company.

Don't Give Your Life Story

Don't:

"Six years ago, I started a career in nursing. I subsequently left to manage the division of a company and later resigned from this lucrative position to pursue my first career, nursing."

Do:

"I have several years' nursing experience and significant business management experience. I am sure that this background would make me well qualified for the Nursing Home Director position."

"Please call today! I'll be waiting by the phone."

"I really, really need this job to pay off medical bills."

"I AM VERY BADLY IN NEED OF MONEY!"

Personal Photos

Unless you're seeking employment in modeling, acting, or other performing arts, it's inappropriate to send a photograph.

Confessed Shortcomings

Some job seekers mistakenly call attention to their weaknesses in their cover letters, hoping to ward off an employer's objections. This is a mistake, because the letter emphasizes your flaws rather than your strengths.

Examples of what not to do:

"Although I have no related experience, I remain very interested in the management consultant position."

"I may not be well qualified for this position, but it has always been my dream to work in the publishing field."

Misrepresentation

In any stage of the job-search process, never, *ever*, misrepresent yourself. In many companies, erroneous information contained in a cover letter or resume will be grounds for dismissal if the inaccuracy is discovered. Protect yourself by sticking to the facts. You're selling your skills and accomplishments in your cover letter. If you achieve something, say so, and put it in the best possible light. Don't hold back or be modest—no one else will. At the same time, don't exaggerate to the point of misrepresentation.

Examples of what not to do:

"In June, I graduated with honors from American University. In the course of my studies, I played two varsity sports while concurrently holding five jobs."

"Since beginning my career four years ago, I have won hundreds of competitions and awards and am considered by many to be the best hairstylist on the east coast."

Demanding Statements

Your cover letter should demonstrate what you can do for an employer, not what he or she can do for you. For example, instead of stating "I am looking for a unique opportunity in which I will be adequately challenged and compensated," say "I am confident I could make a significant contribution to your organization, specifically by expanding your customer base in the northwest and instituting a discount offer for new accounts." Also, since you're requesting an employer's consideration, your letter shouldn't include personal preferences or demands. Statements like "It would be an overwhelmingly smart idea for you to hire me" or "Let's meet next Wednesday at 4:00 P.M., when I will be available to discuss my candidacy further" come across as presumptuous. Job candidates' demands are rarely met with an enthusiastic response.

Missing Resume

Have you ever forgotten to enclose all the materials you refer to in your cover letter? This is a fatal oversight. No employer is going to take the time to remind you of your mistake; he or she has already moved on to the next application.

Personal Information

The same suggestions in Chapter 4 [**Resumes**] about personal information in resumes also apply to cover letters.

Choice of Pronouns

Your cover letter necessarily requires a thorough discussion of your qualifications. Although some applicants might choose the third person ("he or she") as a creative approach to presenting their qualifications, potential employers sometimes find this disconcerting. In general, using the first person ("I") is preferable.

Example A (wrong way): "Bambi Berenbeam is a highly qualified public relations executive with over seven years of relevant experience in the field. She possesses strong verbal and written communication skills, and has an extensive client base."

Don't Be Grandiose
Don't:

"As a recent graduate of Mitzelflick University with a degree in Biology, I am currently launching my career as an environmental campaigner in hopes of reversing global warming and ozone depletion on a world-wide basis . . ."

Do:

"I would like to apply for the position of environmental campaigner due to my strong interest in many environmental causes."

More Cover Letter Don'ts

Following are some actual real-life examples, sent by job seekers, that illustrate what NOT to write in your cover letter:

"I am excited by the prospect of growing with [BLANK SPACE] and look forward to discussing your needs."

"Marketing is in my blood, and I believe that I am genetically predetermined to enter the marketing world . . . I am writing to you about possible job openings in your company in hopes that I can fulfill my destiny there."

"As my resume indicates, I have extensive experience in pubic relations."

Example B (right way): "I am a highly qualified public relations executive with over seven years of relevant experience in the field. I possess strong verbal and written communication skills and have an extensive client base."

Tone Trouble

Tone problems are subtle and may be hard to detect. When reading your cover letter, patrol for tone problems by asking yourself, after each sentence, "Does this statement enhance my candidacy? Could a hiring manager interpret it in an unfavorable way?" Have a second reader review your letter. If the letter's wording is questionable, rewrite it. A cover letter should steer a middle course between extremely formal, which can come across as pretentious, and extremely informal, which can come across as presumptuous. Try to sound genuine, not stilted. When in doubt, err on the side of formality.

Gimmicks

Gimmicks like sending a home video or a singing telegram to replace the conventional cover letter may seem attractive. No matter how creative these ideas may sound, the majority of employers will be more impressed with a simple, well-crafted letter. In the worst-case scenario, gimmicks can even work against you, eliminating you from consideration. Examples include sending a poster-sized cover letter by courier service or a baseball hat with a note attached: "I'm throwing my hat into the ring!" Avoid such big risks; most hiring decisions are based on qualifications, not gimmicks.

Typographical Errors

It's easy to make mistakes in your letters, particularly when you're writing many in succession. But it's also easy for a hiring manager to reject any cover letter that contains errors, even those that seem minor. Don't make the mistake that one job-hunting editor made, citing his attention to detail while misspelling his own name! Here are a few common technical mistakes to watch out for when proofreading your letter:

Misspelling the hiring contact's name or title in the address or salutation or on the envelope.

Forgetting to change the name of the organization you're applying to each time it appears in your application, especially in the body of the letter. For example, if you're applying to Boots and Bags, don't express enthusiasm for a position at Shoe City.

Indicating application for one position and mentioning a different position in the body of the letter. For instance, one candidate applying for a telemarketing position included the following statement: "I possess fifteen years experience related to the marketing analyst opening." Another mistake here is that the applicant didn't use "years" as a possessive: ". . . fifteen years' experience. . . ."

Messy Corrections

Your cover letter should contain *all* pertinent information. If, for any reason, you forget to communicate something to your addressee, retype the letter. Including a supplementary note, either typed or handwritten, will be viewed as unprofessional or, worse, lazy. For example, one candidate attached a "post-it" note to his cover letter, stating his willingness to travel and/or relocate. This and all other information must be included in your final draft. Also, avoid using correction fluid or penning in any corrections.

Omitted Signature

However obvious this may sound, don't forget to sign your name neatly in blue or black ink. Far too many letters have a typed name but no signature. Also, don't use a script font or a draw program on your word processor.

Details, Details . . .

Can and May

No: *I may be reached at (505) 555-5555 (days) and (505) 444-4444 (evenings).*

Better: *I can be reached at (505) 555-5555 (days) and (505) 444-4444 (evenings).*

Fused Participle

No: *I appreciate you taking the time to speak to me is an example of a fused participle and is grammatically incorrect.*

Better: *I appreciate your taking the time to speak to me.*

Serial Comma

Standard editorial practice in a series of items is to use a comma after each item.

No: *". . . lumberjack, lounge lizard and organ grinder."*

Yes: *". . . lumberjack, lounge lizard, and organ grinder."*

CALL HEAD HUNTER

FAX RESUMES

LL HEAD HUNTER

Pick up Suit at Dry Clean

SEND THANK Y
Note

FORMATIO
RNS RES
R OF

RVIE
RN

9 A.M.
INTERVIEW WITH THOM TAN
AT NARD INC.

WEDNESDAY Mercredi/Mittwoch/Me

THURSDAY Jeudi/Donnerstag/Gio

8 A.M.
MEET WITH BILL MacNEILL
DIRECTOR OF CAREER PLANNING
AT BIG RED UNIVERSITY

FRIDAY Vendredi/Freitag/Venerdi/Vi

SATURDAY Samedi/Samstag/Sabato/Sáb

TO DO

ACTION LIST   **DATE:**

Get Sunday Newspaper ✓
WANT-ADS
MAIL/FAX RESUMES ✓

Call Head Hunter ✓

Pick up Suit at
Dry Cleaners ✓

Send Thank You
Notes

ACTION LIST

One Page Per Day Out

HEAD HUNTER

11 INFORMATIONAL MEETING
    BURNS RESEARCH AGENCY
12 TOUR OF FACILITY

1   INTERVIEW WITH KARA FORR
    AT BURNS RESEARCH AGENC

2

3   Commute Home
    * SEND THANK YOU Not
4   GO TO CAREER FAIR

5

6

TUESDAY Ma

OUR, IN
ARCH AGE,

DNESDAY Mercredi/Mittwoch/Me

WITH THOM TANI
ENC.

THURSDAY Jeudi/Donnerstag/Gioued

WWW.CAREERCITY.COM

CHAPTER 8

Cover-Letter Samples

11 INFORMATIONAL M...
BURNS RESEARCH A...
12 TOUR OF FACILITY
1 INTERVIEW WITH KARA H...
AT BURNS RESEARCH AGE...
2
3 Commute Home
* SEND THANK YOU NOTE
4 GO TO CAREER FAIR
5

SEND N...

WWW.CAREERCITY.COM

9 CALL HEAD HUNT...

INFORMATIONAL MEE...
BURNS RESEARCH AGE...
...R OF FACILITY
...EW WITH KARA H...
RESEARCH A...

11 A.M. - 3 P.M.
INFO. MEETING, TO...
T BURNS RESEARCH...

9 A.M. WEDNESDAY
INTERVIEW WITH...
AT NARD INC.

THURSDAY

8 A.M. FRIDAY
MEET WITH BILL M...
DIRECTOR OF CAREER...
AT BIG RED UNIV...
SATURDAY

1547 South Street
Cheeseville, CA 96037
(530) 555-5555
July 21, 1999

Samuel Butcher
Hiring Manager
Davis Accounting Associates
17 Alice Circle
Davis, CA 95616

Dear Mr. Butcher:

   I am seeking an entry-level accounting position in which I can apply expertise in both financial management and customer service. While researching area firms, I became interested in Davis Accounting Associates' esteemed training and development program. To such a program, I would bring the following:

- a Bachelor of Science degree, *cum laude*, in Finance
- four years' of collections experience
- successful collection of 90 percent of company's overdue accounts
- experience in accounts payable and accounts receivable
- knowledge of Lotus 1-2-3, Microsoft Word, and accounting software

   Thank you for your consideration. I look forward to speaking with you.

Sincerely,

George Glass

George Glass

Part-Time Art Instructor

178 Armour Street
Kingsdale, PA 17340
(215) 555-5555
January 28, 1999

Kay Nichols
Principal
Ty-Nee Tots Elementary School
11 Cleese Lane
Knightsville, PA 17052

Dear Ms. Nichols:

I would like to express my interest in applying for the part-time art instructor position advertised in the *Philadelphia Daily News*.

I am a trained elementary art instructor with expertise in arts and crafts instruction as well as program conception and coordination. For four years, I taught art classes on a part-time basis for the Camelot School in Kingsdale. In addition to my teaching and program management activities, I arranged field excursions and produced an annual district-wide arts competition. Also, I hold a State of Pennsylvania Elementary Education Certificate in Art and a Bachelor of Fine Arts in Art Education.

For the past year, I have been spending weekends as arts and crafts program director for the Knightsville Parks and Recreational Association. I create and facilitate programs for children, control a budget, select and purchase supplies, and supervise aides in various duties. Since this work is restricted to weekends, my weeks would be open to fulfill my responsibilities as your art instructor. I am confident I could create and maintain an exciting program at Ty-Nee Tots Elementary School.

My resume is enclosed for your review. I would welcome the opportunity to discuss my relevant experience further in a personal interview. At such a time, I could provide you with several references attesting to my skills, as well as a portfolio of past implemented programs.

I look forward to hearing from you.

Sincerely,

Tim Concorde

Tim Concorde

"Cold" Cover Letter to a Potential Employer

49 Wilson Street
Miami, FL 33054
November 11, 1999

Jenny Ryan
Personnel Manager
Frohman Corporation
6 Smallest Crow Road
Chicago, IL 60605

Dear Ms. Ryan:

After five years as a district sales manager, I am seeking new opportunities and am forwarding my resume for your consideration.

As important as my experience in new business development for multimedia products is my interest in becoming an integral part of a young, aggressively expanding organization like Frohman Corporation. I am confident of my ability to stimulate company growth and profits from successful follow-through on corporate sales and marketing programs.

I can be reached at the above address or by phone at (305) 555-5555. Thank you for your consideration.

Sincerely,

Cesil Ives

Cesil Ives

24 Smalley Street
Miami, FL 33132
September 21, 1999

Julie J. Bugg
Executive Producer
Beta-Um Production Company
2 Pete's Circle
Hialeah, FL 33012

Dear Ms. Bugg:

I am writing to express my interest in the production assistant position advertised in the *Miami Herald*.

I possess extensive experience in all aspects of video production, including positions as writer, researcher, director, and editor. For the past three years, I have been a freelance production assistant working on several commercial and documentary pieces. As chief assistant on "Milk Carton Kids: An American Crisis," I assisted in preliminary research and writing, scheduling location shooting, and screening potential interview candidates. I also helped complete two public service announcements for Miami Child Services, where my duties included camera operation and heavy editing work.

My freelance experience has been diverse and rewarding, but I would like a permanent production position where my skills can be used to greater advantage. I have admired Beta-Um Production Company's work for some time and attended your screening of "Silent Victims" at the Miami Crime Awareness Convention last month. I would like the opportunity to contribute to such remarkable work.

Please contact me at (305) 555-5555 or (305) 444-4444 evenings if you need any additional information or to arrange a meeting.

I look forward to hearing from you.

Sincerely,

Lee Luther Boog

Lee Luther Boog

Freelance Writer

24 Dry Creek Lane
Oklahoma City, OK 73125
(918) 555-5555
e-mail: akohl@rols.com
January 6, 1999

Maureen McGrady
Publisher
Collinsville Publishing Company
40 Bono Road
Collinsville, PA 17302

Dear Ms. McGrady:

    I am a freelance writer of educational and reference materials for college students and adults. My experience is primarily in the areas of careers, self-help, and parenting. Having frequently noticed such books by Collinsville Publishing Company on the best-seller lists, I would like to learn more about your freelance needs.

    My clients tell me I have a facility for synthesizing information and conveying it in a creative and well-organized way. Whether writing textbook materials, teacher apparatus, or ancillary activities and worksheets, I can tailor the tone and approach to a variety of purposes and audiences.

    I wonder if I could speak to you about undertaking some of your projects? I can provide a variety of writing samples and references.

    Thank you for your consideration.

Sincerely,

Augustus Kohler

Augustus Kohler

Marketing Assistant

178 rue Verte
Paris, France
011-331-45-55-55
January 7, 1999

Ms. Helen Sugarson
Director of Human Resources
Small World Corporation
1140 Main Street
New York, NY 10028

Dear Ms. Sugarson:

I am looking for a new association with an international service-oriented organization that can benefit from my multilingual and organizational skills in a marketing position.

I have a Bachelor of Arts degree in French (*summa cum laude*), am fluent in French and Italian, and have strong proficiency in Spanish. In addition, I have experience as an interpreter and translator working on international market research with the International Marketing Department at the University of Paris, Sorbonne. I concurrently worked as an administrative assistant to professors and business executives.

Since 1994, I have been tutoring individuals in foreign languages and English as a Second Language. I am familiar with various cultures and work well with multilingual, multicultural individuals and groups.

The enclosed resume summarizes my experience. I will be in New York from February 14 through February 28 to secure permanent housing arrangements. I would appreciate the opportunity to meet during that time so that we may discuss the mutual benefits of my joining your firm.

I will call the week of February 5 to confirm receipt of my application and to discuss the possibility of an interview. Thank you for your time.

Sincerely,

George Hale

George Hale

22-B Liam Street
El Segundo, CA 90245
(213) 555-5555
e-mail: fasttrack@aon.com
December 14, 1999

Jennifer Quinnie
Director of Marketing
SoCal Corporation
5 Prankster Street
Los Angeles, CA 90089

Dear Ms. Quinnie:

I am currently seeking an entry-level opportunity in a successful marketing department and have learned about SoCal Corporation through the *Los Angeles JobBank*.

As you can see from the enclosed resume, since completion of my Bachelor of Science degree, my professional associations have been extensive and diverse. Throughout my experiences, I have developed several important skills that I believe could benefit your marketing department. I possess solid communication skills, both in person and by phone. I am proficient with Macintosh, PC, and spreadsheet applications, and I can effectively manage all aspects of daily business operations, including inventory management and account maintenance. Above all, I possess a strong work ethic and enthusiasm to learn.

Last month I took an intensive seminar entitled "Marketing for Success!" This investment conclusively confirmed my desire to pursue marketing as a career. I know that, if given the chance, I could quickly prove my worth as a member of your staff.

I look forward to your response.

Sincerely,

Dawn E. Pfaster

Dawn E. Pfaster

2497 Carver Lane
Muckilteo, WA 98275
(206) 555-5555
October 3, 1999

Fred Tripps
Director of Human Resources
Wright-Said Corporation
50 Llama's Way
Farmington, MI 48331

Dear Mr. Tripps:

   I recently learned from your vice president of operations, Clyde Bruckmahn, that you might be in need of a meeting planner to join your management. During the past sixteen years, I have successfully demonstrated solid troubleshooting and problem-resolution skills in management, marketing, and sales. My progressively responsible experience includes:

- corporate/institutional meeting planning
- hospitality service coordination
- destination management/program coordination
- employee/client incentive programs
- sales/customer service

   Could we meet for an interview? I will contact you next week to inquire about a convenient time for further discussion.
Thank you.

Sincerely,

Fred Smyth

Fred Smyth

45 Nickel Street
Provo, UT 84602
(801) 555-5555
January 10, 1999

Thommy Tannin
Controller
Nard Inc.
2 Mudslide Lane
Black Point, ME 04074

Dear Mr. Tannin:

During the past twelve years, my career has been focused on transportation and sales. Seven of these years were spent with the United States Army. Although my recent experience has been in the sale of intangibles, I am interested in resuming a civilian career in transportation operations or in the sale of products or equipment allied to the transportation field.

I have a Bachelor of Science degree, and I am a graduate officer of the U.S. Army Transportation School—the equivalent of a graduate school. In addition to managing all phases of complete civilian and tactical transportation operations (vehicles from two-and-one-half-ton cargo trucks to ten-ton tractor trailers and petroleum tankers), I have taught courses and have trained troops in the total transportation cycle in the United States and abroad.

The enclosed resume summarizes my educational background and experience in the above areas. I feel confident that with my qualifications in the transportation field, I can contribute substantially toward the efficient operation of an in-house traffic, transportation, and distribution function and/or commercial transportation depot.

I would appreciate the opportunity to further discuss my qualifications in the transportation field and the immediate and long-term contribution I could make to Nard Inc.

Sincerely,

Buck Harlow

Buck Harlow

3 Box Street
Scottsdale, AZ 85254
(602) 555-5555
May 13, 1999

Jane Mahone
Manager of Operations
Ishimaruh Airport
2 Leggy Lane
Phoenix, AZ 85021

Dear Ms. Mahone:

I am currently investigating opportunities to which I can apply my knowledge of, and extensive experience in, the management of large parking facilities.

In my most recent position at Parkinson Hotel, my proven abilities and strong work ethic resulted in rapid advancement to a management position after only one year of service as a parking attendant. As supervisor of parking facilities, I oversaw all financial collections, maintained customer service standards, performed troubleshooting, and managed a large staff. Additionally, I administered work schedules and payroll, assigned duties, and interfaced with hotel management.

I am a self-motivated, people-oriented, responsible individual, capable of meeting your expectations for quality supervision. I hope to have the opportunity to further discuss how I can contribute to your parking staff.

Sincerely,

Darren H. Ozwald

Darren H. Ozwald

112 Poet Circle
Pennesauken, NJ 08110
(609) 555-5555
e-mail: tumbleweed@coldmail.com
July 23, 1999

Virgil Canto
President
Dielander Executive Search Firm
1140 Main Street
Pleasantville, NJ 08232

Dear Mr. Canto:

My interest in applying for a position as recruiter at your firm has prompted me to forward the attached resume for your consideration.

My expertise was gained over seven years while recruiting high-technology, support, and marketing personnel. Much of this experience involved extensive travel, training-program development, and networking prospective clients. I possess valuable contacts within the management information systems, software development, and engineering industries that would be a valuable asset to your client base.

I would very much like to apply my skills and knowledge as a member of your recruiting staff. I believe that in a very short time, I could contribute significantly to your success.

I will follow up this inquiry with a phone call in several days. Thank you for your time.

Sincerely,

Len Tumble

Len Tumble

178 Green Road
Brooklyn, NY 11735
(516) 555-5555
April 30, 1999

Joe Chung
District Manager
Kwee Wag Retail Chain
1140 Main Street
Calgary, Alberta T2W 3X6

Dear Mr. Chung:

My interest in joining your dynamic staff in a full-time management position has prompted me to forward the enclosed resume for your consideration.

During the past seven years, I have held progressively responsible positions in retail sales, from salesperson to manager. In my most recent position as store manager for Raintree Designs, I increased branch sales from $.5 to $1.2 million in one year. I possess hands-on experience in sales, inventory control, and product promotion. As assistant manager for Rips, Inc., in Vancouver, I supervised a staff of twelve, oversaw the production of a promotional video, and assisted in the selection of chain-wide promotion techniques.

As my resume indicates, the majority of my retail management experience has been on a part-time basis. At this point in my career, I am ready to apply my skills to a long-term, permanent position. As an employee of Kwee Wag Retail Chain, I would expect to increase sales and promotion and ensure smooth store operations.

After you have had the opportunity to review my qualifications, I would appreciate hearing from you.

Thank you for your time.

Sincerely,

Ray Bloodwurth

Ray Bloodwurth

Broadcast Letter

With a broadcast letter, well-qualified candidates can advertise their availability to top-level professionals in a particular field. The candidate attempts to entice the potential employer to consider his or her impressive qualifications for available positions. Although the broadcast letter discusses a candidate's background in detail, it usually includes a resume. Since this type of letter is used primarily by seasoned executives, its tone should reflect the candidate's experience, knowledge, and confidence in his or her capabilities.

A candidate using the broadcast letter format might begin, "Are you in need of a management accountant who, in her most recent association, contributed to productivity improvements resulting in an annual savings of $20 million?" This attention-grabbing opening is effective only if the reader understands the significance of such an accomplishment. For this reason, broadcast letters are not recommended for candidates conducting widespread job searches, where cover letters may end up in the human resources department rather than in the hands of a fellow industry executive.

Sample Broadcast Letter

14 Interlocken Way
Roswell, NM 88201
(505) 555-5555
January 18, 1999

Mr. J.J. Vicks
Accounting Supervisor
Roland Corporation
1140 Main Street
Roswell, NM 88201

Dear Mr. Vicks:

If your firm is in need of a qualified, seasoned account manager, I would welcome the opportunity to meet with you.

I have over twenty years' of experience as a hands-on manager in all areas of accounting, including general ledger, accounts payable, payroll, budgeting/fore-casting/analysis, and management reporting. I possess a strong background in cost accounting, inventory control, and supervision. Some of my accomplishments include:

- Initiating a department analysis that increased productivity by 20 percent
- Implementing a strong system of internal controls, resulting in a reduction of inventory write-offs from $300,000 per year to $0
- Revising and implementing a revenue accounting system in support of the direct end-customer sales of a Ganubian subsidiary, which resulted in a cost savings of $150,000 per year
- Negotiating policy decisions regarding expenditures and investments across multiple businesses and disciplines
- Writing policies to govern worldwide fiscal processes throughout the company

Thank you for your consideration of this matter. I look forward to speaking with you further concerning possible openings at Roland Corporation.

Sincerely,

Ray Muldrake

Ray Muldrake

Letter to an Employment Agency

When searching for a job, many candidates rely on employment agencies. Letters addressed to employment agencies should focus on who you are, what type of position you're looking for, in what industry, and some of your strongest skills related to that field. For the agency to place you appropriately, mention personal preferences, including geographic and salary requirements. Conclude your letter with a statement about how you can be reached or when you'll follow up on your letter.

Sample Letter to an Employment Agency

362 North Main Street
Reston, VA 22091
(703) 555-5555
December 19, 1999

Natalie Goldword
Representative
Elbonia Employment Agency
7 Bones Street
Taos, NM 87571

Dear Ms. Goldword:

I am searching for a challenging position in the fast-food industry in which work experience and a commitment to excellence will have valuable application.

Currently, I am the manager of a large restaurant in Reston, VA. I am responsible for staffing, inventory, cash receipts, and conflict resolution. I work well in both relaxed or fast-paced, high-pressure environments.

I would like to continue my career in food service upon relocating to your area next month. If you should be aware of any available opportunities, I would appreciate your assistance. Until January 1, I can be reached at (215) 555-5555. After that date, I will be at the above address and telephone number.

Thank you for your time.

Sincerely,

Diana Linsky

Diana Linsky

Response to a "Blind" Advertisement

"Blind" advertisements don't list employer information and generally direct inquiries to a post office box rather than to a company's address. Since you're not provided with a company name in a blind ad, your cover letter should sharply define your knowledge of the industry, position (if mentioned), and how your qualifications match the stated requirements. In other words, tailor your letter to any information given. For example, consider a blind ad that reads "Large law firm in need of paralegal with experience in legal research, writing briefs, and office administration."

Target everything in your response: what you know of the operations of large firms, why you want to be and remain a paralegal, how much experience you have in legal research and writing, and exactly what office skills you have. Avoid long-winded passages that don't follow these guidelines. Keep it brief and to the point.

February 6, 1999

Stupendous Yawpy Staffing Agency
P.O. Box 7777
Bangor, ME 04401

RE: Field Finance Manager

Dear Sir or Madam:

Please accept this letter and enclosed resume as an application for your opening advertised in the *Bangor Daily News*.

I am a 1996 graduate of the University of Maine's Graduate School of Business, with over six years' of business and financial analysis experience. This includes two years' of domestic and international travel as an internal auditor for Botanee Bay Foods, Inc., two years' of credit analysis at Millbury, and a treasury internship at Envirlab. Since graduating, I have worked as a business analyst in the areas of banking, real estate, and restaurant management.

I have been recognized for my creative spirit and ability to identify implementable solutions to current business problems. The following highlights some of my achievements:

- Participated in the due diligence and/or postacquisition reviews of five acquisitions
- Planned, coordinated, and/or participated in the compliance and productivity audits of forty-one independent business units
- Participated in the fraud review of a major business unit
- Researched, developed, and planned a cash collection reorganization that, when implemented, will save $120,000 per year

Based on my job experience and educational qualifications, I am confident I can make an immediate contribution to your firm. I would appreciate the opportunity to further discuss my credentials with you. Thank you.

Sincerely,

David Wuss-Goff

David Wuss-Goff

12 Evans Lane Street
Plymouth, MA 02360
(508) 555-5555
e-mail: sluggo@slicklink.com
April 8, 1999

Derf Harlow
Human Resources Manager
Willuse School District
5 Spitbizz Lane
Oyster Harbors, MA 02655

Dear Mr. Harlow:

In response to last week's advertisement for an English teacher in the *New England Journal of Higher Education*, I have enclosed my resume for your consideration.

I have recently graduated from Boston College with a Bachelor's degree in Secondary Education. I am certified to teach both English and Special Education. In addition to fulfilling my practice-teaching requirement in your district, I participated in a volunteer literacy program to tutor both youths and adults struggling with reading difficulties. I also organized and performed in a variety show at Newton High School that benefited special-needs students.

As I fulfilled my practice teaching requirement, I was continually impressed by the high educational standards in District 5 and the long-standing record of producing students whose SAT scores are among the highest in the nation. I would consider it a great opportunity to teach in such an accomplished district.

I look forward to hearing from you.

Sincerely,

Gil Lajeunesse

Gil Lajeunesse

9 Salon Street
Worcester, MA 01610
(508) 555-5555
June 23, 1999

Steve Byras
Director
Turbo-Direct Agency
1140 Main Street
Salem, MA 01970

Dear Mr. Byras:

Thank you for taking the time to speak with me today. As I mentioned on the phone, I am interested in beginning a career in the field of gerontology.

I am currently a senior at the College of the Holy Cross, majoring in Sociology. I have studied a variety of subjects, including gerontology, where I first became interested in this field. Other related courses I have taken include poverty and crisis, the political economy of health care in the United States, race relations, and women in society. My current grade point average is 3.64, and I am a member of the Phi Beta Kappa honor society.

In addition to my school work, I am an active member of the student-run Volunteers for a Better World program. Some of the experiences I have gained through this organization include serving Thanksgiving dinner to the homeless at a local soup kitchen, tutoring underprivileged junior high students in math and English, and codirecting a successful annual campus food drive. As a contributing writer for the *Angora*, I wrote many articles and editorials concerning various social issues, including the plight of the elderly.

As a result of my classroom studies and my volunteer experience, I feel that I have an excellent grasp of the social and political issues that affect older adults in the United States. I feel that, at your agency, I could make a real difference in the lives of older people.

I've enclosed my resume and a sample article for your perusal. Thank you for your attention to this matter. I look forward to your response.

Sincerely,

Kristie Smith

Kristie Smith

1 Vista Place, #3
Aston, PA 19014
(215) 555-5555
April 4, 1999

Jeff Sklars
Attorney-at-Law
Kronig Law Partners
1140 Main Street
Erie, PA 16563

Dear Mr. Sklars:

Justice Ellen Malone, of Allentown Courthouse, suggested that I contact you regarding an opening you may soon have for a legal assistant.

I will be graduating this May from Temple University with a Bachelor of Arts degree in African-American Studies. In addition to my core studies, I have studied in several areas, including business administration and computer applications. In 1997, I was awarded the prestigious Lieberman Scholarship.

I also offer a strong background in law, having worked in a variety of legal settings throughout my college years. I was a volunteer for Temple's Student Legal Aid, helping students with legal problems. I worked part-time over the past three years as a volunteer probation officer for the Allentown juvenile court. And in addition to being an outside media contact for an Aston Outreach Unified Neighborhood Team, I spent one summer as a research assistant for the Chief County Clerk of Allentown.

All these positions have given me a strong sense of the law and the American legal system. Moreover, this experience convinced me that I would like to pursue a career in law. Justice Malone highly recommends your firm as one that might be a good match for my goals and qualifications.

I will contact you within the week to further discuss the possibilities of securing this position. Thank you for your time.

Sincerely,

Jill Harlow

Jill Harlow

297 Third Street
Columbia, SC 29202
(803) 555-5555
August 14, 1999

David Evergreen
Stage Director
Plunk Production Company
2 Way Street
Nancy, TX 75980

Dear Mr. Evergreen:

Lynne Winchester recently indicated that you may have an opening for a set designer and suggested that I contact you. I am seeking a position involving stage design in television.

I graduated last December from Clemson University with a Bachelor of Arts degree in Theatre Arts and a concentration in Studio Art. In addition to modern drama and music and sound in theatre, I completed courses in set creation and design, intermediate painting, and woodworking. As a member of the drama club, I designed and helped create props for numerous campus productions, including *Dielander* and *Marco Polo Sings a Solo.*

As for my work experience, I co-designed and co-created the props and decorations for a new miniature golf course with a tropical island theme, which turned out to be a big hit. I also gained valuable skills working as an apprentice to a busy carpenter and painting houses for a large company.

Enclosed is my resume as well as some photographs of my work. I have some great ideas for the sets of *The Queen of Exuberance* and *Videos After Dark* and hope to have the opportunity to discuss them with you.

Thank you for your consideration.

Sincerely,

Maya P. Fairs

Maya P. Fairs

Translator

12 Lornado Lane
Chicago Heights, IL 60411
(708) 555-5555
July 5, 1999

Moni L. Trenta
Director
Goth Ltd.
1140 Main Street
Denver, CO 80204

Dear Ms. Trenta:

   I am writing with the hope that you will consider me for the position of translator advertised in today's *Rocky Mountain News*.
   I graduated last month with a Bachelor of Arts degree in International Relations and French Language from Northwestern University. Throughout my university career I was recognized for excellent scholarship, including being consistently on the Dean's list and graduating one year early with honors and advanced standing. I was also active in many extracurricular events and organizations; by my junior year, I had become a Model United Nations Advisor, an Alumni Ambassador, and president of the International Affairs Society.
   In addition, I have work experience in the field of international affairs, having been employed as an interpreter and translator for a Parisian film corporation. In this position, I interpreted for negotiations over film coproductions and translated agreements, film scripts, scenarios, and foreign correspondence. I also worked as the assistant to the Parisian correspondent for Cluseaux Associates, an import/export company.
   I am not limited by location and would enjoy the opportunity to live and work in Denver for Goth Ltd.
   I look forward to hearing from you.

Sincerely,

Laura Rafferty

Laura Rafferty

CHAPTER 9

Other Letters

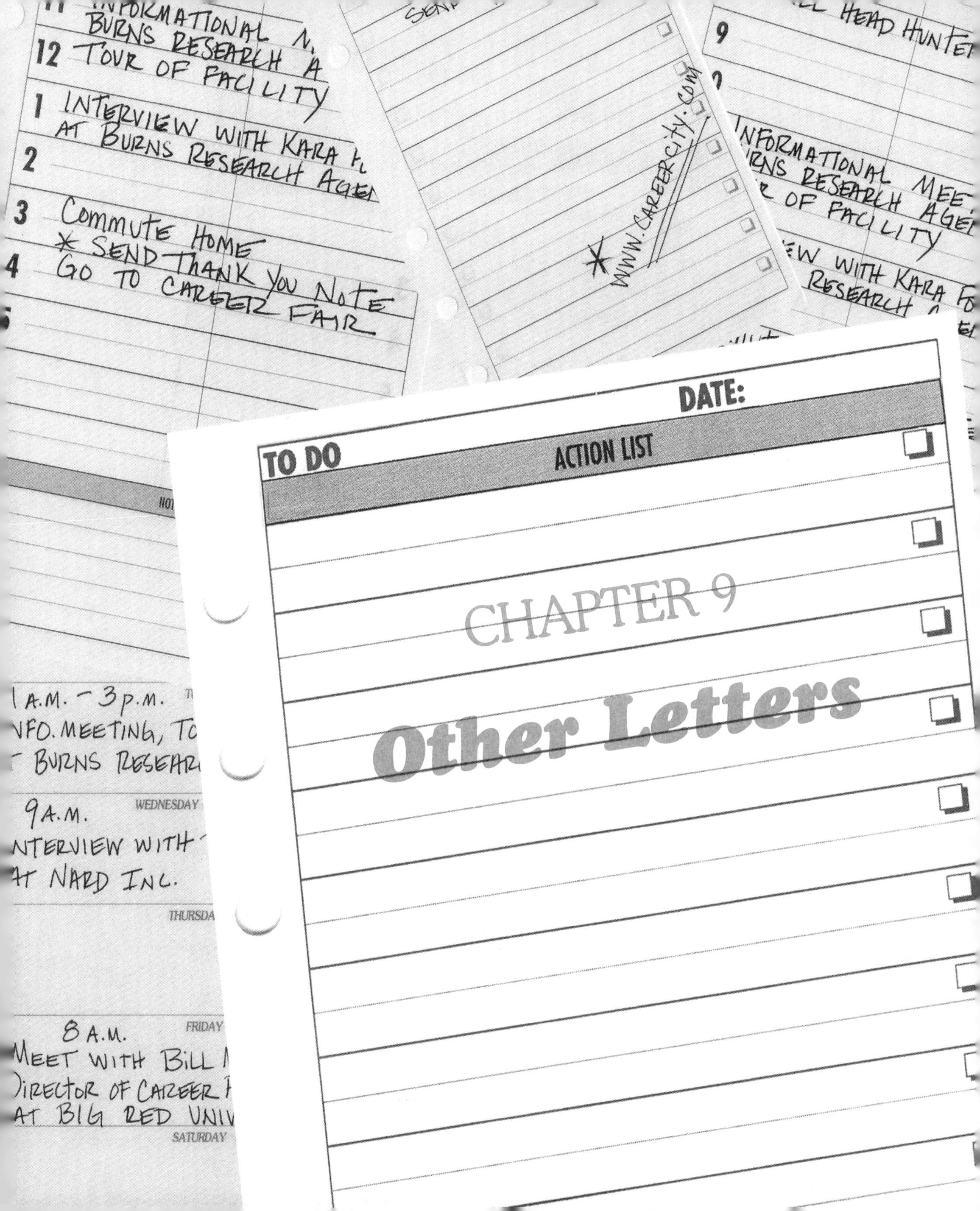

Your correspondence doesn't end with cover letters. Other types of letters, such as mostly thank-you letters, are often appropriate, even obligatory. It's acceptable to handwrite your thank-you letter on a generic blank note card (but *never* a postcard). Make sure handwritten notes are neat and legible. If you're in doubt, typing your letter is always a safe bet. If you met with several people, it's fine to send each an individual thank-you letter. Call the company if you need to check on the correct spelling of their names. Remember to keep the letters short, proofread them carefully, and send them *promptly*.

Thank-You Letters

After a Telephone Conversation

Immediately after a telephone conversation with a potential employer, send a cover letter expressing your gratitude for his or her time. Use this opportunity to reiterate your qualifications and continued interest in the position. Be sure to include your resume.

After a Job Interview

Always send a thank-you letter after an interview, ideally within twenty-four hours. So few candidates do this, yet it's another way for you to stand out. A follow-up letter expresses thanks for the employer's time and emphasizes your continued interest in the position. It can also provide a convenient opportunity to reiterate your unique qualifications.

Mention something specific from the interview and restate your interest in the company and the position. As with resumes and cover letters, avoid catch phrases, and be careful the letter doesn't come across sounding canned or hypocritical. Don't say, for example, "I would like to reiterate my strong interest in this position. I believe it would be an exciting opportunity, and I feel that my track record shows I would be a successful candidate." The letter should be brief (no more than a page; even a few sentences is fine) and personalized.

178 N. Green Street
Chicago, IL 60657
(312) 555-5050
October 2, 1999

Heather Valentine
Personnel Manag
Doubles Corpora
1140 State Stree
Chicago, IL 606

Dear Ms. Valer

    I wanted t .... ut the research assistant
position. I wa .... oration's commitment to
R&D and the .... Iso glad to see that Team
3 is working .... e. Needless to say, I hope
to be able t ....
    If I can .... dacy, please contact me at
the numbe ....
    I look ....

Sincerely

Dante Normun

Dante Normanson

For a Good Reference

During the course of your job search, it may be necessary to call upon personal and professional references to support your credentials. These people are doing you a favor and deserve your written thanks. Thank-you letters also allow you to keep your contacts current.

When writing your letter, you might want to remind the person why you needed the reference and the outcome of his or her efforts. Keep your comments brief and your tone polite.

For a Letter of Recommendation

Potential employers sometimes require letters of recommendation. These may be written by previous employers or, for those with little professional experience, by college professors. Since you requested this person's time, it's only courteous to express your written thanks. By doing so, the person will be more likely to remember you should you require further assistance in the future.

For a Referral

Many jobs are found with the assistance of a networking contact or referral. Throughout your job search, keep track of all your referrals and send each one a personalized thank-you note. Briefly express sincere gratitude for the referral's help on your behalf. If the person's efforts directly led to a positive outcome for you, let him or her know. It may be advantageous to offer your return assistance. In any event, sending a thoughtful thank-you letter is an invaluable career move. If you recognize someone's assistance on your behalf, the person may be more likely to help you again in the future.

After an Informational Interview

Thank-you letters aren't restricted to potential employers. Everyone who assists you in any way during the course of your job search deserves written thanks. Even in the case of an informational interview, a letter is required. Although you're not asking for a job, you've taken a person's time and should thank him or her accordingly.

Consider Susan B., who wrote a timely thank-you letter to an industry executive with whom she met in an informational interview. The executive, impressed by her considerate attention to detail, heard about an appropriate employment opportunity several weeks later and recommended Susan for the job.

Thank-You Letter (After Informational Interview)

178 Green Street
Downers Grove, IL 60515
(708) 555-5555

May 12, 2001

Erika Jorgensen
Occupational Therapist
Any Rehabilitation Center
1140 Main Street
Evanston, IL 60201

Dear Ms. Jorgensen:

Thank you for taking the time to meet with me on Friday. I enjoyed meeting with you and learning about the programs offered at Any Rehabilitation Center.

Our discussion definitely strengthened my interest in occupational therapy as a career path. I am planning to take your advice and enroll in a graduate program in September. In the interim, I will contact the referrals you provided to inquire about summer internship possibilities.

Thank you again for your assistance.

Sincerely,

Andrew Shlenker

Andrew Shlenker

Address or Telephone Number Change

In today's tough market, the job-search process is often lengthy. If your situation has changed since your last correspondence (i.e., a geographical move or phone number change), always inform a potential employer. Keep your correspondence brief. This is a courtesy letter, not a full-page reiteration of your qualifications.

To begin, remind the employer of the position you applied for, and when. State the change in your circumstances and thank the reader for his or her continued consideration. Include an updated copy of your resume. Remember that this letter is not optional. An employer will not waste time trying to track you down.

Resurrection Letter

If several weeks or even months have passed since you mailed your initial inquiry and you haven't received a response, your candidacy may be in need of a jump start. Sending a resurrection letter informs an employer of your continued interest in, and suitability for, a desired position. Begin by reminding the employer of your initial reason for writing. Next, reiterate your most relevant qualifications and stress your desire to join the employer's organization. Be sure to close your letter by clearly stating how and when you can be reached, and enclose another resume for the employer's convenience.

Waiting for a response to your application can be frustrating. If you feel this way, don't let it show in your resurrection letter. A hiring manager is more likely to respond to a polite, upbeat letter.

Resurrection Letter (Physical Therapist)

178 Green Street
Somerville, MA 02145
(617) 555-5555

November 16, 2001

Pat Cummings
Rehabilitation Coordinator
Any Clinic
1140 Main Street
Mansfield, MA 02048

Dear Mr. Cummings:

In a letter dated August 12, I expressed my interest in obtaining a staff position as a physical therapist at Any Clinic. Although I realize there may not have been any suitable openings at that time, I have enclosed a second resume for continued consideration.

Since my initial application, I have been working on an independent research project while continuing my job search. My study evaluated back and shoulder strength of athletes suffering from tendinitis and bursitis. Last week, my results were accepted for publication in the *National Journal of Rehabilitation*. I have enclosed an excerpt of my article for your review.

I would welcome the chance to meet with you should any opportunities for a physical therapist become available.

Sincerely,

Chris Smith

Chris Smith

Response to Rejection

A well-written thank-you note, mailed within one or two days of receiving notice of rejection, makes a positive statement. Admittedly, this technique is less widely used than other thank-you letters, but it can be equally effective.

When writing your letter, emphasize an interest in being considered for future openings. Also, be careful to use an upbeat tone. Although you may be disappointed, you don't want to imply that you don't respect the employer's hiring decision.

Withdrawal from Consideration

If you must withdraw your application from consideration at any point in the hiring process, it's best to inform the employer in writing. This will establish you as a courteous individual worthy of consideration should you reapply for a position in the future. In general, a withdrawal letter should be concise. If you choose to include a reason for your withdrawal, phrase it briefly and in positive terms.

Rejection of an Offer

If you decide to reject an employment offer, inform the employer through a formal letter. Even if you rejected the offer over the phone, confirm your decision in writing. Begin by thanking the interviewer for both the offer and the time extended to your candidacy. Stating a reason for rejection is optional. Above all, keep your letter upbeat—you never know if you'll reapply to the company in the future.

Acceptance Letter

Even if you've been offered the position of your choice, no hiring decision is final until it's in writing. Confirm your acceptance of a job offer with a brief, gracious letter. Express thanks for the organization's decision and your enthusiasm for the new position.

Rejection of Offer (Sales Representative)

178 Green Street
Menomonee Falls, WI 53051
(414) 555-5555

January 30, 2001

Donnie Sloan
Vice-President, Sales
Any Corporation
1140 Main Street
Milwaukee, WI 53202

Dear Mr. Sloan:

I enjoyed our meeting Friday to discuss the possibility of my joining Any Corporation in a sales position. Your staff seems enthusiastic, and I was impressed by your semiannual sales record. That is quite an achievement.

Although I greatly appreciate your confidence in my abilities, I am afraid I must decline your employment offer. I realize that in order to generate the quantity of sales necessary to reach our mutual goals, I would have to invest a great deal of time in travel. At this point, that is not an allowance I am able to make.

Once again, thank you for your consideration.

Sincerely,

Steven Jejackal

Steven Jejackal

Fire Road 34
Weeping Water, NE 68463
(402) 555-5555
May 21, 1999

Andrea Krasker
Human Resources Director
Echo Corporation
1140 Main Street
Chicago, IL 60605

Dear Ms. Krasker:

I would like to express my thanks for your selecting me as the new Benefits Administrator for Echo Corporation. I am pleased to have been offered this opportunity, and I look forward to joining your ranks.

I have submitted my resignation to my present employer and will begin working for you three weeks from today. During the interim, I will remain in contact with both you and Chip Gavin, to ensure a smooth transition.

Again, thank you for your confidence and support.

Sincerely,

David Weissman

David Weissman

Information Request

Requests for information are formal inquiries to organizations or potential employers; common inquiries include requests for membership listings, annual reports, company brochures, and alumni data. When writing an information request, be brief and to the point.

In your cover letter, simply state who you are and ask politely for the information. For example: "I am an experienced paralegal searching for a list of firms specializing in international environmental law." Include a self-addressed, stamped envelope to expedite the process.

2112 Rush Boulevard
Jackson Center, OH 45334
(513) 555-5555
August 10, 1999

Bill MacNeill
Director of Career Planning
Big Red University
1140 Main Street
Richmond, VA 23298

Dear Mr. MacNeill:

I am a 1991 graduate of Big Red University. I have been employed in the social services industry for the last six years. Budgetary cuts within the local youth services agency have prompted me to begin searching for a new position in case management.

Does the university provide a network of alumni in my field—perhaps a local chapter of graduates I can contact? Gaining several new contacts, in the Ohio area especially, would be a valuable asset to my job-hunting research. I would appreciate your forwarding a directory of names or information on how to contact other professionals in social services who are graduates of Big Red University.

Thank you for your assistance.

Sincerely,

Libby Bird

Libby Bird

14 Starbuck Street
San Jose, CA 95134
(408) 555-5555
e-mail: drmoore@slicklink.com
January 27, 1999

Larry Badtuch
Director, Public Relations
Bunk & Train Corporation
1140 Main Street
San Francisco, CA 94120

Dear Mr. Badtuch:

I am currently investigating career opportunities in the San Francisco area. In the course of my research, I found Bunk & Train Corporation to be an industry leader in accounting and financial planning.

Could you send me information concerning your services? I would be especially interested in an annual report. I have enclosed a self-addressed, stamped envelope for your convenience.

Thank you.

Sincerely,

Keith Moore

Keith Moore

CALL HEAD HUNTER

FAX RESUMES

ACTION LIST

9 A.M.
INTERVIEW WITH THOM TAN
AT NARD INC.

WEDNESDAY Mercredi/Mittwoch/Me

THURSDAY Jeudi/Donnerstag/Gio

ALL HEAD HUNTER

PICK UP SUIT AT
DRY CLEAN
SEND THANK Y
NOTE

8 A.M.
MEET WITH BILL MacNEILL
DIRECTOR OF CAREER PLANNING
AT BIG RED UNIVERSITY

FRIDAY Vendredi/Freitag/Venerdi/Vie

SATURDAY Samedi/Samstag/Sabato/Sáb

FORMATIO
RNS RES
R OF

RZVIE
URN

TO DO

ACTION LIST   DATE:

GET SUNDAY NEWSPAPER
WANT-ADS ✓

MAIL/FAX RESUMES

CALL HEAD HUNTER ✓

PICK UP SUIT AT
DRY CLEANERS ✓

SEND THANK YOU
NOTES

YEAR

ACTION LIST

One Page Per Day (Undated)

HEAD HUNTER

11 INFORMATIONAL MEETING
    BURNS RESEARCH AGENCY
12 TOUR OF FACILITY

1   INTERVIEW WITH KARA FORRE
    AT BURNS RESEARCH AGENC

2

3   COMMUTE HOME
    * SEND THANK YOU NOT
4   GO TO CAREER FAIR

5

6

TUESDAY Ma

TOUR, IN
ARCH AGE,

ONESDAY Mercredi/Mittwoch/Me

WITH THOM TAN
NC.

THURSDAY Jeudi/Donnerstag/Gioued

WW.CAREERCITY.COM

11 INFORMATIONAL M...
BURNS RESEARCH A...
12 TOUR OF FACILITY
1 INTERVIEW WITH KARA H...
AT BURNS RESEARCH AGE...
2
3 Commute Home
* SEND THANK YOU NOTE
4 GO TO CAREER FAIR
5

SEND ...

9

WWW.CAREERCITY.COM

L HEAD HUNT...

INFORMATIONAL MEE...
...URNS RESEARCH AGE...
...R OF FACILITY

...EW WITH KARA H...
...RESEARCH A...

I A.M. – 3 P.M.
NFO. MEETING, TO...
T BURNS RESEARC...

9 A.M.   WEDNESDAY
NTERVIEW WITH ...
AT NARD INC.

THURSDA...

8 A.M.   FRIDAY
MEET WITH BILL...
DIRECTOR OF CAREER...
AT BIG RED UNIV...

SATURDAY

DATE:

TO DO   ACTION LIST

CHAPTER 10

Internet Job Search

The Internet consists of four separate areas: the World Wide Web, Usenet, Telnet, and Gopher. These areas include hundreds of thousands of job listings. Bulletin Board Systems (BBSs), which represent a part of cyberspace that doesn't fall into these areas, are also an excellent job-search resource. No surprise, then, that when most people think of electronic job searching, they think of the Internet.

The World Wide Web. The Web is the best-known area of the Internet. It has dozens of excellent electronic career centers that offer all kinds of job-search advice and information, including a growing number of large databases of job listings. The Web has by far the largest collection of job listings found on-line.

Usenet. The User's Network is comprised of more than 20,000 newsgroups, or electronic discussion groups, where people can exchange information, discuss ideas, or just chat. The nature of Usenet makes it a natural for networking—with so many different newsgroups to choose from, you're sure to find one in your field of interest. Usenet is also an outstanding resource for job listings, with over 100,000 offerings.

Telnet. Telnet is the smallest area of the Internet, and getting smaller. Telnet is a good place to look for federal job listings and other information regarding applying for a federal job. It's also useful as a way of connecting to other sites, like a Gopher server.

Gopher. Gopher is a menu-based system of organizing information on the Internet. It was also the first step in making the Internet more user-friendly, with its easy-to-manage menus and powerful search engines, Veronica and Jughead. Because it was developed at the University of Minnesota and quickly became a favorite of academics at other universities, Gopher remains a good source of academic and other specialized job listings. For example, it has one of the few on-line employment resources dedicated to the arts. However, Gopher's popularity is fading in competition with the Web and Usenet newsgroups.

The World Wide Web

The Web is fast becoming the place to look for jobs on the Internet. Dozens of career resources on the Web are devoted to job listings, with more springing up every day. Unlike Usenet newsgroups, which tend to focus on computer-related or other technical positions, the Web has listings for job hunters of all backgrounds.

Major Sites

The Web's job databases vary greatly in both the quality and quantity of job listings. Start with the all-purpose job-search sites described in Chapter 4 [**Resumes**], like Careercity, CareerMosaic, Job Options, and the Monster Board. These are three of the largest and most popular job-search sites on the Web.

A number of listings in the major job databases overlap. The same search performed on the Monster Board and CareerSite, for example, will likely retrieve many of the same listings. Keep careful records, so you don't mistakenly send a resume to the same company twice for the same job.

JOB HUNTING SITES FOR EVERYONE

ADGUIDE'S COLLEGE RECRUITER EMPLOYMENT
   SITE: *www.adguide.com*
AMERICAN JOBS: *www.americanjobs.com*
BEST JOBS USA: *www.bestjobsusa.com*
BLACKWORLD: *www.blackworld.com/careers.htm*
BUSINESS JOB FINDER:
   www.cob.ohio-state.edu/dept/fin/osujobs.htm
THE CAREERBUILDER NETWORK:
   www.careerbuilder.com
CAREERCITY: *www.careercity.com*
CAREER CONNECTION: *www.connectme.com*
CAREER EXCHANGE: *www.careerexchange.com*
CAREER EXPOSURE: *www.careerexposure.com*
CAREERLINK USA: *www.careerlinkusa.com*
CAREERMAGAZINE: *www.careermag.com*
CAREERMART: *www.careermart.com*
CAREERMOSAIC: *www.careermosaic.com*
CAREERPATH: *www.careerpath.com*
CAREER RESOURCE CENTER:
   http://cgi.pathfinder.com/fortune/careers/index.html
CAREER SHOP: *www.careershop.com*
CAREERSITE: *www.careersite.com*
CAREERWEB: *www.careerweb.com*
CAREER WOMEN: *www.careerwomen.com*
CAREERS.WSJ.COM: *www.careers.wsj.com*
CLASSIFIEDS2000: *www.classifieds2000.com*
CLASSIFIED WAREHOUSE: *www.adone.com*
COLLEGE GRAD JOB HUNTER: *www.collegegrad.com*
   CONTRACT EMPLOYMENT WEEKLY:
     www.ceweekly.com
     COOL WORKS: *www.coolworks.com*
     E-SPAN'S JOBOPTIONS:
      www.joboptions.com
      4WORK: *www.4work.com*
      HEADHUNTER: *www.headhunter.net*

HEART: CAREER CONNECTION: *www.career.com*
THE HELP-WANTED NETWORK:
   www.help-wanted.net
HOT JOBS: *www.hotjobs.com*
INTERNET CAREER CONNECTION: *www.iccweb.com*
THE INTERNET JOB LOCATOR: *www.joblocator.com*
THE INTERNET JOB SOURCE: *www.statejobs.com*
THE INTERNET'S EMPLOYMENT RESOURCE:
   www.tier21.com
JOBDIRECT: *www.jobdirect.com*
JOBEXCHANGE: *www.jobexchange.com*
JOBFIND: *www.jobfind.com*
JOBHUNT: *www.job-hunt.org*
JOBS.COM: *www.jobs.com*
JOB-SEARCH-ENGINE: *www.jobsearchengine.com*
JOBTRAK: *www.jobtrak.com*
JOBVERTISE: *www.jobvertise.com*
JOBWEB: *www.jobweb.com*
THE LATPRO PROFESSIONAL NETWORK:
   www.latpro.com
MBA FREEAGENTS.COM: *www.mbafreeagents.com*
MONSTER.COM: *www.monster.com*
NET-TEMPS: *www.net-temps.com*
PASSPORTACCESS: *www.passportaccess.com*
PHILLIPS CAREER CENTER:
   www.phillips.com/careercenter.htm
RECRUITING-LINKS.COM: *www.recruiting-links.com*
WESTECH VIRTUAL JOB FAIR: *www.vjf.com*

JOB OPENINGS—ASIA
ASIA NET: *www.asia-net.com*

JOB OPENINGS—AUSTRALIA
AUSTRALIAN JOB SEARCH:
   http://jobsearch.deetya.gov.au

BYRON EMPLOYMENT AUSTRALIA:
http://employment.byron.com.au

JOB OPENINGS—CANADA
CANADIAN JOBS CATALOGUE: *www.kenevacorp.mb.ca*

JOB OPENINGS—EUROPE
OVERSEAS JOBS EXPRESS: *www.overseasjobs.com*

JOB OPENINGS—INDIA
CAREER INDIA: *www.careerindia.com*
JOB OPENINGS—IRELAND
THE IRISH JOBS PAGE: *www.exp.ie*

JOB OPENINGS—UNITED KINGDOM
JOBSITE GROUP: *www.jobsite.co.uk*
VACANCIES: *www.vacancies.ac.uk*
WORKWEB: *www.workweb.co.uk*

JOB OPENINGS—UNITED STATES
ALASKA JOBS CENTER:
www.ilovealaska.com/alaskajobs
AMERICA'S TV JOB NETWORK: *www.tvjobnet.com*
BOSTON.COM: *www.boston.com*
BOSTON JOB BANK: *www.bostonjobs.com*
BOSTONSEARCH: *www.bostonsearch.com*
THE CALIFORNIA JOB SOURCE:
www.statejobs.com/ca.html
CAREERBOARD: *www.careerboard.com*
CAREERGUIDE: *www.careerguide.com*
CAREERLINK: *www.careerlink.org/index.htm*
CAROLINASCAREERWEB: *www.carolinascareerweb.com*
CLASSIFIND NETWORK: *www.classifind.com*
COLORADOJOBS: *www.coloradojobs.com*
FLORIDA CAREER LINK: *www.floridacareerlink.com*
HOUSTONCHRONICLE: *www.chron.com*
JOBNET: *www.jobnet.com*
KANSAS JOB-BANK: *http://entkdhr.ink.org/kjb/index.html*

MINNESOTA JOBS: *www.minnesotajobs.com*
NEW ENGLAND OPPORTUNITY NOCS:
www.opnocs.org
NEW JERSEY ONLINE: *www.nj.com*
ONLINE COLUMBIA: *www.onlinecolumbia.com*
ORANGE COUNTY REGISTER:
www.ocregister.com/ads/classified/index.shtml
PHILADELPHIA ONLINE: *www.phillynews.com*
THE SILICON VALLEY JOB SOURCE:
www.valleyjobs.com
680CAREERS: *www.680careers.com*
STL DIRECT: *http://directory.st-louis.mo.us*
TOWNONLINE: *www.townonline.com/working*
TRIANGLE JOBS: *www.trianglejobs.com*
VIRGINIA EMPLOYMENT COMMISSION:
www.vec.state.va.us
WASHINGTON EMPLOYMENT WEB PAGES:
http://members.aol.com/gwattier/washjob.htm
WISCONSIN JOBNET: *www.dwd.state.wi.us/jobnet*

INDUSTRY-SPECIFIC JOB OPENINGS
—ACCOUNTING/BANKING/FINANCE—
ACCOUNTING & FINANCE JOBS:
www.accountingjobs.com
ACCOUNTING.COM: *www.accounting.com*
ACCOUNTING NET: *www.accountingnet.com*
AMERICAN BANKER ONLINE'S CAREERZONE:
www.americanbanker.com/careerzone
BLOOMBERG: *www.bloomberg.com*
CFO'S FEATURED JOBS:
www.cfonet.com/html/cfojobs.html
FINANCIAL, ACCOUNTING,
AND INSURANCE JOBS PAGE:
www.nationjob.com/financial
FINCAREER: *www.fincareer.com*
JOBS FOR BANKERS ONLINE: *www.bankjobs.com*
NATIONAL BANKING NETWORK:
www.banking-financejobs.com

—ADVERTISING/MARKETING/PUBLIC RELATIONS—
ADWEEK ONLINE: www.adweek.com
DIRECT MARKETING WORLD: www.dmworld.com
MARKETING JOBS: www.marketingjobs.com

—AEROSPACE—
AVIATION AND AEROSPACE JOBS PAGE:
    www.nationjob.com/aviation
AVIATION EMPLOYMENT:
    www.aviationemployment.com
SPACE JOBS: www.spacejobs.com

—ARTS AND ENTERTAINMENT—
THE INTERNET MUSIC PAGES: www.musicpages.com
ONLINE SPORTS:
    www.onlinesports.com/pages/CareerCenter.html

—BIOTECHNOLOGY/ SCIENTIFIC—
BIO ONLINE: www.bio.com
SCIENCE PROFESSIONAL NETWORK:
    www.recruitsciencemag.org

—CHARITIES AND SOCIAL SERVICES—
THE NONPROFIT TIMES ONLINE:
    www.nptimes.com/classified.html
SOCIALSERVICE: www.socialservice.com
SOCIAL WORK AND SOCIAL SERVICES JOBS
    ONLINE: www.gwbweb.wustl.edu/jobs/index.html

—COMMUNICATIONS—
    AIRWAVES MEDIA WEB:
        www.airwaves.com/job.html

THE JOBZONE:
    www.internettelephony.com/JobZone/jobzone.asp

—COMPUTERS—
COMPUTER:
    www.computer.org/computer/career/career.htm
THE COMPUTER JOBS STORE:
    www.computerjobs.com
COMPUTERWORK: www.computerwork.com
DICE: www.dice.com
DIGITAL CAT'S HUMAN RESOURCE CENTER:
    www.jobcats.com
IDEAS JOB NETWORK: www.ideasjn.com
I-JOBS: www.I-jobs.com
JOBS FOR PROGRAMMERS: www.prgjobs.com
JOBS.INTERNET.COM: http://jobs.internet.com
JOB WAREHOUSE: www.jobwarehouse.com
MACTALENT: www.mactalent.com
SELECTJOBS: www.selectjobs.com
TECHIES: www.techies.com

—EDUCATION—
ACADEMIC EMPLOYMENT NETWORK:
    www.academploy.com
ACADEMIC POSITION NETWORK: www.apnjobs.com
AECT PLACEMENT CENTER:
    www.aect.org/employment/employment.htm
THE CHRONICLE OF HIGHER EDUCATION/
    CAREER NETWORK: http://chronicle.com/jobs
DAVE'S ESL CAFE: www.eslcafe.com
HIGHEREDJOBS ONLINE: www.higheredjobs.com
JOBS IN HIGHER EDUCATION:
    www.gslis.utexas.edu/~acadres/jobs/index.html
LIBRARY & INFORMATION SCIENCE JOBSEARCH:
    www.carousel.lis.uiuc.edu/~jobs
THE PRIVATE SCHOOL EMPLOYMENT NETWORK:
    www.privateschooljobs.com
TEACHER JOBS: www.teacherjobs.com

—ENGINEERING—
ENGINEERJOBS: *www.engineerjobs.com*

—ENVIRONMENTAL—
ECOLOGIC:
   www.rpi.edu/dept/union/pugwash/ecojobs.htm
ENVIRONMENTAL JOBS SEARCH PAGE!:
   http://ourworld.compuserve.com/homepages/
   ubikk/env4.htm
WATER ENVIRONMENT WEB: *www.wef.org*

—GOVERNMENT—
CORPORATE GRAY ONLINE: *www.greentogray.com*
FEDERAL JOBS CENTRAL: *www.fedjobs.com*
FEDERAL JOBS DIGEST: *www.jobsfed.com*
FEDWORLD FEDERAL JOB ANNOUNCEMENT
   SEARCH: *www.fedworld.gov/jobs/jobsearch.html*
THE POLICE OFFICERS INTERNET DIRECTORY:
   www.officer.com/jobs.htm

—HEALTH CARE—
HEALTH CAREER WEB: *www.healthcareerweb.com*
HEALTH CARE JOBS ONLINE: *www.hcjobsonline.com*
HEALTH CARE RECRUITMENT ONLINE:
   www.healthcarerecruitment.com
MEDHUNTERS: *www.medhunters.com*
MEDICAL-ADMART: *www.medical-admart.com*
MEDICAL DEVICE LINK: *www.devicelink.com/career*
MEDZILLA: *www.medzilla.com*
NURSING SPECTRUM CAREER FITNESS ONLINE:
   www.nursingspectrum.com
PHYSICIANS EMPLOYMENT: *www.physemp.com*
SALUDOS HISPANIS WEB CAREER CENTER:
   www.saludos.com/cguide/hcguide.html

—HOTELS AND RESTAURANTS—
ESCOFFIER ONLINE:
   www.escoffier.com/nonscape/employ.shtml

HUMAN RESOURCES/ RECRUITING
HR WORLD: *www.hrworld.com*
JOBS 4 HR: *www.jobs4hr.com*

—INSURANCE—
THE INSURANCE CAREER CENTER:
   www.connectyou.com/talent
INSURANCE NATIONAL SEARCH:
   www.insurancerecruiters.com/insjobs/jobs.htm

—LEGAL—
LAW NEWS NETWORK: *www.lawjobs.com*
THE LEGAL EMPLOYMENT SEARCH SITE:
   www.legalemploy.com
RIGHT OF WAY EMPLOYMENT JOBLINE:
   www.rightofway.com/jobline.html

—MINING/GAS/PETROLEUM—
OIL-LINK: *www.oillink.com*

—PRINTING AND PUBLISHING—
JOBLINK FOR JOURNALISTS:
   http://ajr.newslink.org/newjoblink.html
JOBS IN JOURNALISM:
   http://eb.journ.latech.edu/jobs.html

—TRANSPORTATION—
INTERNATIONAL SEAFRERS EXCHANGE:
   www.jobxchange.com/xisetoc.com
I-800-DRIVERS:
   http://204.32.45.41/final/seek.htm

—RETAIL—
RETAIL JOBNET: *www.retailjobnet.com*

—UTILITIES—
POWER: *www.powermag.com*

Meta-List

This is a "list of lists" found on the Web, with links to sites and other Internet resources on a particular subject, like job hunting. These lists are good time-savers—they generally include a short description or review of the site or service, so you won't waste time visiting irrelevant or low-quality sites. To access a particular site, you need only click on the site name.

Meta-Lists

Also, check out some job-related meta-lists, which contain links to other on-line career resources. The Career Resource Center *www.careers.org* contains thousands of links, broken down into categories like financial services or computers and engineering. Other meta-lists to consult include Stanford University's JobHunt *www.job-hunt.org* and Purdue University's Center for Career Opportunities Sites for Job Seekers and Employers *www.purdue.edu/student/jobsites.htm*. The Riley Guide *www.dbm.com/jobguide* is another superb source of job-related resources on the Web.

Keyword Search

Another way to find job listings on the Web is to perform a keyword search in a search engine like Yahoo! or Lycos. Try using keywords like "employment opportunities," "job listings," or "positions available." Finally, a company's Web page is often an excellent source for job listings.

Commercial On-line Services

These services, which charge users to access their resources, are more recognizable by their brand names: America Online, CompuServe, Microsoft Network, and Prodigy. All these services provide users with full access to the Internet and the vast employment resources available there. America Online (AOL) and CompuServe are the two largest services and, not surprisingly, have the most resources to offer job seekers.

America Online is considered by many to have the strongest and largest collection of job listings available through a commercial on-line service. CompuServe has dozens of high-quality professional discussion groups that are ideal for networking, as well as a number of searchable business databases that offer in-depth information on tens of thousands of companies. Microsoft has worked to get into the game through acquisitions and partnerships with various Internet software companies, and Prodigy also has several quality resources worth checking out. The smaller services—like Delphi and

Preceding the name of any Web site is a long string of seemingly indecipherable words and letters called a Uniform Resource Locator (URL) or Web address. URLs are difficult to type in every time you want to go somewhere on the Web (forget about trying to memorize them), but they're essential if you want to find information. A URL is a standardized system for finding things like files, directories, or other computers connected to the Web. Knowing what the various letters stand for helps users remember the URLs for particular sites and get a feel for the type of information found there.

Every URL has at least two parts: a protocol and a server, or location. The protocol is how computers exchange information. On the World Wide Web, it's called hypertext transfer protocol, since all documents on the Web are written using hypertext. The server is the name of the computer from which information is received. For instance, in the URL *http://www.occ.com*, the server is "occ," for the main computer at the On-line Career Center. (The "http://" is often omitted when identifying Web addresses, as in this book, where the "http://" is automatically assumed unless noted otherwise.)

The United States has six basic codes to identify the type of server: .com (commercial); .edu (educational); .gov (government); .mil (military); .org (organizational); .net (network).

A two-letter code at the end of a location name, like the .uk in *http://www.demon.co.uk/EuroJobs* signifies an international address. These country codes are similar to the country codes assigned in international telephone numbers.

In addition to the protocol and server, URLs will often include a directory, subdirectory, and file name. These are simply added to the end of a URL and are separated by single slashes. So in the URL *http://espnet.sportszone.com/nfl/news/index.html*, "*espnet.sportszone.com*" is the server, "nfl" is the directory, "news" is the subdirectory, and "index" is the file name. (Sometimes, typing in the full address produces an error message. In this case, it may be necessary to delete all but the basic protocol and server information to get to the Web site, then search the home page for directions to the page you're seeking.)

Genie—lack the quantity of resources presently found on AOL or CompuServe.

The following overview indicates the strengths and weaknesses of each service. To find out how to sign up with a service, visit the Web address listed.

America Online *www.aol.com* is the largest commercial on-line service, with more than 17 million households. America Online is well known for its wide range of home and leisure activities for the entire family. Since the creation of the on-line Career Center in 1989, AOL has been the leader among commercial on-line services in the resources it offers job seekers. AOL's employment databases contain thousands of job listings, all of which use the same fairly simple search engine. These listings can be accessed with the keyword "Career Center." For on-line newspapers, click on "Local Resources"; for federal opportunities, click on "Find a Job," then select a relevant site from the WorkPlace site.

America Online now offers a 4.0 version, which provides the ability to spellcheck e-mail and put pictures in e-mail, switch between AOL screen names without signing off, and offers better Internet capabilities than those which were available through AOL 3.0.

CompuServe *www.compuserve.com* was purchased by America Online in 1998, yet it remains a separate and distinct service. A large portion of CompuServe's two and a half million subscribers are businesses, which is a good indication of the service's orientation. CompuServe has by far the best collection of business resources online, including dozens of business-related databases. Job listings are not the primary reason most job seekers like CompuServe. CompuServe's strengths lie in its research capabilities and professional forums—over nine hundred special groups for people of like ideas and interests to gather and exchange information. The recently released CompuServe 2000 offers many of the features found in the new America Online 4.0.

The Microsoft Network *http://home.microsoft.com* has certainly drawn lots of new subscribers due to the popularity of

Internet service providers allow users to access different areas of the Internet, like the Web or Usenet. Commercial on-line services do this as well but also provide access to their own resources—services developed especially for their subscribers.

ISP

- The primary advantage of a direct Internet connection is that you pay only a monthly service charge to your Internet service provider—all your time spent on-line (provided you have a local-access telephone number) costs only as much as a local phone call.

Commercial On-line Services

- Commercial services remain a favorite of families and, to a lesser extent, businesses. They differ in terms of the services they offer—some are more entertainment-oriented, while others are more business-oriented.
- Many people, especially technical neophytes, find commercial on-line services less intimidating to use than the Internet, because information is well organized and easy to find. Additionally, new users can take advantage of on-line tutorials and guided tours to learn how to use the service most effectively.
- Cost is traditionally the biggest drawback of commercial on-line services. Typically, they offer plans that provide customers with unlimited access for about $20 a month. Most recruit new members by giving away trial memberships. They often waive their monthly fee for one month and offer up to ten free hours of connect time. But be careful! In the case of at least one service, that free month is a *calendar* month, so if you sign up on July 24, for example, you'll actually get only one *week* free. Be sure to ask. If you exceed the free hours, you're assessed the regular hourly charge, usually $2–4.
- Some services charge additional fees for entering certain areas or accessing databases, like CompuServe's Dun & Bradstreet business databases.

On-line Strategies

Know what you want to accomplish before you go on-line. Have an agenda prepared, complete with keywords to search for, or the names and addresses of sites you want to visit. This will save you time and money, because you won't be fumbling around on-line for the right keyword or address. Also, having a plan will lessen the chances that you'll get sidetracked into a discussion group.

On the Web, use search engines like Yahoo!, Excite, and Alta Vista to help you find what you need.

(continued)

Microsoft's Windows 95 and 98 operating systems. MSN Members will want to check out its Career Forum, which features a wealth of job search and career advice, tutorials, and information. Specialized forums include those devoted to nursing and theater professions.

In addition to these major services, the following two services are worth mentioning here—although keep in mind that they were once somewhat more prominent than they are today.

Delphi *www.delphi.com* allows free access to its many forums. Searching the "Business/Finance" forums will lead you to a number of career-related forums, though few have job listings. These forums are best used for networking, finding the occasional job lead, or staying up-to-date on discussions in different fields.

Prodigy *www.prodigy.com* was best known in the past as the favorite on-line service of families with young children, mainly because of its educational resources and games. Today, Prodigy's greatest asset is the easy Internet access it provides for its subscribers. Users can easily switch between Prodigy's services, the Web, Usenet newsgroups, and Gopher. Plus, Prodigy's main menu even contains some hypertext links to Prodigy-sponsored Web sites. *Note:* Prodigy offers *Prodigy Classic*, which provides a wide variety of member services, and *Prodigy Internet*, which is distinguished primarily by its faster and more complete access to the Internet, via partnership with Microsoft's Internet Explorer. Prodigy's Career Channel is a good example of the service's ability to incorporate the World Wide Web into a traditional on-line service.

Usenet Newsgroups

Usenet newsgroups are one of the oldest and most misunderstood areas of the Internet. What was once the exclusive territory of this country's brain trust—academics, scientists, and top government officials—has developed into one of the most popular means of exchanging information on the Internet. At the same time, many new users are scared off by what they perceive as an intimidating Usenet culture. But by ignoring the discussion groups on Usenet, you could miss out on hundreds of potential job opportunities.

Getting Started

Usenet newsgroups are accessible either through your Internet carrier or commercial on-line services. In America Online, try keyword: Newsgroups. If you have a regular Internet connection, you'll need the help of a newsreader, like Trumpet Newsreader, to organize the thousands of available newsgroups and allow you to read and post messages. Many Web browsers, like Netscape Navigator, have a built-in newsreader. Netscape's newsreader is called Netscape News. If you can't find a newsreader on your system, call your Internet provider and ask where to find one.

Once you're in Usenet, read the messages in the newsgroups news.newusers.questions and news.announce.newusers. You'll find answers to the most commonly asked questions regarding Usenet, or you can post your own questions about Usenet. You can also find information like a history of the Internet, rules for posting messages, and hints about the Usenet writing style.

This Is a Test

After reviewing the basics of Usenet, post a test message to the newsgroups alt.test or misc.tests. This test allows you to check whether your newsreader is configured properly. If you can't post test messages, ask your Internet carrier or commercial service provider for assistance. If your test goes off without a hitch, you're all set.

A Few Basic Facts

Before you begin posting messages to dozens of newsgroups on the Web, you need to know a few basic facts about Usenet. Different hierarchies and newsgroups have different tones to their discussions. In general, alt. newsgroups are more casual, while the comp. and sci. newsgroups are more formal and factual. And talk. newsgroups discuss serious subjects in a serious manner. It's important to take the time—at least one week—to get a feel for a newsgroup. This can usually be done simply by reading a few days' worth of messages. Doing this should decrease your chances of posting an inappropriate message.

(continued from previous page)

Try going on-line during off-peak hours, either early morning or late night. Services experience less traffic at these times, so it can be much easier to get through. And be sure you're dialing into a local phone number, to save money on your phone bill.

Don't rely on one particular area of the on-line world for all your job information. The Web is glamorous, but don't forget those old reliables like Usenet newsgroups and Bulletin Board Systems, as well as off-line options like joblines and directories. After you spend some time exploring, you'll probably discover that certain resources work best for you. Narrow your efforts to those areas.

How Usenet Newsgroups Are Structured

Usenet is a collection of thousands of individual discussion groups, called newsgroups, that can be accessed through a direct Internet connection or through commercial on-line services like America Online or CompuServe. Anyone with access may post messages to these newsgroups that are broadcasted to interconnected computer systems. In some newsgroups, the message is sent to a "moderator" for approval before broadcasting. The main purpose of the moderator is to ensure that advertising on newsgroups is kept to a bare minimum. Otherwise, messages are generally left uncensored. Usenet allows millions of users worldwide to discuss any topic imaginable—anarchy, current events, Elvis—you name it. Because newsgroups cover such a wide range of topics, they're broken down by hierarchies, or general categories, that enable you to more easily find the topics you want. The main hierarchies are as follows: alt. (alternative); comp. (computers); humanities. (arts, literature, and other humanities); misc. (miscellaneous); news. (news for Usenet users); rec. (recreation); sci. (science); soc. (social issues); talk. (serious discussions about often controversial issues).

There are also dozens of local hierarchies like swnet. (Sweden) which don't fall into any of the above hierarchies. The local hierarchies have newsgroups that cover subjects like local politics, and some are on-line classifieds, with items like cars, bicycles, or kittens for sale.

Newsgroups can be further broken down according to subject. For instance, alt.backrubs is in the alternative hierarchy under the subject "backrubs." And they can get even more specialized: alt.movies.hitchcock and alt.movies.monster are in the alternative hierarchy, under the general subject "movies," discussing the movies of Alfred Hitchcock and the monster genre, respectively.

Finally, each newsgroup contains discussion threads, which are basically a group of messages relating to the same topic. Every time someone posts a message regarding a new topic, a new thread is started. Ironically, this organizational and hierarchal structure turns many people off to newsgroups. They open their newsreader, find a list of newsgroups—with directories and subdirectories of subdirectories—and immediately close it back up. They decide it's simply not worth it for them to figure out how the whole thing works, so they'll just stick with their commercial services and the World Wide Web. Unfortunately, they're missing out on a real jewel of the Internet.

Types of Jobs

Usenet has over one hundred newsgroups dedicated to job postings, each containing dozens, often hundreds, of listings for full-time and part-time positions and short-term, contract, free-lance, or consulting work. A number of newsgroups are dedicated to postings for contractual labor. The majority of job-related newsgroups are local, but you can find plenty of national ones as well. Many, if not most, of the newsgroups place a heavy emphasis on high-tech positions, like computers and engineering. This is not to say that you won't find postings for accountants or secretaries. But job seekers in less technical fields may need to look a little more carefully.

Searching Newsgroups from the Web

Many of the larger job-search Web sites, like CareerMosaic *www.careermosaic.com* provide a search engine that allows you to simultaneously search more than a hundred employment newsgroups for job openings. For that matter, many search engines enable you to conduct searches on the World Wide Web *or* Usenet. Deja News *www.dejanews.com* which searches Usenet newsgroups and forums rather than Web sites, is an excellent search mechanism in its own right. It allows searches by topic and has an extensive classifieds section.

Major Job-Posting Newsgroups

The newsgroups listed here are specifically for the posting of jobs, but you can often find one or two job postings in a newsgroup related to your profession, so you should check in fairly regularly with those types of groups. For instance, if you're a veterinarian, drop in on alt.med.veterinary, just in case something turns up.

The following list will help you find job openings in your region or field.

FAQs

FAQs are frequently asked questions, posted by most newsgroups, mailing lists, special interest groups, and other on-line services for the benefit of new or inexperienced users.

Advantages of Newsgroup Listings

Because so many newsgroups are local, they're an excellent resource for job seekers interested in relocating. If you want to move to another city or even another country, you can get a feel for the job market and send out your resume.

Newsgroup job listings are also valuable because they contain more information than a traditional newspaper help-wanted advertisement. Generally, these listings spell out the requirements and duties of the position in detail. One big reason for this is cost—employers, employment agencies, and professional recruiters can post job listings free!

Australia
aus.ads.jobs—Jobs available in Australia

Bermuda
bermuda.jobs.offered—Jobs available in Bermuda

Canada
ab.jobs—Job opportunities in Alberta
bc.jobs—Employment opportunities in British Columbia
can.jobs—Jobs available in Canada
kw.jobs—Jobs available in Kitchener-Waterloo
ont.jobs—Jobs available in Ontario
ott.jobs—Job opportunities in Ottawa, Ontario
qc.jobs—Jobs available in Quebec
tor.jobs—Jobs available in Toronto, Ontario

Europe
eunet.jobs—Job opportunities in Europe
euro.jobs—More job opportunities in Europe

Ireland
ie.jobs—Jobs available in Ireland

Israel
iijnet.jobs—Job opportunities in Israel

South Africa
za.ads.jobs—Employment opportunities in South Africa

Sweden
swnet.jobs—Employment opportunities in Sweden

United Kingdom
uk.jobs—Job opportunities in the United Kingdom

United States—Northeast/Mid-Atlantic
balt.jobs—Jobs available in Baltimore, MD
conn.jobs.offered—Jobs available in Connecticut
dc.jobs—Employment opportunities in Washington, DC
ithaca.jobs—Job opportunities in the Ithaca, NY area
li.jobs—Jobs available on Long Island, NY
md.jobs—Jobs available in Maryland and Washington, DC
me.jobs—Jobs available in Maine
ne.jobs—Employment opportunities in New England
ne.jobs.contract—Contract labor in New England
niagara.jobs—Jobs available in the Niagara region of New York
nyc.jobs—Employment opportunities in New York City

nyc.jobs.contract—Contract labor and consulting opportunities in New York City

nyc.jobs.misc—Discussion of the New York City job market

nyc.jobs.offered—More jobs available in New York City

pgh.jobs.offered—Jobs available in the Pittsburgh, PA area

pgh.jobs.wanted—Positions wanted in Pittsburgh, PA

phl.jobs.offered—Job opportunities in Philadelphia, PA

phl.jobs.wanted—Positions wanted in Philadelphia, PA

United States—Southeast

atl.jobs—Employment opportunities in and around Atlanta, GA

fl.jobs—Job opportunities in Florida

hsv.jobs—Jobs available in Huntsville, AL

lou.lft.jobs—Employment opportunities in the Lafayette, LA area

memphis.employment—Employment opportunities in the Memphis, TN area

tnn.jobs—Professional job opportunities in Tennessee

triangle.jobs—Jobs available in the Research Triangle of Raleigh, Durham, and Chapel Hill, NC

uark.jobs—Jobs wanted and available at the University of Arkansas

us.sc.columbia.employment—Jobs available in Columbia, SC

va.jobs—Job opportunities in Virginia

United States—Midwest

chi.jobs—Jobs available in the Chicago, IL area

cle.jobs—Jobs available in the Cleveland, OH area

cmh.jobs—Job opportunities in Columbus, OH

il.jobs.misc—Discussion of the job market in Illinois

il.jobs.offered—Employment opportunities in Illinois

il.jobs.resumes—Resume-posting area for jobs wanted in Illinois

in.jobs—Job opportunities in Indianapolis, IN

mi.jobs—Jobs available in Michigan

milw.jobs—Jobs available in the Milwaukee, WI area

mn.jobs—Employment opportunities in Minnesota

oh.jobs—Jobs available and wanted in Ohio

stl.jobs—Jobs available in St. Louis, MO

United States— West/Southwest

austin.jobs—Jobs available in Austin, TX

az.jobs—Jobs available in Arizona

If It's Too Good to Be True . . .

Beware of job postings that sound too good to be true. A number of sites contain job postings with subjects along the lines of "$$MAKE MONEY AT HOME!$$" Stay clear of those types of postings. Unfortunately, a number of unscrupulous characters try to make money from people who are looking for work. Don't assume a job is legitimate simply because it's posted on the Internet.

Dealer's Choice

Each Internet provider and on-line service decides which newsgroups to carry; therefore, not all newsgroups will be available on every service.

ba.jobs.resumes—Resume-posting area for jobs wanted in the San Francisco Bay Area

co.jobs—Jobs available in Colorado

houston.jobs.offered—Jobs available in Houston, TX

la.jobs—Jobs available in Los Angeles, Ventura, and Orange Counties, CA

nm.jobs—Jobs available in New Mexico

nv.jobs—Job opportunities in Nevada

pdaxs.jobs.computers—Computer-related job opportunities in Portland, OR

pdaxs.jobs.engineering—Engineering and technical job opportunities in Portland, OR

pdaxs.jobs.management—Management opportunities in Portland, OR

pdaxs.jobs.retail—Retail job opportunities in Portland, OR

pdaxs.jobs.sales—Sales opportunities in Portland, OR

sat.jobs—Employment opportunities in the San Antonio, TX area

sdnet.jobs—Jobs available in San Diego, CA

seattle.jobs.offered—Job opportunities in the Seattle, WA area

seattle.jobs.wanted—More job opportunities in Seattle, WA

tx.jobs—Jobs available in Texas

ucb.jobs—Employment opportunities at University of California, Berkeley

vegas.jobs—Jobs available in Las Vegas, NV

wyo.jobs—Employment opportunities in Wyoming

United States—Nationwide

bionet.jobs—Job opportunities in biological science

cit.jobs—Computer-related employment opportunities nationwide

dod.jobs—Employment opportunities with the U.S. Department of Defense

misc.jobs.offered—Job opportunities available nationwide

misc.jobs.offered.entry—Entry-level jobs available nationwide

prg.jobs—Computer programming job opportunities available nationwide

sci.research.postdoc—Job opportunities in postdoctoral scientific research

us.jobs—Jobs available in the United States

us.jobs.contract—Contract labor and consulting opportunities in the United States

us.jobs.misc—Employment opportunities in the United States

us.jobs.offered—More employment opportunities in the United States

Bulletin Board Systems

Bulletin Board Systems are an often overlooked on-line resource for job listings. These days, it seems everyone is more interested in the Web and services like CareerMosaic. But job-related bulletin boards can contain up to 10,000 job listings, and Bulletin Board Systems are much easier to connect to than the Web is.

Basically, a BBS is a computer set up with special software that you access by using a telephone line and the communications software on your computer. BBSs were created as a way for people to exchange information and discuss ideas, much like a Usenet newsgroup. Usenet newsgroups, unlike BBSs, require Internet access.

The biggest problem with BBSs is the difficulty in searching for particular boards. To dial up a BBS, you need to have the phone number beforehand for the specific board you want to access. Unlike the Web, you can't connect to a general BBS and do a search for specific BBSs by name or keyword. If you have access to the Web, try a search engine like Yahoo! or a commercial on-line service like America Online to find bulletin boards in your area. Another good resource is the BBS Corner at . . .
http://www.thedirectory.org/diamond/bbslists.htm

After connecting to a new BBS, you'll be required to register to use the services. This helps to discourage casual users from tying up the phone lines. Since most BBSs have a limited number of phone lines (some may have only four or five), the system operators, or sysops, limit the number of minutes users can spend on the system in one day. The systems listed here allow a maximum of one hour per day.

BBSs of job listings are quickly becoming a thing of the past. The most reliable sites are maintained by the federal government and are also available on the Web.

Exec-PC (414-789-4210)—This is an enormous BBS, with thousands of files available for download, including job listings nationwide. Also contains local access numbers for users dialing long-distance.

Federal Job Opportunities Board (FJOB) (912-757-3125 or by Internet telnet: *telnet://jobentry.opm.gov*)—Sponsored by the U.S.

Tech and Fed Jobs on BBSs

Job seekers interested in finding technical positions or jobs in federal, state, or local governments should take special notice of the number of BBSs dedicated to those areas.

The Meter Is Running

Remember that while these services are free, you'll be charged the cost of a regular long-distance call while connected to the BBS. Try calling during off hours to minimize your phone bill.

Office of Personnel Management, this BBS contains federal job listings and other employment information.

OPM Mainstreet (202-606-4800)—Includes federal job listings from the Office of Personnel Management as well as access to other federal job BBSs and employment-related mailing lists and Usenet newsgroups.

Networking On-line

While some may think that top executives and industry insiders are the only people to benefit from networking, that is not the case. The development of specialized on-line discussion groups has made it easier for all job seekers to meet and interact with other professionals in the same field or industry.

Job seekers should look at three main areas as potential networking resources: Usenet newsgroups, mailing lists, and special interest groups on commercial on-line services. Gopher, Telnet, and the Web don't lend themselves well to networking, since they weren't designed for two-way communication. Newsgroups, mailing lists, and SIGs, on the other hand, were designed expressly for the purpose of disseminating and receiving information. The dozens of career-related discussion groups available cover fields like accounting, education, journalism, and microbiology.

Also keep an eye out for Web sites of industry organizations and associations. While they don't have the ability to accept posted messages, field-specific Web sites are still a good way to stay current with the latest developments in a field.

Don't expect to be besieged with job offers and contact names simply because you logged on to a professional discussion group and posted a message full of intelligence and insight. Networking on-line is a slow process, since in the on-line world, as in real life, relationships don't form overnight. It may be months before any job leads materialize. That's why it's advisable to maintain a continual presence in appropriate discussion groups, even when you're happily employed, since the opportunity of a lifetime may turn up when it's least expected.

Networking on Usenet Newsgroups

Newsgroups are a terrific place for networking, with discussion groups to suit almost every interest. They also tend to have the harshest rules of netiquette, in part because their participants are more technologically savvy than the on-line world as a whole. At the same time, their users are helpful to those who have taken the time to learn the rules.

The following are some that you should know about:

alt.journalism.moderated—Moderated discussion group for journalists

bionet.women-in-bio—Discusses issues relevant to women in the field of biology

bionet.microbiology—Discussion of issues related to microbiology

hepnet.jobs—Discussion of issues relating to high-energy nuclear physics

k12.chat.teacher—Discussion group for teachers, from kindergarten to 12th grade

misc.business.consulting—Discusses the consulting business

misc.education—General discussion of the educational system

misc.jobs.contract—Discussion of both short- and long-term contract labor

misc.jobs.misc—General issues of employment and careers

misc.legal—Discussion group for lawyers and other legal professionals

misc.writing—Discussion group for writers of all types

sci.med—Discussion group for those interested in science and medicine

sci.med.pharmacy—Discusses the pharmaceutical field

sci.research.careers—Discusses the various careers relating to scientific research

Networking with Mailing Lists

Like newsgroups, mailing lists, also known as list-serves or e-mail discussion groups, allow users to post and read messages that contain threads of discussions on various topics. What sets

Advantages of On-line Networking

Discussion group participants often include human resources representatives and hiring managers, who lend their expertise by discussing the qualities they look for in employees. Many recruiters report visiting field-specific discussion groups to look for potential job candidates.

Participating in on-line discussion groups brings far greater exposure than, for instance, going to a meeting of a local industry group. A discussion group's audience is most often nationwide and may even include participants from around the world.

Monitoring discussion groups makes it easy to determine what skills and experiences employers are looking for. It's also a good way to find out which companies are hiring and what the hot topics are in the field.

The Importance of Netiquette

"Netiquette" is a combination of the words "network" (or Internet) and "etiquette," and refers to the widely accepted do's and don'ts for on-line discussion groups. It is essential that new users, or "newbies," be familiar with the netiquette of a group before joining the discussion; otherwise, they may get "flamed" (criticized and ridiculed by established group members).

The easiest way to avoid getting flamed is to spend time observing and reading the group's posted messages before joining the discussion. Each discussion group, especially those on Usenet, have a particular tone and rules. "Lurking" (reading messages but not posting your own) will give you a good sense of the group's personality. This is also a good way to ensure that a group fits your interests.

When you're ready to join the discussion, don't simply post a general message along the lines of "Hi, I'm new here and just wanted to drop in and say hello!" Post a message asking for specific advice or introduce an original thought or comment to the discussion. A boring, generic posting with headers like "Help!" or "Hire Me!" will be ignored at best and will get you flamed at worst. If you do get flamed—something bound to happen to every new user once or twice—just ignore it. Unless you violated a sacred rule of netiquette, someone was probably just having a bad day.

Following are some other basic rules of netiquette, as well as some general guidelines for professional discussion groups:

- Write in complete sentences, and be sure spelling, punctuation, grammar, and capitalization are correct.

- Don't type messages in capital letters, because that's the on-line equivalent of SHOUTING.
- Don't use "emoticons," like :) [happy face] or : ([frown] or common abbreviations like BTW (by the way) or IMHO (in my humble opinion), which are commonly used in recreational discussion groups. These types of cutesy shorthand are out of place in a professional discussion group. For more information, visit the following sites:

  www.mire.co.uk/emote.html
  www.netsurf.org/~violet/Smileys
  www.utopiasw.demon.co.uk/emoticon.htm
  www.ultranet.com/support/netiquette/
    emoticons.shtml
  www.accessmagazine.com/scripts/articles.
    cfm?articleid=265

- Understand the appropriate times to post or e-mail a reply to a particular message. Many new and experienced users alike are often unsure of when to direct an e-mail to the message's author and when a reply should be posted to the group. In general, post a reply if your message is something the group as a whole could appreciate and learn from, but use e-mail if your comment concerns only the poster. This is important because no one wants to participate in a discussion that is little more than a dialogue between two or three people.
- Use your best manners. Respect and be tolerant of others' ideas and opinions.

mailing lists apart from newsgroups is that instead of users logging in to a specific group and posting and reading messages on-line, subscribers both receive new messages and post messages to the group via e-mail. Many users like mailing lists because it's possible to monitor discussion groups simply by checking one's e-mail.

To subscribe to a mailing list, send an e-mail to the list's system administrator. The administrator makes sure all messages are sent to subscribers and moderates the content, ensuring that postings are relevant to the topic. Like other discussion groups, each mailing list has its own rules, so be sure to contact the administrator for details.

Tens of thousands of mailing lists cover subjects like arts, business, health, politics, and religion. To find the ones that match your interests, consult one of the following on-line directories. Each directory contains contact information, like the system administrator's e-mail address, for over 50,000 mailing lists.

Liszt: The Mailing List Directory (www.liszt.com) claims to be the largest directory of mailing lists, and it just may be, with 84,792 lists available for searching. The site also allows you to search by keywords.

Publicly Accessible Mailing Lists (www.neosoft.com/ internet/paml) contains hundreds of subject classifications and is searchable by name or subject. Check under "jobs" or "employment" for job-related mailing lists, but check out lists in your field as well. This list is also posted to the Usenet newsgroups news.lists and news.answers around the end of each month.

Networking through Special Interest Groups (SIGs)

SIGs are found only on commercial on-line services, like America Online, CompuServe, and Prodigy. These groups are called different names on each service—forums, bulletin boards (not to be confused with Bulletin Board Systems), roundtables—and are known collectively as SIGs.

SIGs differ from newsgroups in a number of ways. First, SIGs have smaller audiences, because fewer people subscribe to commercial on-line services than have access to the Internet. Also, most SIGs have moderators, called sysops, or system operators, who monitor the discussions to be sure that the comments are relevant to the specific group. They also make sure the discussions don't get out of hand—which, despite netiquette, can occasionally happen. And in most special interest groups, the main subject is subdivided into smaller directories, which makes it easy to pinpoint the topic you want to discuss.

If you can't find a forum here that fits your interests, browse the newsgroups and mailing lists directories for a group that seems more appropriate.

America Online

In addition its outstanding career resources, America Online has a number of forums for networking with other professionals. Most of the services described in this section are not forums in the strictest sense, because they offer other valuable information in addition to their message boards. To find a complete list of America Online special interest groups, search for the keywords "clubs" and "forums" in the Directory of Services.

Health Professionals Network (Keyword: HRS or Better Health). Choose "Health Professionals Network" from the main menu. The Network contains over seventy-five topics for all types of health professionals, including physicians, physician assistants, and physical therapists.

Legal Information Network (Keyword: LIN) offers networking resources for paralegals, family law specialists, social security specialists, women lawyers, and law students.

Professionals Forum (Keyword: places). P.L.A.C.E.S. is a discussion group for professionals in all disciplines including landscape, architecture, construction, engineering, education, financial services, and many more.

The Teacher's Lounge (Keyword: teacher's lounge). This SIG allows teachers of kindergarten through the twelfth grade to trade ideas and discuss relevant issues.

The Writers Club (Keyword: writers) offers writers the opportunity to exchange information, like how to find a publisher or secure freelance work, and offers writing workshops and advice.

CompuServe

With over nine hundred forums, CompuServe has by far the most discussion groups for professionals, with forums in a wide range of fields. CompuServe is well known for the quality of its forums and the participants therein. Its forums have three basic components: the message section, where users can post and read messages; conference areas that allow users to participate in real-time chats and scheduled meetings or conferences with other users; and libraries, which enable users to search for archival information like conference transcripts and articles related to the forum's topic. Most forums require you to join them, but there is no fee for membership. Often, forums may restrict nonmember access; in some, for instance, you may not have access to the libraries or conference rooms if you haven't joined.

Following is a list of some of the best professional forums CompuServe offers. To find additional forums, select Find from the Services menu or click on the Index icon and type in your desired subject area. You'll then be presented with a list of related forums.

Architecture & Building Forum (Go: ArchBldg) allows for discussion and the exchange of information between architectural professionals.

Broadcast Professionals Forum (Go: BPForum) allows professionals in radio and television to share news and views about the industry.

Computer Consultants (Go: Consult) allows computer professionals to discuss issues related to the field, including networking and business development.

Court Reporters Forum (Go: Crforum) is a networking forum for court reporters that includes information from the National Court Reporters Association and the *Journal of Court Reporting*.

Desktop Publishing Forum (Go: DTP) is a discussion group for professionals in the field of electronic publishing, design, writing, and printing.

Education Forum (Go: Edforum) is open to teachers at all levels, administrators, college and university personnel, and educational publishers for the discussion of issues relevant to education.

Health Professionals Forum (Go: MedSIG) is open to all professionals in the health-care field to discuss medical issues and exchange information regarding such topics as new advances in medicine.

Journalism Forum (Go: Jforum) is a place for journalists of all kinds—print, radio, television, even freelancers. You can discuss issues of the day, look for jobs, and talk about the business of news.

Photo Professionals (Go: Photopro). Imaging professionals and all those interested in entering the field are welcome to join in a wide range of discussions regarding imaging and photography.

ProPublishing Forum (Go: Propub) is open to anyone in publishing or the graphic arts to discuss issues relating to the field. This forum charges members a small monthly fee.

Public Relations Forum (Go: Prsig). This discussion group for marketing and PR professionals is great for networking and finding contacts. It also offers its members a huge library of information.

Writers Forum (Go: Writers). Here, writers of all experience levels can make contacts, get advice, receive support, or have their work critiqued. This site is especially helpful for writers who are looking to break into freelancing.

Microsoft Network

The Microsoft Network has been playing catch-up in many on-line service areas. However, one forum is definitely worth checking out for job seekers: Career Forum (Go: Careers), featuring career chats, answers to specific questions, and advice from experts. Job-search tips are also available.

CHAPTER 11

CD-ROM Job Search

DATE:

TO DO — ACTION LIST

Business directories on CD-ROM contain a tremendous amount of information for anyone looking for a job. Most give you the same basic information: company name, description, address, phone and fax numbers, and number of employees. Virtually all directories list one or more contacts, so you know exactly whom to call for information or where to send your resume. Others give you the name of the parent company or subsidiaries, e-mail or Web site address, product information, biographical information on key personnel, and financial information. Some directories are broad and include companies of all sizes and industries; others are specialized, according to industry, size, or company revenue.

Search Options

Standard & Poor's Register alone has over fifty search possibilities. The most basic are by geographic location or industry, so you can look for all the companies in your field that are located in your city or state. Other common search options are company size or revenue, SIC (which stands for Standard Industrial Classification), or zip code. Some databases can be searched by job title, parent company name, stock symbol, or where key personnel went to undergraduate or graduate school. In the *Martindale-Hubbell Law Directory*, for instance, you could search for the names of all attorneys born in 1950 who went to Harvard Law School.

The Databases

Most of these databases cost upwards of $500 and are designed for use by businesses or libraries, so don't expect to find them at your local software store. Nor will every library have every database. Call to determine what resources are available or where you can get them. Many can be found in the offices of career counselors or outplacement specialists and are used as part of their service.

American Big Businesses Directory CD-ROM (800-555-5211) is available through InfoUSA. This resource provides profiles of 189,000 privately and publicly held companies employing over 100 people. The CD-ROM contains company descriptions that include company type, industry, products, and sales information. Also included are contact names for each company, with a total of over 645,000. You can search by industry, SIC, sales volume, employee size, or zip code. Available only through libraries. Note: The company information on this CD-ROM is formatted in all capital letters.

American Business Disc (800-555-5211) is available through InfoUSA. This CD-ROM contains extensive information on more than ten million U.S. companies. The profiles provide contact information, including contact name and title, as well as the industry and company size, in terms of both employee size and sales volume. The profiles also indicate whether a company is public or private, as well as detailed information regarding the company's products. A number of search methods, including key word searches by industry, SIC, geographic area, or number of employees. Available only through libraries.

American Manufacturer's Directory (800-555-5211) is available through InfoUSA and lists over 622,000 manufacturing companies with 20 or more employees. This resource contains product and sales information, company size, and a key contact name for each company. The CD-ROM is searchable by region, SIC, sales volume, employee size, or zip code. Note: The print version of this product lists 161,000 companies, while the CD-ROM lists all 622,000 companies; however, the directory and disk are sold as a set, Available only through libraries.

Corptech EXPLORE Database on CD-ROM

www.corptech.com contains detailed descriptions of over 50,000 mostly private technology companies. It also lists the names and titles of executives—CEOs, sales managers, R&D managers, and human resources professionals. Web and e-mail addresses are also available. In addition to contact information, job seekers can find detailed information about each company's products or services and annual revenues. The CorpTech EXPLORE Database also lists both the number of current employees and the number of employees one year prior. Some companies also list the number of employees they project having on staff in one year. Job seekers can

Know What You're Looking For

Before using an employer database, have a pretty clear picture of the type of company you want to work for. While employer databases can be great tools for job seekers, they're virtually worthless if you have no idea what you want to do.

search the database using more than thirty-three different criteria, such as the type of company, geographic location, or sales revenue. You can also create a more personalized search by entering in criteria for all fields. This database can be found in many public and university libraries.

D&B Million Dollar Database *www.dnbmdd.com* provides information on over 1.25 million companies covering many different industries. The listings include information on the number of employees, sales volume, name of the parent company, and the corporate headquarters or branch locations. Also included are the names and titles of top executives, as well as biographical information, including education and career background. Searches can be done by location, industry, SIC, or executive biography. This database, which is updated quarterly, can be found at many colleges and universities, as well as some public libraries.

Gale Business Resources CD-ROM (800/877-GALE) is geared more towards businesses than job hunters. However, there is still plenty of valuable information for job seekers within the database. The CD-Rom is compiled from several different databases, and contains information on more than 448,000 companies worldwide. Job seekers can find contact names, number of employees, and type of industry. Also included is information on company products and revenues. This product is available at public and university libraries.

Harris Database CD-ROM *www.harrisinfo.com/aboutdat.htm.* Produced by Harris InfoSource, this database of manufacturers profiles more than 360,000 companies. Although the majority of the companies listed are in the United States, the database also provides listings for some companies in other countries. Besides contact information, job seekers can find the number of employees, plant size, and sales revenue. Updated annually, this directory is available in CD-ROM format, and can be found in libraries and universities. Also available in smaller regional or state editions.

Hoover's Company Capsules on CD-ROM
www.hoovers.com/hoov/store/electronic_frame.html gives in-depth profiles of more than 11,000 companies and 30,000 executives. The in-depth corporate profiles include detailed information on the company history, products, and growth prospects. The profiles also include information taken from company financial statements. Subsidiary profiles include information on industry averages and projected growth for the industry. Updated quarterly, Hoover's Company Capsules on CD-ROM can be found at public and university libraries.

Martindale-Hubbell Law Directory on CD-ROM
www.martindale.com/products/law_dir_cd.html is a directory of over 900,000 lawyers and law firms. Searches are possible using more than twenty criteria, including area of practice, firm name, law school attended, and field of law. While it does list some international law firms, the database consists mainly of U.S. firms. This CD-ROM is available for job seekers at many law libraries, as well as some university and public libraries.

Moody's Company Data
www.fisonline.com. This CD-ROM has detailed listings for over 10,000 publicly traded companies. In addition to information such as industry, company address, or phone and fax numbers, each listing includes the names and titles of top officers, company size, number of shareholders, corporate history, subsidiaries, and financial statements. Job seekers can conduct searches by region, SIC, industry, or earnings. This CD-ROM is updated monthly. Available at public and university libraries.

Standard & Poor's Compustat Research Insight CD-ROM
www.compustat.com/products/univ_mkt.htm is priced at $79/semester, or $129/year for students at schools with a network subscription. This database lists thousands of top international companies, including more than 10,000 active and 9,000 inactive companies, and up to twenty years of market history for those companies. This database is available through university libraries.

CALL HEAD HUNTER

ADS
FAX RESUMES

LL HEAD HUNTER

PICK UP SUIT AT
DRY CLEAN

SEND THANK Y
NOTE

ACTION LIST

FORMATIO
RNS RES
R OF

RVIE
URN

9 A.M.
INTERVIEW WITH THOM TAN
AT NARD INC.

WEDNESDAY Mercredi/Mittwoch/Me

EARCH AGEN

THURSDAY Jeudi/Donnerstag/Gio

8 A.M.
MEET WITH BILL MACNEILL
DIRECTOR OF CAREER PLANNING
AT BIG RED UNIVERSITY

FRIDAY Vendredi/Freitag/Venerdi/Vi

SATURDAY Samedi/Samstag/Sabato/Sõh

TO DO

ACTION LIST
DATE:

GET SUNDAY NEWSPAPER
WANT-ADS
MAIL/FAX RESUMES ✓

CALL HEAD HUNTER ✓

PICK UP SUIT AT
DRY CLEANERS ✓

SEND THANK YOU
NOTES

ACTION LIST

YEAR

One Page Per Day (Un

HEAD HUNTER

11 INFORMATIONAL MEETING
    BURNS RESEARCH AGENCY
    TOUR OF FACILITY

12 INTERVIEW WITH KARA FORRE
1   AT BURNS RESEARCH AGENC

2

3   COMMUTE HOME
    * SEND THANK YOU NOT
4   GO TO CAREETZ FAIR

5

6

TUESDAY Ma

TOUR, IN
EARCH AGE

NESDAY Mercredi/Mittwoch/Me

WITH THOM TANI
ENC.

THURSDAY Jeudi/Donnerstag/Giou

W. CAREERCITY.COM

CHAPTER 12

Employment Services

M any people turn to temporary agencies, permanent employment agencies, or executive recruiters to assist them in their respective job searches. At their best, these resources can be a valuable friend—it's comforting to know that someone is putting his or her wealth of experience and contacts to work for you. At their worst, they're more of a friend to the employer or to more experienced recruits than to you personally. For this reason, it's best not to rely on them exclusively.

Employment services fall into several categories, each of which is described below.

Temporary Employment Agencies

Temporary, or "temp," agencies can be a viable option. Often they specialize in clerical and support work, but it's becoming increasingly common to find temporary assignments in other areas, like accounting or computer programming. Working on temporary assignments will provide you with additional income during your job search and will add experience to your resume. It may also provide valuable business contacts or lead to permanent job opportunities.

Temporary agencies are listed in *The JobBank Guide to Employment Services* (Adams Media Corporation), found at your local public library. If you choose to go through a temp agency, be prepared to take a number of tests before a job placement is potentially made.

Contract Services Firms

Firms that place individuals on a contract basis commonly receive job orders from client companies for positions that can last anywhere from a month to over a year. Most often, contract services firms specialize in placing technical professionals, though some do specialize in other fields, including clerical and office support. Most contract services firms don't charge a fee to the candidate.

For more information on contract services, visit *Contract Employment Weekly* at *www.ceweekly.com*

Permanent Employment Agencies

Permanent employment agencies are commissioned by employers to find qualified candidates for job openings. The catch is that their main responsibility is to meet the employer's needs—not necessarily to find a suitable job for the candidate.

This is not to say that permanent employment agencies should be ruled out altogether. Permanent employment agencies specializing in specific industries can be useful for experienced professionals. However, they're not always a good choice for entry-level job seekers. Some will try to steer inexperienced candidates in an unwanted direction or offer little more than clerical placement to experienced applicants. Others charge a fee for their services—a condition that job seekers should always ask about up front.

Some permanent employment agencies dispute the criticisms mentioned above. As one recruiter puts it, "Our responsibilities are to the applicant and the employer equally, because without one, we'll lose the other." She also maintains that entry-level people are desirable, saying that "as they grow, we grow, too, so we aim to move them up the ranks."

Finding an Agency

If you decide to register with an agency, your best bet is to find one recommended by a friend or associate. Barring that, names of agencies across the country can be found in *The Adams Executive Recruiters Almanac* (Adams Media Corporation) or *The JobBank Guide to Employment Services* (Adams Media Corporation). Or you can contact the National Association of Personnel Services (NAPS) at 703-684-0180.

Making Contact

Call the firm to find out if it specializes in your area of expertise and how it will go about marketing your qualifications. After selecting a few agencies, send each one a resume with a cover letter. Make a follow-up call a week or two later and try to

Make Sure It's for Real

Be aware that there are an increasing number of bogus employment service firms, often advertising in newspapers and magazines. These "services" promise even inexperienced job seekers top salaries in exciting careers—all for a sizable fee. Others use expensive 900-prefix numbers that job seekers are encouraged to call. Unfortunately, most people find out too late that the job they were promised doesn't exist. Check out any agency you're interested in with the local chapter of the Better Business Bureau (BBB).

schedule an interview. Once again, be prepared to take a battery of tests.

Above all, don't expect too much. Only a small portion of all professional, managerial, and executive jobs are listed with these agencies. Use them as an addition to your job-search campaign, not a centerpiece.

Executive Search Firms

Also known as "headhunters," executive search firms seek out and carefully screen (and weed out) candidates, typically for high-salaried technical, executive, and managerial positions (although lower-salaried positions are handled by many such firms as well). These firms are paid by the employer; the candidate is generally not charged a fee. Unlike permanent employment agencies, they often approach candidates directly, rather than waiting for candidates to approach them. Some prefer to deal with employed candidates.

Whether you're employed or not, don't contact an executive search firm if you aren't ready to look for a job. If a recruiter tries to place you right away and finds you aren't really looking yet, it's unlikely he or she will spend much time with you in the future.

Types of Executive Search Firms

There are two basic types of executive search firms—retainer-based and contingency-based. **Essentially, retainer firms are hired by a client company for a search and paid a fee by the client company, regardless of whether a placement is made. Contingency firms receive payment from the client company only when their candidate is hired. Some firms conduct searches of both types.** The fee is typically 20 to 35 percent of the first year's salary, with retainer firm fees at the higher end of that scale, according to Ivan Samuels, president of Abbott's of Boston, an executive search firm that conducts both types of searches.

Retainer Firms

Generally, companies use retainer firms to fill senior-level positions, with salaries over $60,000. In most cases, a company will

hire only one retainer firm to fill a given position, and part of the process is a thorough, on-site visit by the search firm to the client company, so the recruiter can check out the operation. These search firms are recommended for a highly experienced professional seeking a job in his or her current field.

Confidentiality is more secure with these firms, since a recruiter may use your file only in consideration for one job at a time, and most retainer firms will not freely circulate your resume without permission. This is particularly important to a job seeker who is currently employed and insists on absolute discretion. If that's the case, make sure you don't contact a retainer firm used by your current employer.

Contingency Firms

Contingency firms make placements that cover a broader salary range, so these firms are preferable for someone seeking a junior or mid-level position. Unlike retainer firms, contingency firms may be competing with other firms to fill a particular opening. As a result, they can be quicker and more responsive to your job search. In addition, a contingency firm will distribute your resume more widely. Some require your permission before sending your resume to a company; others ask that you trust their discretion. Inquire about this with your recruiter at the outset, and choose according to your needs.

Finding an Agency

Look for firms that specialize in your field of interest or expertise as well as generalist firms that conduct searches in a variety of fields. You don't need to limit yourself to firms in your geographic area, as many firms operate nationally or internationally. Once you've chosen the specific recruiter or recruiters to contact, keep in mind that they're working for the companies that hire them, not for you. Attempting to fill a position—especially among fierce competition with other firms—means your best interests may not be the recruiter's only priority. For this reason, contact as many search firms as possible to increase your chances of finding your ideal position.

Making Contact

A phone call is your first step, during which you should speak with a recruiter and exchange all relevant information. Ask whether they operate on a retainer or contingency basis (or both) and some brief questions, if you have any, regarding the firm's procedures. Offer the recruiter information about your employment history and the type of work you're seeking. Make sure you sound enthusiastic but not pushy. The recruiter will ask you to send a resume and cover letter.

Occasionally the recruiter will arrange to meet with you, but most often this won't occur until he or she has received your resume and found a potential match. James E. Slate, president of F-O-R-T-U-N-E Personnel Consultants, advises that you generally not expect an abundance of personal attention at the beginning of the relationship with your recruiter, particularly with a large firm that works nationally and does most of its work over the phone. You should, however, use your recruiter's inside knowledge to your best advantage. Some recruiters will coach you before an interview, and many are open to giving you all the facts they know about a client company.

Keep in mind that it's common for recruiters to search for positions in other states. For example, recruiters in Boston sometimes look for candidates to fill positions in New York City, and the reverse is true as well. Names of search firms nationwide can be found in *The Adams Executive Recruiters Almanac* or *The JobBank Guide to Employment Services*, or by contacting the Association of Executive Search Consultants (AESC) at 212-398-9556. You may also wish to contact Top Echelon *www.topechelon.com* a cooperative placement networking service of recruiting firms.

Letter to an Executive Search Firm

Although executive search firms actively recruit candidates for client companies, don't let this discourage you from writing. A well-crafted cover letter can alert an otherwise unknowing recruiter to your availability. Remember, this is your chance to shine. Highlight your most impressive accomplishments and attributes and briefly summarize all relevant experience. If you have certain preferences, like geographic location, travel, and salary, mention them in your cover letter. Generally, if executive search firms are interested, they'll call you, so keep your closing succinct.

"Cold" Cover Letter to an Executive Search Firm

1441 Pistash Park
Flandreau, SD 57028
March 4, 1995

Heidi Button
Director
First Search Corporation
1140 Main Street
Chicago, IL 60605

Dear Ms. Button:

During the past ten years I have worked in the liability insurance field, in positions ranging from transcriber to senior field claims representative. Currently, I am seeking a new position with an underwriter or a corporate liability insurance department with a need for expertise in claims settlement, from fact-finding analysis to negotiation.

I am hoping that among your clients, one or two may be looking for someone knowledgeable in the area of corporate liability insurance. If so, I would like to explore the opportunity. I can be reached at (605) 555-5555.

I look forward to hearing from you.

Sincerely,

Jennifer-Anne Kelly

Jennifer-Anne Kelly

Outplacement Services

Unlike many nonprofit organizations that offer free or inexpensive job-counseling services (see below), for-profit career or outplacement counseling services (also called "employment marketing services") can charge a broad range of fees, depending on the services they provide. These include career counseling, outplacement, resume development and writing, interview preparation, assessment testing, and various workshops.

Whereas employers pay agencies, *you* pay an outplacement service (often thousands of dollars) to help you find a job. These companies will send out letters, make phone calls for you, and basically do the things you should be doing in your job search. If you go out and do it yourself, not only will you save a great deal of money, you'll gain important experience and probably make invaluable contacts.

Outplacement fees can range from $170 to over $7,000! As results are not guaranteed, you may want to check on a firm's reputation through the local Better Business Bureau.

Community Agencies

Many nonprofit organizations—colleges, universities, private associations—offer free or inexpensive counseling, career development, and job placement services. Often these services are targeted to a particular group—for example, women, minorities, the blind, and the disabled. Many cities and towns have commissions that provide services for these special groups.

For Students and Recent Graduates

Employment Services

If you're just starting out fresh from academia, don't expect headhunters to help you out. Executive search firms are paid by employers, and your lack of professional experience puts you straight into the unprofitable bin. Consider this resource later on down the line, once you've added some kick to your resume.

Permanent employment agencies are probably more your speed at this career juncture. The reputable agencies are usually compensated by employers, so if you're asked to pay up front, make for the door.

Temporary agencies are a great way to get in on the corporate ground floor; just make sure you request placement with a company specializing in your area of interest. Once so installed, you can make all the right contacts while watching for a more upscale position to become available.

Outplacement Services

Outplacement services were discussed previously. If you really feel you need help finding a job and don't know where to turn, try your college placement office before you sign on with an outplacement service. Most colleges will assist you in your job search even if you graduated some time ago.

Agencies for Special Groups

Women:
Wider Opportunities for Women
www.w-org-w.org

Minorities:
National Association for the Advancement of Colored People (NAACP)
www.naacp.org

The blind:
Job Opportunities for the Blind Program
Phone: 410-659-9314

The disabled:
President's Committee on Employment of People with Disabilities
Phone: 202-376-6200

CALL HEAD HUNTER

INFORMATIO
URNS RES
UR OF

RVIE
URN

ADS
FAX RESUMES

LL HEAD HUNTER

PICK UP SUIT AT
DRY CLEAN

SEND THANK
NOTE

9 A.M.
INTERVIEW WITH THOM TAN
AT NARD INC.

WEDNESDAY Mercredi/Mittwoch/
THURSDAY Jeudi/Donnerstag/Gi

8 A.M.
MEET WITH BILL MACNEILL
DIRECTOR OF CAREER PLANNING
AT BIG RED UNIVERSITY

FRIDAY Vendredi/Freitag/Venerdi/
SATURDAY Samedi/Samstag/Sabato/Sch

TO DO

GET SUNDAY NEWSPAPER
WANT-ADS
MAIL/FAX RESUMES ✓

CALL HEAD HUNTER ✓

PICK UP SUIT AT
DRY CLEANERS ✓

SEND THANK YOU
NOTES

HEAD HUNTER

One Page—1

11 INFORMATIONAL MEETING
BURNS RESEARCH AGENCY
TOUR OF FACILITY

12 INTERVIEW WITH KARA FOR
AT BURNS RESEARCH AGEN

1

2

3 COMMUTE HOME
* SEND THANK YOU NO
GO TO CAREER FAIR

4

5

6

TUESDAY Ma

TOUR, IN
EARCH AGE.

NESDAY Mercredi/Mittwoch/Me

WITH THOM TAN
NC.

WW.CAREERCITY.COM

THURSDAY Jeudi/Donner

11 INFORMATIONAL M...
BURNS RESEARCH A...
12 TOUR OF FACILITY

1 INTERVIEW WITH KARA H...
AT BURNS RESEARCH AGE...

2

3 Commute Home
* SEND THANK YOU NOTE
4 GO TO CAREER FAIR

5

9

...BALL HEAD HUNTE...

INFORMATIONAL MEE...
...URNS RESEARCH AGE...
...R OF FACILITY

...EW WITH KARA F...
...RESEARCH A...

1 A.M. - 3 P.M.
NFO. MEETING, TO...
- BURNS RESEAR...

9 A.M. WEDNESDAY
NTERVIEW WITH ...
...T NARD INC.

THURSDA...

8 A.M. FRIDAY
MEET WITH BILL ...
DIRECTOR OF CAREER P...
AT BIG RED UNIV...
SATURDAY

DATE:

TO DO ACTION LIST

CHAPTER 13

Researching Companies

Once you've scheduled an interview with a targeted company, you'll need to begin your in-depth research. To prepare yourself for an interview, you need to know the company's products, types of customers, subsidiaries, parent company, corporate headquarters or regional locations, rank in the industry, sales and profit trends, whether the company is publicly or privately held, and current plans. You need to find out everything you can about the industry, the firm's principal competitors and their relative performance, and the direction in which the industry and its leaders are headed.

While many electronic employer databases will give you much of this information, you need to take your research a step further. Reading relevant articles about the company or the industry will enable you to enter your interview with more confidence. Also, the interviewer will be impressed if you can speak intelligently about industry trends or the company's plans.

Unless you're interviewing with a high-profile corporation, company and industry news can be hard to find. This is especially true if you have an interview in a distant city or state, for which you're less likely to have access to local information.

The information you need is available on business periodical databases, on the Internet, and directly from Adams Media Corporation, the publisher of this book and the *JobBank* series. Each of these sources is discussed below.

Business Periodical Databases

Business periodical databases can contain hundreds of thousands of articles on business and industry. Most contain either full articles or abstracts (summaries) from hundreds of national, regional, and local business publications. From these articles, you can learn about what products a company is developing, marketing strategies, personnel moves, and financial condition—all the information you should know for an interview. Since these databases are updated as often as once a month, you'll find the most current information. You can also find articles dating back one or two years, which allows you to track a company's performance. Other databases contain financial statements, Securities and Exchange Commission filings, or press releases from individual companies.

As with electronic employer databases, you can search business periodical databases in a number of ways: by company name, industry, region, or topic. Conducting a topic or industry search can often be a way to learn valuable information about a company's market share and competitors.

Look for these business periodical databases at your local public library. Not every library will have every database. Call to determine what resources are available or to find out where you can get them. Most colleges and university libraries carry them as well.

ABI/Inform Global *www.bellhowell.infolearning.com* is a CD-ROM database containing abstracts from over 1,000 international business periodicals, including business, management, industry, and trade publications. This database is helpful to job seekers looking for information on a national level about hundreds of different industries. You can find information regarding industry trends, business conditions, products and services, and a number of other topics. The abstracts range from 25–150 words and contain bibliographic citations to more in-depth information. ABI/Inform can be searched by company, industry, topic, or region and is updated monthly.

Business and Company ProFile (800-419-0313) contains information on business topics like management, international business, business law, mergers and acquisitions, marketing and advertising, small and emerging companies, and new technologies and products. The database also contains directory information (name, address, phone number, and more) for over 180,000 public and private companies. It contains abstracts of approximately 900 business periodicals, including full text for 460 of those. Some of the journals included are the *Wall Street Journal*, the *New York Times* financial section, local business journals, and economic publications, as well as trade publications in every industry segment that report on developments at over 50,000 companies. The database can be searched by keywords or subject.

Business Dateline Ondisc (800-521-0600) is a source for regional and local business news.

It contains full articles from more than 450 local and regional publications, including the business sections of local daily newspapers, and business newswire services. Job seekers can learn in detail about the growth prospects for smaller, local companies in a wide range of industries as well as the economic outlook for the region or state. The database helps job seekers target a particular area that's experiencing solid growth and determine which companies are hiring and expanding. Updated monthly, the database can be searched by company, industry, region, or topic.

Investext on InfoTrac (800-419-0313) is compiled by the Information Access Company, the same company that produces Business and Company ProFile. The Investext database is a valuable resource for detailed financial information about a company. Job seekers can use it to analyze a company's line of business, locate current and historical financial information, or perform competitive analysis on products and companies. The database contains indexing and full text of more than 50,000 company and industry reports on more than 11,000 U.S. and international companies, and is searchable by both subject and keywords. The reports are compiled by 300 leading Wall Street, regional, and international brokerage, investment bank, and research firms in the United States, Canada, Europe, and Asia.

JobBank List Service (800-872-5627), e-mail: jobbank@adamsonline.com, Web site: *www.adamsjobbank.com* A compilation of company information derived from the *JobBank* series of career directories. This database of private and public companies nationwide is frequently updated to ensure the most current information and a high degree of accuracy. Company information is provided in ASCII comma-quote-delimited text format either by e-mail or on disk.

Each order is quickly compiled according to criteria determined through a consultation (by phone or e-mail) between a *JobBank* editor and the customer. There is no minimum order. Criteria for companies or employment agencies can be specified geographically, by industry, by occupation, or any variation/combination desired by the customer.

The *JobBank List Service* contains the most current information on public and private companies nationwide. Industries covered include:

Accounting and Management Consulting; Advertising, Marketing, and Public Relations; Aerospace; Apparel, Fashion, and Textiles; Architecture, Construction, and Engineering; Arts, Entertainment, Sports, and Recreation; Automotive; Banking/Savings and Loans; Biotechnology, Pharmaceutical, and Scientific R&D; Charities and Social Services; Chemicals/Rubber and Plastics; Communications: Telecommunications and Broadcasting; Computer Hardware, Software, and Services; Educational Services; Electronic/Industrial Electrical Equipment; Environmental and Waste Management Services; Fabricated/Primary Metals and Products; Financial Services; Food and Beverages/Agriculture; Government; Health Care: Services, Equipment and Products; Hotels and Restaurants; Insurance; Manufacturing; Mining/Gas/Petroleum/Energy; Paper and Wood Products; Printing and Publishing; Real Estate; Retail; Stone, Glass, Clay, and Concrete Products; Transportation; Utilities; Miscellaneous Wholesaling; and many others.

Internet

One of the increasingly popular tools for researching companies is the Internet. Company Web sites, while not always up-to-date, generally contain a lot of helpful information. CompuServe, in particular, has many excellent resources for researching both national and international companies. Usenet newsgroups, Telnet, or Gopher sites, though extremely helpful in other areas of job hunting, generally contain little information that would be useful in researching companies and potential employers.

What Information Do You Need?

Which databases you search depends on the information you're seeking. If you'd like to find a list of all financial consulting firms in Chicago, a database like the Web's Big Book is most likely adequate. But if you're preparing for a job interview as a high-level financial analyst, you need to have a solid grasp of the company's finances. You can easily gather that type of information through a service like Dun & Bradstreet.

Some information comes in the form of employer databases, where you can conduct searches according to criteria like geographic location and industry. Many Web sites contain a list of companies, with links to each company's own home page. General job-hunting sites, like Monster.com, include employer profiles of companies with listings at the site. Other databases, both on the Web and through commercial on-line services, contain much more in-depth information regarding a company's history, financial standing, or products and services.

Compare the Results

Companies are often listed in two or more databases. You may be tempted to disregard the additional information and move on to a company you don't have information about. However, it's wise to compare the information contained in the different databases. If the information is consistent, it's probably correct. If the two sources conflict, try to find a third source. Different databases also contain different types of information—one may have financial information, another may have a list of the chief executives. Take care to note the timeliness of the information; most on-line databases are updated frequently, but this isn't always true.

On-line Databases

New resources for researching potential employers pop up regularly on the Web. To find additional resources, use a search engine like Yahoo! or AltaVista and type in the keyword "companies" or "employers." You can also tap into job-search meta-lists, like Purdue University's Center for Career Opportunities Sites for Job Seekers and Employers *www.purdue.edu/student/jobsites.htm*, which provides links to numerous other career resources.

Listed below are some databases that can be searched for employers. They can be accessed free, although others may charge a small fee.

Researching companies on-line has many advantages:

• First is convenience: you can search right from your own home instead of going to the library or employment service.

• Second, you can research companies whenever it's convenient to you—the Internet is available twenty-four hours a day. This convenience is especially valuable for last-minute job interviews.

    Say you receive a call at three o'clock asking you to come in for an interview the next day. In the past, you might have panicked because you wouldn't have had adequate time for research. But with the Internet, the information is right at your fingertips, with many companies updating their information daily. Finally, researching companies can go much faster on the Internet. Once you know where to look, the information is only a few keystrokes away. You no longer have to carve out a large part of your day to go to the library and do research.

As for disadvantages, well, there really aren't that many:

• In most cases, accessing this information is free (except for your on-line monthly charges).

• While some services—especially those found only on commercial on-line services—charge for accessing some information, there's generally enough free information out there so that looking in fee-based databases isn't always necessary.

America's Employers *www.americasemployers.com.* The philosophy behind America's Employers is that since most job openings are never advertised, the best way to find jobs is through direct contact with targeted companies. This extensive database has a search engine that allows you to search by state (either alone or in combination with another state), industry, or company name. America's Employers doesn't really give you in-depth information about a particular company; instead, you'll find names, addresses, and telephone numbers. It does provide links to each listed company's Web site, when applicable.

Big Book *www.bigbook.com.* While not specifically designed for job seekers, Big Book contains the names, addresses, and phone numbers of hundreds of thousands of businesses throughout the country. You can search the extensive database by category, company name, state, and city. Big Book can be tremendously useful for job interviews: by selecting a company in your targeted list, you'll see a detailed map of the area near the business, with the company's location highlighted (not available for all listings). Big Book also has a classifieds section with employment listings (through a link with www.classifieds2000.com).

CareerCity *www.careercity.com.* To reach the company profiles, choose the "27,000 U.S. Employers" link from the main page. You'll find company names, addresses, phone numbers, and brief descriptions, as well as links to companies' Web sites or e-mail contacts. The employers are searchable by state, industry, and keyword. In addition, 7,000 employment services are searchable by agency type. Company information listed here is available in book format through the JobBank Series *www.adamsjobbank.com* and electronically through the JobBank List Service *www.adamsjobbank.com*

CareerMagazine *www.careermag.com.* To reach the detailed company profiles, select "Employers" from the main menu, which provides a list of over 100 companies to choose from. Click on a specific company and you'll see in-depth information regarding a company's structure, philosophy, and career opportunities.

CareerMosaic *www.careermosaic.com.* CareerMosaic's employer database contains over 200 international companies, with more added every day. You may choose from a list of employers, or search the database by job title, description, and location. The list of employers acts as a link to each company's home page; therefore, the information you find on a company will depend on the content of its home page.

E-Span's JobOptions *www.espan.com.* To access, choose "Search Employers" from the main menu. You can search for employers by location (a maximum of five), industry (a maximum of five), and keywords.

EDGAR Database of Corporate Information *www.sec.gov/edgarhp.htm.* EDGAR, the Electronic Data Gathering, Analysis, and Retrieval system, is the electronic filing arm of the Securities and Exchange Commission (SEC). All publicly traded companies, and many others, are required by law to file certain documents with the SEC. Some international companies also file with EDGAR, but this is not mandatory. Job seekers can search the database for companies and are likely to find information like forms 10K and 10Q (annual and quarterly reports), Form 144 (notice of proposed sale of securities), and other financial information.

Job Web *www.jobweb.com.* To access, choose "Employment Information" from the main menu, and then search "Employer Profiles." You can search the database of companies by name or region, including international searches. Choose a company from your search results and you'll find a description of the company, along with its philosophy and a summary of available job opportunities.

Lexis-Nexis *www.lexis-nexis.com* offers a variety of services that are available in books, on CD-ROM, through an on-line dial-up connection, and on the World Wide Web. Overall, the Lexis-Nexis database offers access to two billion documents and 8,700 individual databases, derived from nearly 25,000 sources. More than 1.5 million subscribers conduct more than 400,000 searches on the service daily. The service offers information on industries worldwide (from aerospace to health care, and more) and professions (from financial analyst to journalist, and more). NEXIS is the part of the service that is responsible for developing and selling business, financial, and public records information to businesses and the government. NEXIS is one of the largest on-line services of its type.

Monster.com *www.monster.com.* To access, select "Research Companies" on the opening screen. You can search by state or company name. Each company's profile includes information on products and services, benefits, and corporate culture and environment. Some profiles include a link that allows you to search for job opportunities in a particular company. For international searches, choose "International," then select the appropriate country.

Company Web Sites

A company's home page on the Web is often one of the best sources of information for job seekers. You can learn the company's history and read its mission statement, which generally provides the names of its chief executives. Many sites for larger, public companies include information for stockholders, like financial statements, annual reports, earnings reports, and stock quotes. Many Web sites also contain press releases where you can read about recent developments within the company, like new product launches, changes among executives, and other important information.

The tone of a home page can also be a good way to get a feel for the company's corporate culture. For instance, Ben & Jerry's lighthearted depiction of cows and dancing skeletons is consistent with the laid-back, easygoing culture the company promotes. Arthur Andersen's home page, on the other hand, has a professionalism and polish appropriate for an international accounting firm.

For many job seekers, the most valuable information on a Web site concerns employment. Web sites that don't contain job listings usually include information on how to apply, like a street or e-mail address. Others go into a little more detail, outlining requirements for common positions and describing the departments within the company. In either case, this is usually more information than you can get from most employer databases or from speaking to a human resources representative within a company.

You can't look up a company's URL in the phone book, as you can an address or telephone number, but you can use Web search

engines and directories to find the URLs of thousands of companies. The following information should help you get started.

Career Resource Center *www.careers.org.* This meta-list of job-search resources contains over 17,000 links to employers, job listings, reference materials, and more. The Employers Links section has links to more than 5,000 international companies. You can either perform a search of all companies or browse through the more manageable category lists, like technology companies or financial services.

JobHunt *www.job-hunt.org.* Another meta-list of job hunting resources available on the Internet, this site contains a list of international companies that post job openings on their Web sites as well as lists of resume banks, reference materials, and job listings.

Open Market's Commercial Sites Index *www.directory.net.* This huge site contains over 35,000 international companies, commercial services, products, and information that can be accessed through the Internet. Since the information is so dense, you can perform a keyword search to find what you're looking for. If you have specific companies in mind, you can search the list alphabetically. Each listing is a link to that particular company's (or service's or product's) Web site.

Yahoo! *www.yahoo.com/text/Business_and_Economy/Companies/.* Yahoo!'s search engine is a standout resource for company information. The site has thousands of international links to companies in dozens of categories—accounting, advertising, computers, consulting—you name it. You can also search for firms in your field by typing in keywords like "health care" or by using the company name in your keyword search.

On-line Periodicals

The Internet and commercial on-line services are also excellent resources for researching companies in periodicals. Today, most of the country's largest newspapers (including the *New York Times* and the *Wall Street Journal),* as well as magazines, trade publications, and regional business periodicals, have on-line versions of their publications. Many have their own Web sites or are available through an on-line service like The Microsoft Network or America

Online. If you're looking for information on a company, you can type in the company's name and search the publication for references to that company. Many publications allow you to search their archives going back several years, although they may charge a fee to download these articles.

Commercial On-line Services

Services like America Online and CompuServe are gold mines of valuable information for job seekers. Costs of the services vary. Most databases on CompuServe charge a search fee in addition to CompuServe's monthly access fee. It typically costs around $45 to obtain full company profiles for five companies. America Online has a smaller selection of business resources, but the information is free. You may find that you don't need the in-depth financial information from the more expensive databases on CompuServe.

America Online

Hoover's Business Resources (Keyword: hoover). Calling itself "The Ultimate Source for Company Information," Hoover provides profiles for over 13,000 international companies, including information on company officers, annual sales, and number of employees. Each company profile even allows you to search the Web for references to that company. You can also find information on the top fifty companies for selected U.S. cities, which companies are in the *Fortune* 500, and links to over 3,500 corporate Web sites. Searching the database carries no fees in addition to the connect time charges from America Online.

CompuServe

Business Database Plus (Go: busdb) contains five years' worth of articles from over 750 business magazines, trade journals, and regional business newspapers. You can also find articles—dating back two years—from more than 500 specialized business newsletters. Updated weekly, this comprehensive database can provide you with timely, in-depth information on business and industry trends from throughout the world. The database also contains detailed company profiles and industry descriptions. In addition to

CompuServe charges, there's a $1 charge per article that's read or downloaded.

Corporate Affiliations (Go: affiliations). This extensive database contains company profiles for most large public and private companies worldwide and their subsidiaries. A company profile can contain an address, phone number, and description, as well as names of directors and executives, total sales, assets, net worth, liabilities, and, if applicable, the exchange on which the company's stock is traded. Some listings contain the corporate family structure, parent company name and location, and more. Published by the National Register Publishing Company and made available by Dialog Information Services, Corporate Affiliations charges $4 per search and $7.50 for a full company reference. These charges, in combination with the connect charges from CompuServe, can add up to some pretty hefty research fees.

Disclosure SEC (Go: disclosure). Job seekers scanning the Disclosure database can find financial information for over 10,500 companies. The information is gathered from the 10K (annual) and 10Q (quarterly) documents that publicly traded companies are required to file with the Securities and Exchange Commission. Among the most valuable resources for a job seeker is the management discussion, which generally indicates the future direction and financial health of a company. You'll also find annual income statements, balance sheets, and ratio reports (some going back as far as eight years); quarterly income statements; ownership information (including the names, holdings, and transactions of the company's principals and institutions); the letter the president sends to all shareholders; and more. Charges for reports vary, depending on how much information you want. There's no charge for a company's name and address, but it costs $4 for a company profile and $8 for a company's financial statements. You can get all reports, including the company profile, financial statements, management discussion, president's letter, officers, and directors, for $23.

Dun's Electronic Business Directory (Go: dunsebd). Dun's database provides directory information on over 8 million U.S. businesses and individuals, including public and private companies of all sizes and types. Company information includes the address, telephone number, type of business, number of employees, industry, SIC, and Dun's number. An entry for an individual most likely will

not contain all this information. In addition to CompuServe's connection charges, you'll spend $7.50 for a search that retrieves up to five companies, and an additional $7.50 for five more companies. Full company references are extra.

Dun & Bradstreet Online (Go: duns) contains six additional databases that yield more substantial information than you'll find in Dun's Electronic Business Directory. These databases contain directory information on almost 12.5 million U.S., Canadian, and international companies, as well as business reports with financial information on additional companies. Again, these databases carry transaction charges in addition to the regular CompuServe fees. Charges range from $7.50 for a search of Dun's Market Identifiers to $100 for a copy of the financial records and summary financial for a European company in Dun's Financial Records Plus Summary Financials.

D & B Dun's FRP History/Operations Reports cover over 2.7 million publicly and privately held U.S. companies and 2.5 million Western European businesses. In addition to company names, addresses, and telephone numbers, you can find sales figures, number of employees, date of incorporation, corporate family hierarchy, and name of the chief executive. For U.S. companies, you'll also find a short company history. Expect to pay $10 for your search, $50 for a full company report ($25 for a European company).

D & B Dun's FRP Summary/Financials Reports are useful if you're researching European companies, because the information for U.S. companies is the same as in Dun's FRP History/Operations Reports. For European companies, however, you'll also find a financial summary that includes total assets, liabilities, and net worth. Again, you'll pay $10 for a search, which can yield up to five companies, and $75 for a full company report ($100 for a European company).

D & B Dun's Market Identifiers contains information on more than 10 million U.S. companies (both public and private), government organizations, and schools and universities. You'll find the name, address, and telephone number for all companies. Other information you're likely to find includes sales revenue, number of employees, net worth, incorporation dates, and names and titles of company executives and officers. Searches cost $7.50, plus another $7.50 for each full reference.

D & B Dun's Canadian Market Identifiers covers over 500,000 Canadian companies. Listings include name, address, telephone number, sales revenue, and name of the chief executive officer. Cost is the same as for Dun's Domestic Market Identifiers.

D & B Dun's International Market Identifiers contains information on over 4.7 million public, private, and government-controlled companies in Asia, Africa, Europe, the Middle East, South America, Australia, and the Pacific Rim—120 countries in all. Most entries include name, address, telephone number, cable or telex number, type of business, size (by number of employees and sales), name of the chief executive, and the parent company name. Cost is the same as for Dun's Domestic Market Identifiers.

Dun & Bradstreet Business Reports include three types of financial and credit reports containing information on over ten million companies. These reports are the Business and Information Report, the Payment Analysis Report, and the Supplier Evaluation Report. The reports contain such information as the Dun & Bradstreet rating, company history, payment filings, public filings, and other financial information. While there's no charge for a search that retrieves no results, fees for successfully retrieved reports range from $45 to $360.

InvesText (Go: invtext). Here, job seekers will find in-depth reports on more than 8,200 public U.S. companies and over 2,300 public foreign corporations as well as industry reports for over fifty industry groups, like consumer goods and services, real estate, and finance. Compiled by fifty leading Wall Street, regional, and international brokerage houses and research firms, the reports contain company profiles and a detailed financial history, including revenues, earnings, stock performance, and an analysis and projection of future performance. Costs range from $7.50 for a search by topic or report number to $20 for a report title search. Full page citations also cost $15 each.

Thomas Register Online (Go: thomas) provides job hunters with profiles for almost 150,000 U.S. and Canadian manufacturers and service providers. Each record contains the company name, address, telephone number, and the type of products or services provided. Some records also contain the number of employees, names and titles of chief executives, names of parent or subsidiary companies, asset rating, and more. Searches cost $5 to retrieve up to five companies, $5 for each additional set of five companies, and $5 to view a full company record.

CALL HEAD HUNTER

...AD'S
FAX RESUMES

...LL HEAD HUNTER

Pick up Suit at
Dry Clean...
Send Thank Y...
Note

9 A.M.
INTERVIEW WITH THOM TAN...
AT NARD INC.

WEDNESDAY Mercredi/Mittwoch/M...

THURSDAY Jeudi/Donnerstag/G...

8 A.M.
MEET WITH BILL MacNEILL
DIRECTOR OF CAREER PLANNING
AT BIG RED UNIVERSITY

FRIDAY Vendredi/Freitag/Venerdi/...

SATURDAY Samedi/Samstag/Sabato/Sôv...

...NFORMATIO
...RNS RES
...UR OF

...RVIE
...URN

TO DO

ACTION LIST

DATE:

Get Sunday Newspaper
WANT-ADS ✓
Mail/Fax Resumes

Call Head Hunter ✓

Pick up Suit at
Dry Cleaners ✓
Send Thank You
Notes

TEAR

ACTION LIST

One Page B

...HEAD HUNTER

11 INFORMATIONAL MEETING
    BURNS RESEARCH AGENCY
12 TOUR OF FACILITY

    INTERVIEW WITH KARA FORR...
1   AT BURNS RESEARCH AGEN...

2

3   Commute Home
    * SEND THANK YOU Not...
4   GO TO CAREER FAIR

5

6

...UESDAY Ma...

...OUR, IN
...EARCH AGE.

...NESDAY Mercredi/Mittwoch/M...

...WITH THOM TAN...
...NC.

THURSDAY Jeudi/Donnerstag/Glovedi...

VW.CAREERCITY.COM

11 INFORMATIONAL M
    BURNS RESEARCH A
12 TOUR OF FACILITY

1   INTERVIEW WITH KARA H
    AT BURNS RESEARCH AGEN

2   _____

3   COMMUTE HOME
    * SEND THANK YOU NOTE
4   GO TO CAREER FAIR

5   _____

SEND

9

WWW.CAREERCITY.COM

9

INFORMATIONAL MEE
URNS RESEARCH AGE
R OF FACILITY

EW WITH KARA H
RESEARCH AGE

NOT

11 A.M. - 3 P.M. T
NFO. MEETING, TO
T BURNS RESEARC

9 A.M. WEDNESDAY
NTERVIEW WITH
AT NARD INC.

THURSDA

8 A.M. FRIDAY
MEET WITH BILL M
DIRECTOR OF CAREER P
AT BIG RED UNIV

SATURDAY

| TO DO | ACTION LIST | DATE: | ☐ |

CHAPTER 14

Interviewing

At last, you've reached the long-sought goal. All your efforts spent writing the resume and cover letter, answering job listings, networking, and researching companies have paid off—you've been called for an interview! As with these previous steps, certain techniques will increase your chances of success. Follow these techniques to maximize your chances of landing the job.

Know the Company

As each interview is arranged, begin your in-depth research. You should arrive at an interview knowing the company upside down and inside out. You need to know the company's products, types of customers, subsidiaries, parent company, principal locations, rank in the industry, sales and profit trends, type of ownership, size, current plans, and much more. By this time, you've probably narrowed your job search to one industry. Even if you haven't, you should still be familiar with common industry terms, the trends in the firm's industry, the firm's principal competitors and their relative performance, and the direction in which the industry leaders are headed.

Dig into every resource you can! Surf the Internet. Read the company literature, the trade press, the business press. If possible, speak to someone at the firm before the interview, or if not, speak to someone at a competing firm. The more time you spend, the better. Even if you feel extremely pressed for time, set aside several hours for pre-interview research.

Practice Your Presentation

The more you use your interview muscle, the stronger it will become. Recruit as many people as possible to run through test interviews with you. Also keep in mind that your first interview will probably be your worst, so try not to have it with the company you most want to work for. Getting the first interview under your belt when you haven't interviewed in a long time usually makes you more at ease at subsequent interviews.

Telephone-screening interviews are becoming more commonplace, because companies want to reduce their hiring costs by avoiding travel at screening stages in interviews. Using phone interviews, recruiters can quickly weed out most candidates and decide on the best candidates to pursue.

Here's why planning for a telephone interview is important: Unlike a planned first interview, for which you've done lots of preparation, a telephone interview can come at any time and from any company. Also, once you begin to network, a phone interview may result when all you expected was possible leads. Sometimes recruiters will call to schedule an interview later, but more often they'll call hoping to catch you and interview you on the spot. (This is a good argument for using an answering machine.)

Here are some tips for handling a phone interview:

- If you feel unprepared or uncomfortable with your phone skills, practice with a friend. Role-play and ask your friend to question you over the phone.
- Keep a copy of your resume by the phone, along with a list of keywords representing the themes you think are relevant to the industry or job category you're pursuing.

- You can't count on clues from an interviewer's body language, eye contact, or other such signs. You'll have to pay close attention, instead, to his or her voice pattern, and you must use your own voice—simple, direct, enthusiastic responses—to keep the conversation interesting and easy to follow.
- Listen carefully and maintain your highest level of concentration. Have a phone set up where you can sit more or less as you'd sit for an interview. Keep a pen and paper near the phone, along with your resume and notes. Take careful notes about what you're asked and what seemed most critical to the recruiter. (This information will help you follow up later with a letter.)
- Avoid long pauses; provide quick summaries of your key themes or points with clear examples of how you've made positive contributions where you've been and how you could contribute to this company.
- Make sure you get the name (spelled correctly), number, and address of the person who called.
- Reaffirm your interest—if you're interested after this first round. Find out what happens next and what you can do to make yourself competitive. Follow up with a thank-you note, just as you would for a screening interview. Your goal is to get face-to-face in the next round.

Attire

How important is proper attire for a job interview? Buying a complete wardrobe, donning new shoes, and having your hair styled every morning aren't enough to guarantee you a career position as an investment banker. On the other hand, if you can't find a clean, conservative suit or won't take the time to wash your hair, you're wasting your time by interviewing at all.

Men applying for any professional position should wear a suit, preferably in a conservative color like navy or charcoal gray. It's easy to get away with wearing the same dark suit to consecutive interviews at the same company; just wear a different shirt and tie for each interview.

Women should also wear a businesslike suit. Professionalism still dictates a suit with a skirt, rather than slacks, as proper interview garb for women. This is usually true even at companies where pants are acceptable attire for female employees.

The final selection of candidates for a job opening won't be determined by dress, but inappropriate dress can quickly eliminate a first-round candidate. So while you shouldn't spend a fortune on a new wardrobe, be sure your clothes are adequate. The key is to dress at least as formally and conservatively as the position requires, or slightly more so.

Grooming

Personal grooming is as important as finding appropriate clothes for a job interview. Careful grooming indicates both a sense of thoroughness and self-confidence. Women should not wear excessive makeup, and both men and women should refrain from wearing perfume or cologne. (It only takes a small spritz to leave an allergic interviewer with a fit of sneezing and a bad impression of your meeting.) Men should be freshly shaven, even if the interview is late in the day.

How to Stay in the Game

"The interviewer's job is to find a reason to turn you down; your job is to not provide that reason."
—John L. LaFevre, author,
How You Really Get Hired

Reprinted from the 1989/90 *CPC Annual*, with permission of the National Association of Colleges and Employers (formerly College Placement Council, Inc.), copyright holder.

What to Bring

Everyone needs a watch, a pen, and a notepad. Finally, a briefcase or a leatherbound folder (containing extra, unfolded copies of your resume) will help complete the look of professionalism.

Sometimes the interviewer will be running behind schedule. Don't be upset—be sympathetic. Recruiters are often under pressure to interview a lot of candidates to quickly fill a demanding position. Come to your interview with good reading material to keep yourself occupied and relaxed.

The Crucial First Few Moments

The beginning of the interview is the most important, because it determines the tone. Do you smile when you meet? Do you establish enough eye contact, but not too much? Do you walk into the office with a self-assured and confident stride? Do you shake hands firmly? Do you make small talk easily, without being garrulous, or do you act formal and reserved, as though under attack? It's human nature to judge people by that first impression, so make sure it's a good one.

Do you wait for the recruiter to invite you to sit down before doing so? Alternatively, if the recruiter forgets to invite you to take a seat, do you awkwardly ask if you may be seated, as though to remind the recruiter of a lapse in etiquette? Or do you gracefully help yourself to a seat? As you can see, much of the first impression you make at an interview will be dramatically affected by how relaxed and confident you feel. This is why it's important to practice for each interview.

Interview Formats

Interviews fall into one of two categories: structured and unstructured. In a structured interview, the recruiter asks a prescribed set of questions, seeking relatively brief answers. In an unstructured interview, the recruiter asks more open-ended questions, to prod you to give longer responses and reveal as much as possible about yourself, your background, and your aspirations. Some recruiters mix both styles, typically beginning with more objective questions and asking more open-ended questions as the interview progresses.

Try to determine as soon as possible if the recruiter is conducting a structured or unstructured interview, and respond to the questions accordingly. As you answer, watch for signals from the recruiter as to whether your responses are too short or too long. For example, if the recruiter is nodding or looking away, wrap up your answer as quickly as possible.

Setting the Right Tone

The interviewer's decision about whether you'll be invited back for an additional interview will probably be influenced by your attitude and personality as much as your qualifications. So don't concentrate too much on trying to project the perfect image. Just try to relax and visualize yourself as smooth and confident. Also remember that some things are beyond your control—some interviews go well without any effort on your part (and you still may not get the job), and others go awry no matter how poised you are (and sometimes you're offered the job anyway). Generally, you should try to stress the following qualities in your choice of words, tone of voice, and body language:

- Capability
- Confidence
- Dependability
- Easygoing manner
- Enthusiasm
- Flexibility
- Resourcefulness
- Strong work ethic

After the Small Talk

Often the interviewer will begin, after the small talk, by telling you about the company, the division, the department, and the position.

Because of your detailed research, the information about the company should be repetitive for you, and the interviewer would probably like nothing better than to avoid this regurgitation of the company biography. So if you can do so tactfully, indicate that you're familiar with the firm. If the interviewer seems intent on providing you with background information despite your hints, then acquiesce. And if you can manage to generate a brief discussion of the company or the industry at this point without being forceful, great. It will help build rapport, underscore your interest, and increase your impact.

Make an Impression

As the interview progresses, the interviewer will probably mention some of the most important responsibilities of the position. If applicable, draw parallels between your experience and the demands of the position as detailed by the interviewer. Describe your experience the same way you do on your resume: emphasize results and achievements, don't merely describe activities. But don't exaggerate—be on the level about your abilities.

The first interview is often the toughest, where many candidates are screened out. If you're interviewing for a competitive position, you'll have to make an impression that will last. Focus on a few of your greatest strengths that are relevant to the position. Develop these points carefully and re-emphasize them where possible.

Remember to keep attuned to the interviewer and make the length of your answers appropriate to the situation. If you're really unsure as to how detailed a response the interviewer is seeking, ask.

Avoid the Negative

Try not to be negative about anything during the interview, particularly any past employer or previous job. Even if you detest your current or former job or manager, don't make disparaging comments. The interviewer may construe this as a sign of a potential attitude problem and not consider you a strong candidate.

Some Common Interview Questions—Be Ready!

- Tell me about yourself.
- Why did you leave your last job?
- What excites you in your current job?
- Where would you like to be in five years?
- How much overtime are you willing to work?
- What would your previous/present employer tell me about you?

**More Common
Interview
Questions**

- Tell me about a difficult situation that you faced at your previous/present job.
- What are your greatest strengths?
- What are your weaknesses?
- Describe a work situation where you took initiative and went beyond your normal responsibilities.
- Why should we hire you?

Emphasize the Positive

Take some time to really think about how you'll convey your work history. Present "bad experiences" as "learning experiences." Instead of saying "I hated my position as a salesperson because I had to bother people on the phone," say "I realized cold-calling wasn't my strong suit. Though I love working with people, I decided my talents would be best used in a more face-to-face atmosphere." Always find some sort of lesson from previous jobs, as they all have one.

Money: Don't Ask

It's usually best to avoid talking finances until you receive the offer. Otherwise you'll look like you care more about money than putting your skills to work for the company. Your goals at an interview are simple: 1) to prove to the recruiter that you're well-suited to the job as you understand it, and 2) to make sure you feel comfortable with the prospect of actually doing the job and working in the environment the company offers. Even if you're unable to determine the salary range beforehand, don't ask about it during the first interview. You can always ask later. Above all, don't ask about fringe benefits until you've been offered a position. (Then be sure to get all the details.)

If you're pressed about salary requirements during an interview and you feel you must name a figure, give a salary range instead of your most recent salary. Naming a salary range gives you a chance to hook onto a figure that's also in the range the company has in mind. In fact, many companies base their offers on sliding salary scales. Therefore, if you name a range of, say, $25,000–30,000, it may be that the company was considering a range of $22,000–28,000. In this case, you'll be more likely to receive an offer in the mid-to-upper end of your range. Of course, your experience and qualifications also play a part here. If you're just starting out and have little experience, the recruiter may be more likely to stick to the lower end of the scale.

Handling Impossible Questions

One of the biggest fears candidates harbor about job interviews is the unknown question for which they have no answer. To make matters worse, some recruiters may ask a question knowing full well you can't answer it. They don't usually ask such questions because they enjoy seeing you squirm—they want to judge how you might respond to pressure or tension on the job. If you're asked a tough question you can't answer, think about it for a few seconds. Then, with a confident smile and without apology, simply say "I don't know" or "I can't answer that question."

You'll find some of the toughest of these questions later in the chapter, under "Zingers."

Asking Your Own Questions

As the interview winds down, the recruiter will probably say something like "Are there any questions you'd like to ask?" It's essential to have a few questions to ask at this point—otherwise you won't seem serious about pursuing a career at that company. Some of your planned questions may already have been covered by the time your reach this stage of the interview, so have some extra questions ready.

Use the questions you ask to subtly demonstrate your knowledge of the firm and the industry and to underscore your interest in a long-term career position at the firm. But don't allow them to become an interrogation—pose only two or three thoughtful questions. Don't ask questions the recruiter will find difficult or awkward to answer. This is not the time to ask, for example, "Does your company use recycled paper for all its advertising brochures?" And, of course, avoid reading directly from your list of questions.

After the Interview

You've made it through the toughest part—but now what? First, breathe a sigh of relief! Then record the name and title of the person you interviewed with, as well as the names and titles of anyone else you may have met. Ideally, you'll have collected their business cards. Don't forget to write down what the next agreed-upon step will be. Will the recruiter contact you? How soon?

Don't Forget to Write

Write a follow-up letter immediately afterward, while the interview is still fresh in the interviewer's mind. Not only is this a thank-you, it also gives you the chance to provide the interviewer with any details you may have forgotten (as long as they can be added tactfully). If you lost any points during the interview, this letter can help you regain your footing. Be polite and make sure to stress your continued interest and competence to fill the position. Just don't forget to proofread it thoroughly. If you're unsure of the spelling of the interviewer's name, call the receptionist and ask.

Keep in Touch

Allow the interviewer five to ten business days to contact you after receiving your letter. If you haven't heard anything after that time, follow up with a phone call. Express your continued interest in the firm and the position and ask whether a decision has been made or when you'll be notified.

In the meantime, it's important to keep your candidacy fresh in the interviewer's mind. Send work that intrigued the interviewer (for example, brochures or writing samples). If the conversation during the interview provided any possibilities for follow-up, like reading an article or book, drop the interviewer a note mentioning how much you learned from the piece.

Taking the Next Step

Don't be discouraged if you don't receive an immediate response from an employer—most companies interview many applicants before making a final decision. Take advantage of this time to contact other firms and schedule more interviews, so that if a rejection does come, you have other options. Continuing to job-search and interview is a good idea, even if you end up receiving the offer. Ultimately, you may have a number of opportunities to

choose from, and you'll be in a better position to negotiate terms. So keep plugging away!

Handling Rejection

Rejection is inevitable, and it's bound to happen to you, just as it happens to all other job seekers. The key is to be prepared for it and not take it personally.

One way you can turn rejection around is by contacting each person who sends you a rejection letter. Thank your contact for considering you for the position and request that he or she keep you in mind for future openings. If you feel comfortable about it, you may want to ask the person for suggestions to help you improve your chances of getting a job in that industry or for the names of people who might be looking for someone with your skills—something like "Do you have any suggestions about whom else I might contact?"

Two cautions are in order: First, don't ask employers to tell you why they didn't hire you. Not only will this place a recruiter in an awkward position, you'll probably get a negative reaction. Second, keep in mind that if you contact employers solely for impartial feedback, not everyone will be willing to talk to you.

A Thank-You Note

A well-written thank-you note, mailed within one or two days of receiving notice of rejection, makes a positive statement. When Danny P. was turned down for a position as a publicity director, he wrote his interviewer a letter that expressed his disappointment at not being offered the job and also his thanks for the company's consideration of his qualifications. The interviewer was so impressed by Danny's initiative that she provided him with several contact names to assist in his continued search.

In your letter, emphasize an ongoing interest in being considered for openings. Also, be careful to use an upbeat tone. Although you may be disappointed, you don't want to put the employer on the defensive or imply that you don't respect his or her decision. Above all, don't give up! Stay positive and motivated, and learn from the process.

If Your Skills Aren't Appropriate . . .

If it looks as though your skills and background don't match the position the interviewer was hoping to fill, ask him or her if another division or subsidiary could perhaps profit from your talents.

Strategies for Later Interviews

When filling professional career positions, few companies make a job offer after only one interview. Usually the purpose of the first interview is to narrow the field to a small number of promising candidates. During the first meeting, therefore, the ideal strategy is to stand out from a large field of competitors in a positive way. The best way to do this is to emphasize subtly one or two of your key strengths as much as possible throughout the interview.

During later interviews, the competition for the position will drop off, and employers will look not for strengths but for weaknesses. At this point, focus on presenting yourself as a well-balanced choice for the position. Listen carefully to the interviewer's questions, so you can determine his or her underlying concerns and try to dispel them. On the other hand, if later interviews are primarily with people who are in a position to veto your hiring but not to push it forward, focus primarily on building rapport, as opposed to reiterating and developing your key strengths.

Usually you can count on attending at least two interviews for most professional positions, or three for high-level positions. Some firms are famous for conducting a minimum of six interviews for all professional positions. Though you should be more relaxed as you return for subsequent interviews, the pressure will still be on. The more prepared you are, the better.

Tougher Questions

Another way in which second interviews differ from first interviews is that the questions become much more specific and technical. The company must now test the depth of your knowledge of the field, including how well you're able to apply your education and work experience to the job at hand. At this stage, the interviewer isn't a recruiter. You may have one or more interviewers, each of whom has a job related to the one you're applying for. Typically, these interviewers will represent your potential boss, professional peer group, or executives who oversee the work group.

The second round of interviews can last one to two days, during which you might meet with as few as several people or as many as fifteen or more over the course of the visit. These interviews typically last longer than initial interviews. For many executive positions, you may also have meetings around breakfast, lunch, or dinner.

In all cases, remember—you're still in an interview. You may be having a dinner conversation about a recent topic of concern to the industry as a whole. Be ready with opinions and equally ready to listen and ask good questions. You may be asked to demonstrate how you'd go about performing some aspect of the job. Be ready in case you're presented with a tough problem and are asked to tackle it as though you'd already started your first day on the job. Use what you said in the screening interview as an outline (It's gotten you this far!), but be prepared to build on this outline in meaningful ways with more developed details, examples, and ideas.

Developing Your Personal Themes

Too many job seekers jump into a full-scale search without much preparation other than putting together a resume. A serious mistake! Although your resume may get you interviews, to win offers, you must prepare yourself further. It's vital to distinguish yourself in some positive way from other candidates. One way is to develop themes to which you refer throughout the interview. This enables you to emphasize your strongest points and ensures that you'll leave a positive impression.

Recruiters seek certain types of information. Knowing these points and being able to discuss how they relate to you will make you better prepared and more in control. Think of your themes as sales messages. Each is designed to showcase your best skills and qualifications. Together, they make up a strategy that will enable you to sell your qualifications in virtually any interview.

Read through the following topics. Develop a personalized approach to each and practice talking about it. Think of specific examples in your background that correspond to each topic. You can't be prepared for every situation, but once you've developed your messages, you'll be able to apply them to almost any interview question. A large number of practice questions and answers based on an expanded discussion of these themes can be found

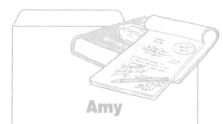

Amy

I was exasperated with looking for work. I was perfectly qualified for a position at a record company. I had completed two internships and worked at a record store practically since birth. But it seemed that everybody knew somebody in the business, and I was definitely out of the loop. The industry was so tightly saturated that I couldn't even score a seat by the phones. All the while, I'm thinking that I went to college, Phi Beta Kappa, and he wonders if I can answer a phone?! How humiliating. The future seemed really grim, and I was tired of waiting tables just to support myself. So I decided to focus on finding another job. One day this guy sits down in my section and starts to chat me up. He's asking me whether I'm an actress, and I'm thinking he's another tool trying to be cute. I wanted a tip, so I asked him what he did. Lo and behold, he worked at Electra Records, and knew of some entry-level positions. With his recommendation, I finally broke into the industry.
—Amy, Columbia University

in *The Adams Job Interview Almanac,* published by Adams Media Corporation.

Try to answer each question aloud, incorporating the themes you've developed. Then evaluate your progress. You may discover that you need more practice to become comfortable discussing the topics clearly and concisely. Nothing you say for the first time will come out the way you like. Practice delivering your messages aloud until the words come easily in an organized yet comfortable, conversational way.

Interest in the Business

Ask yourself "Why am I interested in working in this field and for this company?" Give examples of the things that interest you. These could be anything from the challenge of meeting increasingly higher sales goals to the satisfaction of developing a product from creation to final production. Offer personal experience where possible. Have you used the company's products or talked to its customers or competitors?

Skills and Experience

Consider your key skills and how you'll use them in this job. Avoid clichés and generalities—offer specific evidence. How well do your qualifications fit the requirements of the position? Your answer should incorporate the positive aspects of recent jobs. Think about your weaknesses and how you can minimize and balance them with your strengths. Avoid sounding either arrogant or defensive.

Offer proof, with examples, of your problem-solving ability. How have you resolved difficult issues in the past? Are you practical in how you apply technical skills? Are you realistic? Offer examples in which you've delivered more than expected.

Don't give long descriptions of situations—focus your answer on the action you took and the positive results you obtained. Focus on real issues, on logical, value-added solutions, on practical outcomes of your work, and on realistic measures of judging these outcomes. What can you contribute to the organization?

Professionalism and Leadership

Describe your professional character, including thoroughness, diligence, and accountability. Give proof that you persevere to see important projects through and that you achieve desired results. Demonstrate how you gather resources, predict obstacles, and manage stress. Offer proof of your effectiveness, including creativity, initiative, resourcefulness, and leadership. What examples can you provide for each?

Focus on how you overcome problems, how you take advantage of opportunities that might otherwise be overlooked, and how you rally the support of others to accomplish goals. Talk about the management style and the interpersonal skills you use with peer groups and leaders. What kind of boss, colleague, and employee will you be?

Personality

Consider your personality on the job. How do you fit in with other types of personalities? What types of people would enjoy working with you for hours at a time? How would the company's customers or clients react to you? Your goal is to develop responses that make the interviewer feel confident there won't be any surprises about your personality on the job.

Do you have a balanced lifestyle? Is your personality reflected in the type of job you choose as well as in the outside activities you pursue? Are your personal and career interests compatible? The interviewer may also be interested in your community involvement, to see how commendably you'd reflect the company's image.

Zingers!

Following are some of the most challenging questions you'll ever face. If you're able to answer these questions, you'll be prepared to handle just about anything the recruiter comes up with.

Tell me about yourself.

I'm a production assistant with a B.A. in communications and three years of solid broadcasting and public-relations experience. I

have extensive experience developing and researching topics, preinterviewing guests, and producing on-location videotapings. I have a tremendous amount of energy and love to be challenged. I'm constantly trying to take on additional responsibilities and learn new things. I've been watching your station for some time now, and I've been impressed with your innovative approach and your fast growth. I'd like to be a part of that winning team.

This is a perfect opportunity to "sell" your qualifications to the interviewer. After developing your sales messages in the previous section, condense them into a summary you can use in situations like this. Briefly describe your experience, skills, accomplishments, goals, and personal qualities. Explain your interest in the company and how you plan on making a contribution. If you're a recent college graduate, be sure to discuss your educational qualifications as well, emphasizing the classes you took that are relevant to the position.

What is your biggest weakness?

I admit to being a bit of a perfectionist. I take a great deal of pride in my work and am committed to producing the highest-quality work I can. Sometimes if I'm not careful, though, I can go a bit overboard. I've learned that it's not always possible or even practical to try to perfect your work—sometimes you have to decide what's important and ignore the rest to be productive. It's a question of trade-offs. I also pay a lot of attention to pacing my work, so I don't get too caught up in perfecting every detail.

This is a great example of what's known as a negative question. Negative questions are a favorite among interviewers, because they're effective at uncovering problems or weaknesses. The key to answering negative questions is to give them a positive spin. For this particular question, your best bet is to admit to a weakness that isn't catastrophic, inconsistent, or currently disruptive to your chosen professional field, and emphasize how you've overcome or minimized it. Whatever you do, don't answer this question with a cop-out like "I can't think of any" or, even worse, "I don't really have any major weaknesses." This kind of response is likely to eliminate you from contention.

Tell me about a project in which you were disappointed with your personal performance.

In my last job for a manufacturing company, I had to ana-lyze all the supplier bids and present recommendations to the vice president of logistics. Because the supplier bids weren't in a uniform format, my analysis often consisted of comparing dissim-ilar items. This caused some confusion in my final report, and by the time I'd reworked it and presented it to the vice president, we'd lost the critical time we needed to improve our approval process for these bids. In hindsight, I should have taken a sim-pler approach to the problem and not tried to make it so com-plex or all-inclusive. Ever since, I've paid more attention to making recommendations in a timely manner.

Describe roadblocks and what you've done to try to get around them. How have your skills come into play? In hindsight, what could you have done differently? What lessons have you learned?

Tell me about your most difficult work or personal experience.

One time a coworker went through rehab for six months after a wreck, and I picked up a lot of additional work to help him out. I know he would've done the same for me, and it's important for me to have that kind of trust among the mem-bers of my work group.

The interviewer will want to know how you hold up under pressure. Describe a situation, either personal or professional, that involved a great deal of conflict and challenge and placed you under an unusual amount of stress. What, specifically, were the problems, and what did you do to resolve them?

What was your greatest challenge in your last job?

I had to get longtime employees with few or no computer skills to embrace a new e-mail system. I started by explaining the need for less paper in everyone's job. Then I decided to create a temporary e-mail account with one daily riddle on the system; everyone who responded correctly got his or her name put in a weekly drawing. Each week for one month a person from the drawing won a dinner for four at a nice local restaurant. This idea worked well as a device to get people to use the system.

Describe a problem area that you improved in your last job, emphasizing the solution you devised. If you're relatively inexperienced and can't boast of solving a tremendously difficult or involved problem, like saving the company from a hostile takeover, that's okay. Describe a relatively minor problem you've solved creatively, as this candidate does.

Tell me about the most difficult problem you've dealt with.

That would be the time I was promoted to manage a new department. A coworker in the department resented me from the beginning. I soon learned that her best friend had been turned down for the position. I actually confronted her about it; I explained that I had once put a relationship of my own to the test, working too closely with a friend—we found that we spent all our leisure time talking about work. A few weeks after our talk she admitted that she'd never thought about the potential results of working too closely with a friend. Our working relationship was fine after that.

Discuss the problem briefly, then focus on what actions you took and the results you obtained. Be revealing: Why was this problem personally hard for you? How did you remain objective and professional?

Describe a time when you failed to resolve a conflict.

I wasn't able to keep a good employee once who'd been in our manufacturing facility for ten years. His job description was rewritten to require computer skills. I offered to send him to night classes, but he refused the help. I had no option but to replace him. In retrospect, if I'd encouraged him and other employees to acquire new training periodically, he might not have been overwhelmed by the time his position was reworked. Now I'm vigilant about encouraging my group to attend seminars and courses to enhance their job skills and to avoid becoming outdated.

The ideal solution here is to discuss a conflict that wasn't yours to solve in the first place. If you must discuss a personal conflict, focus on the positive steps you'd take if you could go back and do it over again. What have you learned as a result of this experience?

How have you handled criticism of your work?

The first time I had a complaint from a client, I found it difficult to keep the complaint separate from my professional service of the account. The client was upset about the downtime on ATM machines. I learned that showing empathy usually calms an unpleasant situation. I also learned that no client is going to be happy with everything, even if that client's overall experience is positive.

The interviewer is looking for an indication of the candidate's accountability and professional character. Describe a specific project or work habit that caused you a problem until you faced up to it and overcame it. Alternatively, you might describe a time you responded objectively and professionally to particularly harsh or unreasonable criticism of your work.

What aspects of your work are most often criticized?

I remember in my first job as marketing assistant, I spent endless hours analyzing a particular problem. I came up with a revised marketing plan that was extremely well received. Unfortunately, when it came time to present the plan to top management, I hadn't prepared the fine points of the presentation—overheads and slides—and the proposal was turned down. I'd failed to make clear the savings that would result from the plan. I spent the next two weeks working on my presentation. On my second try management approved it, and my recommendations were carried out to everyone's satisfaction.

Allan

My interview was held in a very small room. The partners sat me in the middle of the room and they sat on opposite sides of me. They began bombarding me with questions, purposely not giving me the chance to answer. When they gave me a chance to answer, the questions were absurd: "Is today Tuesday?"

My response: "No, today is Friday."

Their response: "Why?"

This was obviously a pressure interview and they were looking to see if I lost it and started swearing my head off at them. They wanted to see if I could remain cool under pressure.

This question is similar to the question on weaknesses. Try to give an example from a job early on in your career. Discuss what you did to overcome the situation and to improve your work. You could also discuss how the failure has inspired you to pay more careful attention to detail in all your work.

Give an example of how you've handled rejection.

The answer to the previous question could also be used here. Ideally, you should cite an example from an early stage in your career. Explain why you met with rejection and describe how you managed to overcome it. Demonstrate your improvement in that area over the years.

What might your current boss want to change about your work habits?

I'm a morning person, and she's a night owl. I like to come into the office at least an hour early, usually by seven, to get a jump start on my work. My boss likes to come in after nine and work late into the evening. So I think if she could change one thing about me, she'd probably make me into a night owl, too, so I'd be available during many of the same hours she likes to work.

The interviewer will want to know how you'll fit in with your future boss and coworkers and will also want to feel confident that he or she has uncovered any surprises about your corporate style. One good way to answer this question is to point out minor differences of preference. Alternatively, you might describe a weakness of yours that you and your boss have worked on and improved.

Tell me about one or two aspects of your last job you'd never want to repeat.

I'm glad I have experience in credit collections, because it's enabled me to make better risk assessments. I really didn't enjoy the work, though, and it isn't something I want to do again.

In a constructive way, describe one or two things you've done that you didn't especially enjoy or that didn't play to your strengths. Then describe your strengths and their relevance to the job you're applying for.

Tell me about a situation that frustrated you at work.

I was frustrated once when one of my clients, who'd insisted on a high-growth stock, called in a panic because the stock price had dropped more than twenty points in one day. I had a hard time convincing him to ride it out rather than cut his losses. This happened despite my attempts from the beginning to explain the short-term volatility of that stock.

This is another question designed to probe the candidate's professional personality. The interviewer will want reassurance that you're able to hold up under pressure. Describe how you've remained diplomatic, objective, or professional in a difficult situation.

Tell me about one of your projects that failed.

I've always had the tendency to be a workaholic and to have the attitude that I can tackle anything and achieve good results. During the hurricane of 1992, my insurance company was inundated with claims. I immediately thought I could handle all the claims in my area, and I jumped in with both feet to work eighteen-hour days. I quickly realized there was no way I could complete all the claims on time, and I had to start to delegate some of the responsibility to my investigators. This experience showed me that no matter how efficient and competent you are, sometimes you must either delegate responsibility or ask for help.

Demonstrate the ability here to be humble and learn from your mistakes. In hindsight, what could you have done differently? How has your leadership style changed because of the experience?

Tell me about a time when your employer wasn't happy with your job performance.

That would be during my first week on the job as a paralegal. I gave her two letters that had typos in them. Frankly, I'd simply been a little sloppy—but that's the only example that comes to mind. Ms. Heilman did tell me regularly that she was very happy with my work.

Again, be sure to discuss a relatively minor incident here. Also, show a willingness to accept responsibility for the problem—don't blame others or make excuses. Simply describe what happened and how you successfully resolved the situation.

Have you ever been passed up for a promotion you felt you deserved?

A couple of times in my early career I thought I was unfairly passed up for a promotion. However, in retrospect I now realize that in all likelihood I wasn't ready to perform in those jobs. In fact, the additional training experience I gained remaining where I was proved invaluable in the last few years, as I've made significant progress moving up the corporate ladder. I've also learned to appreciate that being ready for a promotion doesn't necessarily mean it'll happen. Many external factors influence the nature and timing of promotions, aside from a person's performance and capabilities.

The interviewer wants to gauge the candidate's self-confidence as well as his or her objectivity about personal or professional limitations. Give evidence here that you have enough patience to learn what's important before you get bored or frustrated. After you've mastered your own job, would you stay motivated long enough to be productive?

Have you ever been fired?

During one of my summer internships while in college, I worked for a software consulting company. Midway through the summer, a new president was appointed because of some financial difficulties, and he requested the resignation of my entire group. I was swept out with everyone else, even though my work performance had never been criticized.

If you've never been fired, of course, this is a simple question to answer. But if you have been fired, you'll need to be prepared to discuss the situation in detail and possibly answer a series of specific follow-up questions. If the termination was a result of a situation beyond your control, like corporate downsizing, most interviewers will be understanding. But if you were fired due to poor performance or some other problem, you'll need to admit your fault and convince the interviewer you've corrected the problem. Although this may be a difficult question to answer, you should be completely honest. If you aren't, and the recruiter finds out as much from your references, you may be subject to immediate dismissal, or your job offer may be revoked.

Why have you changed jobs so frequently?

My frequent job changes over the last five years have been due to the rapid changes in my profession. My jobs have been based on government contracts, and over the last several years congressional appropriations have been up and down, causing some companies' contracts to be canceled, while other companies land huge, unexpected contracts. This volatility creates some good opportunities, but it also creates a lot of uncertainty. Because your business is based mostly on consumer products and not on government products, I welcome the opportunity to work in an environment where the business cycle is more stable and predictable.

Be candid here. Personal growth, a larger budget, or other career-enhancing experiences are all valid reasons for moving on. Convince the interviewer that you're interested in his or her company for the long haul.

Why did you stay in your last job so long?

I was in my last job over seven years. During that time, I completed an advanced technical degree at an evening university and also had two six-month assignments in which I was loaned out to different departments. As a result, I acquired some additional skills that normally aren't associated with that job. Therefore, I think I've made good progress and am ready to accept the next challenge.

Dawn

I was excited for my interview because the H.R. person seemed really enthusiastic about my resume and told me she would pass it on to the hiring manager. At my interview, the hiring manager told me that it was "a waste of my time to interview there unless I knew someone." When I asked why, she said it was because the position was already filled. Obviously, I was upset. It was probably illegal of them to be interviewing me for a closed position and we were just going through the motions. I wound up taking a job with one of their direct competitors.

The interviewer may be curious about your interest in personal improvement, tackling new assignments, and so on. He or she may also be concerned about whether you have a tendency to get too comfortable with the status quo. Demonstrate how you've developed job responsibilities in meaningful new ways.

Tell me about a problem you've had getting along with a work associate.

I'm pretty easygoing and tend to get along with most people. But I remember one time when we brought in a new associate who was very bossy—to the point where he offended one of our interns with his attitude. I actually pulled him aside and told him that I found it more productive to ask people for help than to give orders. Unfortunately, my advice didn't seem to help much, but we were more careful when we hired new staff after that.

Avoid discussing a personality clash; focus instead on a difference in work ethic between you and an associate or something else with which the interviewer is likely to empathize. For example, you might describe someone whose standards of excellence were less stringent than yours.

Tell me about your least favorite manager or professor.

Well, I've been pretty fortunate as far as managers go, and I didn't have any problems with my professors. In my first job out of college, I worked with a manager who was pretty inaccessible. If you walked into his office to ask a question, you got the sense that you were bothering him, so we just learned to get help from each other instead. I wouldn't say he was my least favorite manager, because he was a good manager in a lot of ways, but I would have preferred that he'd been more available to us and given us more direction.

Answering this question will be a little bit like walking across a minefield, so beware! Keep in mind that the interviewer doesn't want to learn about your former supervisors; he or she does want to learn about the way you speak about them. Though the interviewer may bait you to make a negative statement about your former employer, doing so can create a host of problems. Even if your claim is completely true and entirely justified, the recruiter may conclude either that you don't get along well with people or that you shift blame to others. The best way around this dilemma is to choose an example that's not too negative, touch upon it briefly, then focus the rest of your answer on what you learned from the experience.

Who's the toughest employer you've ever had, and why?

That would be Ms. Paddock, at the Leachfield Project. She'd push people to their limits when things got busy, and she was a stickler for detail. But she was always fair, and she rewarded good, hard work. I'd call her a tough boss but a good boss.

Again, at all costs avoid making negative statements about your previous employers. Turn the question around with a positive, upbeat response, as this candidate does.

Have you ever had to work with a manager who was unfair to you or just plain hard to get along with?

Actually, I've never run into that. Of course, my current boss has to work under time constraints, just like everyone else, and she sometimes has to phrase things succinctly if our department is going to meet its goals. But I've never considered that unfair or hard to handle. It's just part of the job. My supervisors and I have always gotten along quite well.

Never, under any circumstances, criticize a current or former employer, no matter how many times the interviewer gives you the opportunity to do so. What the interviewer is trying to find out here is not whether the candidate has worked for difficult people, but if he or she is willing to badmouth them.

What are some of the things your supervisor has done that you disliked?

The only thing I really don't like is to get feedback in front of others. I want to hear good or bad feedback in private, so that I have time to think and react to the issue without other distractions. I believe that's the fair way to improve learning or to change future behavior.

Bring a Good Book

The Corporate Controller at one large company makes everyone wait for at least one hour before he will interview them. He feels his time is more valuable than anyone else's. This is where you have to ask yourself: "How much do I really want this job—especially if I have to report to this person?"

Again, avoid being overly negative when talking about your ex-boss or manager. Discuss a relatively minor example or one with which the interviewer is likely to empathize. Put a positive spin on your answer by describing what you learned from this difficult situation.

How do you handle tension with your boss?

The only tension I've ever felt was once when we both got too busy to keep each other informed. My boss overcommitted me with a short deadline, not knowing I was bogged down with another client problem. I believe firmly in the importance of staff meetings, so coworkers can respect the demands on each other's time.

The safest ground here is to describe an example of a miscommunication in your early relationship with a boss and how you resolved it. The interviewer will want to know how you avoided a recurrence of the problem.

What are your salary requirements?

I'd expect a salary that's comparable to the going rate for someone in my field. What figure do you have in mind?

Recruiters want to weed out people whose financial goals are unrealistic. This question is a direct hit—it forces a response about a touchy subject. If you mention a salary that's too low, you may seem uninformed or desperate; too high, and you may eliminate yourself from further consideration. It's best to turn the question back on the recruiter. Ask the salary range for the position, then ask the recruiter to consider how your qualifications compare to the average requirements for the position. If the recruiter avoids answering and repeats the question, state a range and say that your salary needs will also take into account any benefits offered.

What is your current salary?

I currently earn an annual salary of twenty-five thousand dollars with full benefits.

By all means, if you're asked about your salary history, don't embellish. More and more companies are starting to verify applicants' pay history, some even demanding to see W–2 forms. If you get the job, a falsehood discovered even years later may be grounds for immediate dismissal. Don't leave yourself open to this kind of trouble.

Would you be willing to relocate to another city?

I'd prefer to be based here, but it's certainly a possibility I'd be willing to consider.

You may, even in some first interviews, be asked questions that seem to elicit a tremendous commitment on your behalf, like this one. Although such questions may be unfair during an initial job interview, you may well conclude that you have nothing to gain and everything to lose with a negative response. If you're asked such a question unexpectedly during an initial job interview, simply say something like "That's certainly a possibility" or "I'm willing to consider that." Later, if you receive an offer, you can find out the specific conditions and then decide if you wish to accept the position. Remember, at the job-offer stage you have the most negotiating power, and the employer may be willing to accommodate your needs. If that isn't the case, you might wish to explain that upon reflection, you've decided you can't (for instance) relocate, but you'd like to be considered for other positions that might open up in the future.

Does the frequent travel required for this work fit into your lifestyle?

The frequent travel in this consulting position is no problem for me or my family. I was recently married, but my wife is an airline flight attendant, so neither of us follows the typical nine-to-five routine.

If you're comfortable divulging information about your family situation, now is the time to do so. The interviewer is

concerned here that the candidate may not be able to travel as much as the job requires. To alleviate these concerns, emphasize your flexibility or explain why travel wouldn't be a problem.

Would you be able to work extended hours as necessary to perform the job?

I'm accustomed to working long hours during the week. I usually work until at least six-thirty, because I get a lot done after the office closes at five. I can make arrangements to be available on weekends if necessary, though I do prefer to have at least twenty-four hours' notice.

Your response should match closely the position you're applying for and should reflect a realistic understanding of the work and time required. Ask about seasonality of work if you're unsure, and show a willingness to work occasional extended hours.

Sell me this stapler.

This is a professional-quality stapler, designed to be functional as well as attractive. It will help you reduce clutter on your desk by enabling you to fasten pages together. And since papers relating to the same subject will now be attached, you'll be more efficient and will save time searching for papers. Finally, its sleek shape and black color are coordinated to match the rest of your office furniture.

With this kind of question the interviewer will want to determine how quickly you think on your feet, as well as your ability to communicate effectively and succinctly. Be prepared to give a thirty-second speech on the benefits and advantages of virtually any common office object, from a paper clip to a telephone, particularly if you're interviewing for a sales position.

Why should I hire you?

I offer over fifteen years of expertise in management, including electronic assembly for a major computer manufacturer and injection-molding operations for a prominent plastics company. Because I have the ability to adjust and learn new skills quickly, I've often been called upon to start new operations. I'm confident, on the basis of my skills and experience, that I can help improve production by leading a team effort directed at achieving your company's goals.

You'll usually encounter this question toward the end of a job interview; how you answer it can make or break your candidacy. Instead of reiterating your resume, emphasize only a few of your strongest qualifications and relate them to the position in question.

Prove to me that your interest is sincere.

I know that a lot of people want to get into television because of the money or because they just want to be on camera. But to me, communicating well is an art, and the television industry is the ultimate test of how well one communicates. Working in television isn't like working for a newspaper, where if a reader misses a fact, he or she can just go back and reread it. A television news story can go by in a flash, and the challenge is to make sure the audience understands it, learns from it, and, in a broader sense, can use the information to better their lives or their situations. It's the way television can evoke action that's always made me want to be a part of the industry. I'm particularly interested in this station because I like your focus on the community. Though the on-air products have a great nineties look, the station seems to remain focused on the tradition of local news and what matters to its audience. The special reports that emphasize town politics, that go on location each week to a different town for a live shot, that explain the big issues facing a community, make the viewer feel that the station is a part of the community. In my opinion, this is a great way to maintain a loyal audience.

Being unprepared to answer this question can eliminate you from further consideration. On the other hand, if you're able to demonstrate a strong interest in the company and in the position, you'll have an advantage over the competition.

What would you do if I told you I thought you were giving a very poor interview today?

Well, the first thing I'd do is ask you if there were any part of the interview you thought I mishandled. After that, I'd think back and try to remember if there had been any faulty communication on my part. Then I'd try to review possible problems I had understanding your questions, and I'd ask for clarification if I needed it. Finally, if we had time, I'd try to respond more fully and appropriately to the problem areas you identified for me.

Interviewers like to ask stress questions like these to see how well you hold up under pressure. Your best bet is to stay calm, relaxed, and don't allow your confidence to be shaken.

You have seven minutes to convince me why you're the best candidate for this position. Go.

Instead of following a traditional question-and-answer format for a job interview, some recruiters have been known to ask no more than this one question. Only the most prepared candidates will survive this type of interview. If you run into this question, your best bet is to discuss the themes you developed, emphasizing throughout one or two of your strongest qualifications for the position.

How would you respond to a defaulted form Z–65 counterderivative renewal request if your manager ordered you to do so, and if the policy under which the executive board resolves such issues were currently under review?

Sometimes recruiters ask seemingly impossible questions just to see how you'll respond. No matter how you may feel at the time, being subjected to a ridiculous question like this one is probably a good sign. If you're asked a tough question that you can't answer, think about it for a few seconds. Then, with a confident smile, simply say something like "I don't know, but if you hire me, I'll sure find out for you."

Special Situations

Interviewing can be even more stressful when you find yourself in a "special situation." Perhaps you lack paid job experience, have been out of the workplace to raise children, are concerned about possible discrimination because of age or disability, or are trying to enter a field in which you have no practical experience. Not to worry! The key to improving your chances in an interview is to emphasize your strengths. Focus on your marketable skills (whether they were acquired in the workplace or elsewhere) and highlight impressive achievements, relevant education and training, and/or related interests. Downplay or eliminate any information that may be construed as a weakness.

For example, if you're a "displaced homemaker" (a homemaker entering the job market for the first time), you can highlight the special skills you've acquired over the years, while downplaying your lack of paid job experience.

Questions for Career Changers

For those of you who've devoted your careers exclusively to one profession or industry, work experience really isn't an issue. You have lots of experience—but none of it relates to your current job objective. No problem! Instead of emphasizing your job history, emphasize the skills you've acquired that apply to the job you're seeking. For example, suppose your career has been in real estate and, in your spare time, you like to run in marathons. Recently you heard about an opening in the sales-and-marketing department at an athletic-shoe manufacturer. What you need to do is emphasize the skills you have that the employer is looking for. Not only do you have strong sales experience, you're familiar with the needs of the company's market, and that's a powerful combination!

Why do you want to leave your current position?

I've learned quite a bit about the plastics industry in my current position and am very glad to have had the opportunities I've had at Fiske, Inc. However, I've found that my interests really lie in research and development, which Fiske has recently decided to phase out over the next two years. That's why I'm so

Sometimes You're the Pigeon . . .

Suddenly, in the middle of the interview, they asked me: "Do you really think you're going to get this job?" I said "Yes, of course." And fortunately, I was right. I got the job.

— Jere

Sometimes You're the Statue . . .

A headhunter contacted me for a fantastic job with a major company in New York. To this day, I don't know how this headhunter found me, but I accepted the interview. I arrived at the interview, was called in to his office, and before I could even sit down he said "Do you consider yourself a loose cannon?" I am haunted by that question to this day—I don't know where it came from and it threw me so badly that by the end of the interview I knew that I wouldn't get the job.

—Jere

interested in this organization. As I understand it, Randy Corporation places a great deal of emphasis on R&D and is also a highly respected leader in the industry.

The interviewer's foremost concern with career changers will always be why they want to switch careers. Show the interviewer that your decision has been based on careful consideration. Explain why you decided on this particular position and how the position will allow you to further your natural skills and interests.

Why would you want to leave an established career at an employment agency for an essentially entry-level position in marketing?

I've enjoyed my work at the agency and have gained many valuable skills from it. At the same time, I feel as if I've stopped growing. I'm no longer challenged by my work. I've thought about this for a long time, and I'm confident it's time for a change. As for my interest in marketing, last year my teenage children and some of the other neighborhood kids decided to design and sell t-shirts to benefit a local family who'd lost their home to a fire. I pitched in by designing and distributing posters, placing advertisements in local newspapers, and selling shirts outside grocery stores and shopping malls. At first I really didn't give the project a lot of thought, but when I saw the fruits of my labor, I began to get excited about it. I learned that you can have a great product and a great cause, but if nobody knows about it, you're dead in the water. I finally felt as if I were making a difference—and I was good at it, too. Since then, I've taken two introductory marketing courses and am planning to enroll in a part-time degree program this fall. Furthermore, I'll be able to use many of the skills and abilities I've gained at the employment agency in the marketing field. After all, working for an employment agency is marketing—marketing the agency to corporate clients and job seekers, and marketing job seekers to corporate clients.

The interviewer is trying to determine two things: the candidate's motivation for choosing a new career and the likelihood that the candidate will be comfortable in a position where he or she will probably have less power and responsibility than in previous jobs. To dispel the interviewer's fears, discuss your reasons for switching careers and be sure to show that you have a solid understanding of the position and the industry in general. Many candidates expect to start their new careers in a job comparable to the one they held previously. But the truth is that most career changers must start in lower, if not entry-level, positions in their new company to gain basic experience and knowledge of the field.

Questions for Candidates Re-entering the Job Market

No doubt about it, if you've been out of the workforce for a while, you're facing some troubling issues. You may be feeling anxious, wondering if you've still got what it takes to make it out there. The key is to make sure all of your skills are up-to-date. If they aren't, consider retraining, which might mean learning a new computer program or taking a class at the local college. What you'll need to emphasize is your previous job experience and skills, ways you've kept up during your leave (reading trade journals, doing freelance work, attending seminars), and the skills you've learned at home that can be transferred to the workplace.

Your resume doesn't list any job experience in the past few years. Why not?

I took five years off to raise my son, Jason, who's now in kindergarten. It was a difficult decision for me, but at the time I decided I wouldn't be able to commit myself a hundred percent to my career with such tremendous responsibilities at home. And I didn't think it would be fair to my employer to give any less than my complete and total commitment. I believe it was the right decision for me at the time, but now I feel refreshed and ready to devote myself full-time to my career.

Whatever the reason for your hiatus, be honest. Discuss the decisions behind your absence, whether they were to stay home and raise a family or to recuperate from a debilitating injury. Tell the interviewer why you're now ready to return to work. Most important, emphasize your eagerness to resume your career.

I see you've been out of work for a while. What difficulties have you had in finding a job that's compatible with your interests?

It's true that I've been out of my field for the last four years, but I've had a number of tempting offers to jump back in. However, I thought it was important to stay home with my new baby and also continue a part-time family business, which I ran out of our home while my husband was completing law school. Now that that's behind us, I'm ready to return to my career in the entertainment industry.

The real question behind the interviewer's curiosity here is why someone else hasn't taken this candidate off the market. Why isn't the candidate in greater demand? Is he or she being unrealistic or perhaps going after a position just because it's available, without having given it much thought? Is there something in the job seeker's past that others have discovered? You'll need to alleviate such concerns by frankly discussing your situation. Be sure to emphasize how you've remained involved in your career during your sabbatical as well as your eagerness to rejoin the workforce.

Your resume indicates that you've been working for the past two years as a part-time clerk at Groom Lake Insurance Brokers. How will this experience help you in your banking career?

Groom Lake was in the process of computerizing its files, and I was hired primarily to check the computerized files for accuracy against the manual files. I recorded premium payments, prepared bank deposits, and sorted payables. Not only did this work help me keep my accounting skills current, I also learned valuable computer skills that will certainly help me become even more efficient and productive in my next position in banking.

The interviewer may be concerned here that the candidate is simply applying for any available job rather than for a specific position in a specific field. Explain how your experience relates to the position you're applying for and discuss any skills you've gained that are transferable to the position and company.

Illegal Questions

Illegal interview questions probe into your private life or personal background. Federal law forbids employers from discriminating against any person on the basis of sex, age, race, national origin, or religion. For instance, an interviewer may not ask you about your age or your date of birth. However, she or he may ask you if you're over eighteen years of age. If you're asked an illegal question at a job interview, keep in mind that many employers simply don't know what's legal and illegal.

One strategy in such cases is to try to discover the concerns behind the question and then address them. For instance, an employer who asks about your plans to have children may be concerned that you won't be able to fulfill the travel requirements of the position. Try to get to the heart of the issue by saying something like "I'm not quite sure I understand." If you can determine the interviewer's concerns, you can allay them with a reply like "I'm very interested in developing my career. Travel is definitely not a problem for me—in fact, I enjoy it tremendously."

Alternatively, you may choose to answer the question or to gracefully point out that the question is illegal and decline to respond. Avoid reacting in a hostile fashion—remember that you can always decide later to decline a job offer.

Any of the following responses is an acceptable way to handle these situations. Choose the response that's most comfortable for you, keeping in mind that adhering to your principles may cost you the job.

What religion do you practice?
Answer 1: I make it a point not to mix my personal beliefs with my work, if that's what you mean. I assure you that I value my career too much for that.

Be Resourceful

This is, believe it or not, a true story: One job candidate finally got a call for a job he really, really wanted. Unfortunately, he was deathly ill with the flu, but he accepted. When he arrived the next day, he was still sick. But he was determined to get through the interview.

Just after the interview started, the manager's phone rang and he excused himself for a few minutes. Our hero sat there waiting in his best suit. Suddenly, the worst happened. He realized he was going to be sick to his stomach. Not soon, but right now. The possibilities flashed through his mind. No time for the bathroom. He didn't see a trash barrel. And he couldn't just get sick on the carpet.

He carefully got sick in to his jacket, folded it up, placed it beneath his chair, and recomposed himself. A few minutes later, the manager returned. And, believe it or not, he got the job.

Answer 2: I'm not quite sure I understand what you're getting at. Would you please explain to me how this issue is relevant to the position?

Answer 3: That question makes me uncomfortable. I'd really rather not answer it.

How old are you?

Answer 1: I'm in my fifties and have over thirty years of experience in this industry. My area of expertise is in . . .

Answer 2: I'm not quite sure I understand what you're getting at. Would you please explain to me how this issue is relevant to the position?

Answer 3: That question makes me uncomfortable. I'd really rather not answer it.

Are you married?

Answer 1: No.

Answer 2: Yes, I am. But I keep my family life separate from my work life so that I can put all my effort into my job. I'm flexible when it comes to travel and late hours, as my references can confirm.

Answer 3: I'm not quite sure I understand what you're getting at. Would you please explain to me how this issue is relevant to the position?

Answer 4: That question makes me uncomfortable. I'd really rather not answer it.

Do you have children?

Answer 1: No.

Answer 2: Yes, I do. But I keep my family life separate from my work life so that I can put all my effort into my job. I'm flexible when it comes to travel and late hours, as my references can confirm.

Answer 3: I'm not quite sure I understand what you're getting at. Would you please explain to me how this issue is relevant to the position?

Answer 4: That question makes me uncomfortable. I'd really rather not answer it.

Do you plan to have children?

Answer 1: No.

Answer 2: It's certainly a consideration, but if I do, it won't be for some time. I want to do the best job I can for this company and have no plans to leave just as I begin to make meaningful contributions.

Answer 3: I can't answer that right now. But if I ever do decide to have children, I wouldn't let it detract from my work. Becoming a parent is important, but my career is certainly important to me, too. I plan on putting all of my efforts into this job and this company.

Answer 4: I'm not quite sure I understand what you're getting at. Would you please explain to me how this issue is relevant to the position?

Answer 5: That question makes me uncomfortable. I'd really rather not answer it.

For Students and Recent Graduates

Being So Positive That It Hurts

Many inexperienced job candidates kill their chances for a job by making negative comments during an interview. A college student or recent grad should never make a negative statement about a former boss or teacher—even if it's completely true and fully justified. If the recruiter asks why you had an unsatisfactory grade in a particular course, don't say "The professor graded me unfairly" or "I didn't get along with the professor."

A recruiter would rather hire someone who gets and deserves an unsatisfactory grade in a course than someone who either doesn't get along with people or shifts blame to others. On the other hand, you can greatly increase your chances of getting any job by projecting a positive, upbeat attitude. This is one of the best ways to stand out from the competition. You can project this image by smiling from time to time during the interview; by responding to interview questions with enthusiasm; by demonstrating excitement

Skirt versus Pants for Women

For those women who are still convinced that pants are acceptable interview attire, listen to the words of one career counselor from a prestigious New England college: "I had a student who told me that since she knew women in her industry often wore pants to work, she was going to wear pants to her interviews. Almost every recruiter commented that her pants were 'too casual' and even referred to her as 'the one with the pants.' The funny thing was that one of the recruiters who commented on her pants had been wearing jeans!"

about your past accomplishments; and by showing optimism about the prospect of starting your career.

Commonly Asked Questions

Whether you're graduating from high school or college, those of you with little or no work history face the same dilemma: it's tough to get a job without experience, and it seems impossible to gain experience without getting hired. But, as you'll see, there are ways to get around this problem—by emphasizing your strengths and educational achievements.

The following responses to interview questions are listed as examples to show you how questions should be handled. They should not be used as the basis of "canned" or scripted answers. Adapt these responses for your own circumstances, but remember that, especially for college students or recent grads, how an answer is given can be more important than what's said. Be positive, project confidence, smile and make eye contact with the interviewer, listen carefully, and go with the flow!

About School Grades

It's likely that if you've made it to the interview stage, you fulfill the basic criteria for the position, including the education requirements. The recruiter is probably trying to judge here how well the candidate handles adversity. It's important not to get defensive or to place blame. Instead, try to put a positive spin on the question—for example, by concentrating on what you learned and the extra effort you put in rather than on the grades you received.

Why are your grades so erratic?

I never hesitated to sign up for a course just because it had a reputation for being difficult. In fact, my American History professor, whose course I enjoyed tremendously, is notorious for giving out only one "A" for each class. You may have noticed that while my major is English, I did take four courses in physics, because I thought they were important to round out my education, and I enjoyed the challenge they presented. Almost everyone else in these courses was a physics major.

About Academics

What was your favorite class?

Outside of my major, one of the classes I particularly enjoyed was an introductory course in economics that I took last semester. It was a completely new subject area to me, and I enjoy new challenges! I was particularly fascinated with macroeconomic theory, where complex mathematical equations can be combined with psychology to explain past economic events and predict future trends.

What course did you find most challenging?

Initially, I was completely overwhelmed by the introductory chemistry course I took last year. No matter how hard I studied, I seemed to be getting nowhere. I failed the first three quizzes. So I tried a new approach. Instead of just studying by myself, I had a friend—a chemistry major—help me with my studies. I also began to get help after class from the professor from time to time. And I found that more time spent in the lab was critical. I ended up with a B+ in the course, and I felt I achieved a solid understanding of the material. More than that, I learned that tackling a new field of study sometimes requires a new approach, not just hard work, and that the help of others can be crucial!

The interviewer will want to see how well you respond to difficult situations. Demonstrate that you won't fold in the face of difficulty and that you're willing to put in the extra effort to meet a challenge.

How do you organize yourself for a large project like writing a term paper?

My first step is to read a book that presents a survey of the time period involved and work up a tentative one-page outline. Then I gather all the appropriate books for reference and begin compiling notes onto index cards. I organize the index cards as logically as possible and tentatively form my thesis statement in my mind. After that, I compose a revised and much more

detailed outline. Finally I put my thoughts on paper, following both my outline and index cards.

How do you prepare for a major examination?

Well, let's take a recent exam I had in Twentieth-Century Art as an example. First, I skimmed the material from two lessons that I felt particularly weak in. Then I went through my class notes again, and I went through the chapter summaries in the textbook for every lesson except those I had just read this week.

Why did you decide to major in history?

It was a difficult choice, because I was also attracted to government, international relations, and economics. But the study of history allowed me to combine all three, especially since I focused on economic history. I also found several of the professors in the department exceptionally knowledgeable and stimulating.

Show that you have solid, logical reasons for choosing your major. If you can't defend your choice of major, the interviewer will wonder how much thought you've put into choosing a career. You should also be sure that your reasons for choosing your major are compatible with your career choice. For instance, if you're applying for a position as a banker, don't say you were an English major because you love literature and writing.

I see the title of your senior thesis is "A Comparative Study of Causal Analyses of the Great Depression." Tell me about your thesis and the conclusions of your study.

It's fascinating to me that even today, there is tremendous disagreement among scholars about the relative importance of various factors leading to the Great Depression. I examined the methodologies used in some of the most prominent works and critically compared their ability to explain this phenomenon. I concluded that the most meaningful analysis gave essentially equal weight to psychological and economic factors.

About Extracurricular Activities

Why did you participate so little in extracurricular activities?

I wanted to give as much effort as possible to my studies. I came from a high school in a small town, where I received mostly As, but this didn't prepare me well for college. So I studied very hard. However, I've found time to explore the city and make new friends, and I do enjoy informal socializing on weekends.

The interviewer may be worried that if you don't have many outside interests, you may eventually suffer from burnout. Employers like candidates who are well-rounded and have interests outside work. If you didn't participate in formal extracurricular activities in college, you still may want to talk about some of your interests, like reading or exercising, that you participated in on a more informal level. For instance, you may have a passion for running, even if you weren't on the college track team.

You seem to have participated a little bit in a lot of different extracurricular activities. Didn't any of them really hold your interest?

I've always felt it was important to have a well-rounded education, and I looked at extracurricular activities as an important part of that education. That's why I participated in many different activities—to broaden my experience and meet new people. I did particularly enjoy the drama club and the cycling team, but I made a conscious effort not to spend too much time on them and to try new and different activities.

You're certainly a talented athlete. You won a schoolwide singles Beer Die championship, you have a low handicap at golf, and you participate in horseback-riding competitions.

competitions. But I'm surprised you don't list any team sports on your resume.

I'm the kind of person who enjoys staying with an activity for a long period and becoming proficient at it. While I do play team sports on a pickup basis, I've chosen to focus on sports I can play for years to come, long after I've left college.

I see you made the football team as a sophomore. Why didn't you play varsity football your junior or senior years?

While I enjoyed the comradeship and being part of the team, I did find practices and drills to be tedious and unchallenging. I was always assigned to play guard, and how many different ways can you block a rusher? Instead, I joined the Drama Club and was able to give more time to my studies. While I didn't become a great actor, it was an enriching experience.

Where would you like to be in five years?

I plan to remain in the banking industry for the foreseeable future. I hope that within five years, I'll have developed a successful track record as a loan officer, first perhaps with consumer loans, then switching to business loans. Ideally, I'd hope that within five years I'd also have advanced to servicing middle-market-size companies.

About Tough Academic Situations

Your transcript reads "incomplete" for your second semester sophomore year courses. Why?

I was suspended from school for the second half of the semester for being at a party where there was excessive drinking and damage to school property. While I didn't cause any damage to school property myself, I accept responsibility for the incident, I paid the penalty, and I learned my lesson. I was grateful for the opportunity to return to school. I applied myself with vigor to my studies and have never been involved in any other incident.

I see that you failed two courses your last semester freshman year and then took a year off before returning to school. I assume there's a connection?

Four years ago, as a freshman, I didn't know what I wanted to study, what career I wanted to pursue, or what direction I was headed in. The year off from school was one of the most constructive experiences of my life. After working as a dishwasher in a restaurant for much of the year, I developed a lot of respect for the value of a college education. I came to school completely refreshed, embarked on a major in English, and committed myself to pursuing a career where I could use my mind a little more and my hands a little less.

About Work Experience

Did you enjoy your summer job as a dishwasher at Lake Ogabohgee Grill?

I wouldn't want to do it for the rest of my life, but it was fine for a summer job. The work was more interesting than you might think, I enjoyed my coworkers, and I had a great rapport with my boss!

I see you worked as a lifeguard one summer, mowed lawns another summer, and did babysitting the two other summers. Which job did you find most interesting?

Actually, by far the most interesting job I held wasn't a summer job but a part-time job I had at school. I did research for my political science professor's just-published book, The Disaffected Electorate. *It's based on extensive surveys that show that most people feel state and federal politicians aren't responsive to their constituents. I conducted hundreds of door-to-door interviews to compile the information and helped tabulate the results. It was fascinating to be part of this study almost from start to finish, and at the same time it was dismaying to see, from the results, how disenfranchised people feel.*

I see you've been working as a waitperson at Double-D's Bar & Grill since graduation. How much notice would you have to give them if I offered you this position?

I'd feel obliged to offer my current employer two weeks notice. But if my boss doesn't object, I may be able to leave earlier.

About Lack of Work Experience

I see that while you returned to your hometown each summer, you worked at different companies. Why didn't you work the same job two summers in a row?

My career goal is to get a job in business after graduation. Because I attend a liberal arts college, I can't take any courses in business. So even though I was invited back to each summer job I held, I thought I could develop more experience by working in different positions. Although I didn't list high school jobs on my resume, I did work for almost three years at the same grocery store chain.

I see that you traveled each of the last two summers rather than taking a summer job. Do you expect to be traveling a lot after you graduate from college?

I figured that once I graduate from college, I'll spend the next forty years of my life working, so I might as well get in some extended travel while I have a chance. I hope to begin a career position immediately upon graduating, and I plan to stay with that company for some time.

About Future Plans

Do you plan to attend graduate school?

Definitely not on a full-time basis. At some point I might like to take courses at night that could contribute to my work performance.

HELP
THIS WAY

I see that you grew up in Hawaii. That's a long way away. Do you plan on going back there to live sometime in the future?

No. I'd prefer to be based in a large mainland city, like here, but I'd be perfectly happy to go wherever my career might take me.

About Your Work Preferences

Why do you want to work in retailing?

I've been fascinated by the retail trade as long as I can remember. To me, each store is a stage or theater for its merchandise; the same merchandise can be sold in an infinite variety of ways. I know it's a challenging field, too. Merchants need to think about current fashion trends, the needs of local consumers, building a niche in the market, and all the other aspects of running a business. Also, retail is a field that's changing quickly, and I want to see firsthand in what direction retailing is going.

What other types of positions are you interested in, and what other companies have you recently applied to for work?

Actually, I've definitely decided to pursue a career as a restaurant manager, so I'm applying only for restaurant management training programs. I've recently had interviews with several other large national fast-food chains, including Shayko Chicken, The Peach Pit, and Salient Greene's Eating Emporium.

Have you thought about why you might prefer to work with our firm as opposed to one of the other firms to which you've applied?

Yes. I like your policy of promotion from within. I think the company's growth record is impressive, and I'm sure it will continue. Your firm's reputation for superior marketing is particularly important to me, because I want to pursue a career in marketing. Most important, it seems that your firm would offer a lot of opportunities—not just for possible advancement but also to learn about many different product lines.

About You As a Person

Tell me about yourself.

It takes me about thirty minutes in the morning to wake up, but after that I'm all revved up and ready to go. I have a tremendous amount of energy and love challenges at school, at work, and at home. This is true even when I'm performing mundane tasks, like when I worked at a direct-mail house last summer stuffing brochures into envelopes. I set up a challenge for myself to have the highest pace of anyone in the office, and I succeeded on every day but four during the entire summer. I also enjoy being around other people, working with them, and helping them. For example, I really enjoyed tutoring freshmen in math.

How would you like other people to think of you?

I like people to think I'm there when they need me. But more than that, I want to be thought of as fair, considerate, and evenhanded. I want everyone I come in contact with to be able to say afterward that it was a positive experience.

Planner notes

11 INFORMATIONAL M...
BURNS RESEARCH A...

12 TOUR OF FACILITY

1 INTERVIEW WITH KARA H...
AT BURNS RESEARCH AGE...

2

3 Commute HOME
* SEND THANK YOU NOTE
4 GO TO CAREER FAIR

5

9

WWW.CAREERCITY.COM

*

... HEAD HUNTE...

INFORMATIONAL MEE...
...URNS RESEARCH AGE...
... OF FACILITY
...EW WITH KARA H...
... RESEARCH A...

11 A.M. - 3 P.M.
NFO. MEETING, TO...
T BURNS RESEARC...

9 A.M. WEDNESDAY
NTERVIEW WITH...
AT NARD INC.

THURSDA...

8 A.M. FRIDAY
MEET WITH BILL...
DIRECTOR OF CAREER...
AT BIG RED UNIV...

SATURDAY

Action list

DATE:

TO DO   ACTION LIST

CHAPTER 15

Computerized Job Interviews and Tests

Computerized Job Interviews

Just when you thought the whole job search process couldn't get any more high-tech, along comes the computerized job interview. Computerized interviews are used by companies that traditionally hire large volumes of workers, like banks, hospitals, hotels, and retailers. Many of these companies are now having candidates complete a computerized job interview in place of an initial screening interview with a human resources representative.

As in the traditional screening interview, the computer asks the candidates questions regarding their work history, background, skills, and qualifications, usually in the true/false or multiple choice formats. Once the interview is complete, the computer provides the interviewer with a summary of the candidate's answers. Among other things, this summary might recommend a face-to-face interview and give the interviewer a list of follow-up questions.

A Structured Interview

Computerized job interviews are based on the principle of the structured job interview. Structured job interviews, long valued by human resources professionals, are interviews where each candidate is asked the same set of questions. (This is usually used only for the initial screening interviews; second interviews tend to be less structured and more of a conversation.) Advocates of the structured interview say it brings a consistency and fairness to the hiring process that's lacking when nonstructured interviews are used—the standardized format of the interview allows recruiters to more easily compare candidates' responses. Also, each question is carefully phrased, so the interviewer doesn't have to worry about breaking any employment laws. One final advantage—structured interviews gather more information in less time than nonstructured interviews.

What to Expect

A computer-assisted interview proceeds in much the same way as a traditional interview. You receive a call, schedule a mutually convenient time, come into the office, and meet with a human resources representative. However, instead of the traditional

Advantages and Disadvantages of Computer-Assisted Job Interviews

Candidates who have taken computer-assisted interviews give high marks to the computer; many report being less nervous during the interview. Human resources professionals like the system because it streamlines the hiring process and makes it more effective. Companies that use computer-assisted job interviews report higher productivity, improved customer service, lower employee turnover and absenteeism, and less theft in the workplace.

(continued)

screening interview, you're led to a computer workstation and are given instructions on how to proceed. Most interview programs are intuitive and, providing you're computer literate, easy to navigate. You're generally given a time limit, usually about thirty minutes, to finish the interview.

Expect to be asked about a hundred questions regarding your educational background, employment history, job skills, work ethic, and more. Following is an example of questions you might expect from the ApView computer-assisted interview from SHL Aspen Tree Software:

Are you currently employed?
A. Yes
B. No

Why did you leave your last job, or why do you want to leave your present job?
A. I was dismissed
B. I was laid off
C. To take a better job
D. Relocation
E. To go to school
F. I am not leaving my present job
G. Other reason

How often do/did you experience conflict with your coworkers?
A. Often
B. Sometimes
C. Rarely
D. Never
E. Cannot say

What kind of recommendation do you think your present or most recent supervisor would give you?
A. Outstanding
B. Above average
C. Average

(continued from previous page)

Computer-assisted interviews also have a few major shortcomings. First, some people say that the questions in these programs are biased against certain groups, especially women and minorities. Also, a computer is not always able to take into account certain special circumstances, like a history of unemployment because of a disability or family obligations, and will provide a negative report to a recruiter. Finally, a computer is not, obviously, a person. It can't discern the intangibles that make us who we are—it can't measure eagerness and enthusiasm or, alternatively, negativity and pessimism.

D. Below average

E. I don't know

Bob, on previous jobs were you able to develop new or better ways of doing the work assigned to you?

A. Most of the time

B. Usually

C. Sometimes

D. Seldom

E. Never

In the past, most computerized job interviews consisted entirely of multiple-choice or true/false questions, but some now require more extended, written responses. ApView, for example, offers its customers the option of open-ended questions instead of, or in addition to, multiple-choice questions. Naturally, these types of answers are reviewed by a recruiter or hiring manager, not a computer. Most computer-assisted interviews are custom-made for each company or position. Generally, the interview is developed to address specific issues for a position or family of positions. This eliminates your being asked questions that are irrelevant to the position.

Accuracy Counts . . .

Answer the questions in a computer-assisted interview just as you would in a traditional interview. Don't exaggerate your skills and accomplishments. For instance, don't tell a computer you have five years' experience in retail if, in reality, you have experience only as a seasoned shopper. Remember, a computer-assisted interview is just the first step; if you're selected for a face-to-face interview, the interviewer will see from your application and resume that you were lying to the computer, which will eliminate you from contention.

It's important to be *more* accurate with computerized interviews, because computers, unlike their human counterparts, immediately pick up on inconsistencies in your responses. A human interviewer may be distracted and fail to note contradictions during an interview, but a computer is programmed to flag inconsistencies for the interviewer.

... But Don't Bare Your Soul

At the same time, don't be *too* honest with the computer. Several studies have shown that people are more honest with a computer because the computer is unbiased and not judgmental. People are likely to tell a computer facts about themselves they wouldn't dream of telling a human interviewer, especially in sensitive areas. However, before you bare your soul, remember that the computer will feed your answers to a human as soon as the interview is over. In short, never tell a computer anything you wouldn't tell a real interviewer.

What the Computer Tells the Interviewer

Once you've completed the interview, the recruiter will explain the next steps in the interviewing process. Generally, the program analyzes your responses and presents a summary. The recruiter reads the report and decides whether you have the qualifications to warrant a second interview. Among other things, the report summarizes basic background information, like education level and length of employment with your past or current company. It also highlights questions where you had an abnormally long pause before responding. This is done because several studies have shown that it takes longer to lie than to tell the truth. The report also flags inconsistencies and contradictions in your responses. For instance, some systems may have tricks worked in, so if you gave a certain response to a particular question or set of questions, the computer flags those responses. Most programs also provide a list of follow-up questions based on your answers. For instance, in the sample questions listed earlier, the follow-up to question number five is, "Give me an example of something you developed on a previous job that enhanced a work assignment."

Some programs also compare the results of your interview with a standardized employee profile developed for the company. By comparing your answers with those of successful hires, the computer can predict—usually with measurable success—whether you'll be a successful employee.

Internet Job Interview

This method of interviewing is quickly gaining popularity, especially for long-distance job searches. For instance, say you're applying for a position with a company in Chicago but you live in San Francisco. If you're hooked up on-line, you can complete a screening interview on your home computer. Companies use this because it saves them time, although there's some debate as to how helpful it is compared to actually talking to someone on the phone.

The process starts like any other: You're contacted for an initial screening interview, but instead of a telephone or face-to-face interview, you're provided with a password that gives you access to the company's in-house computer system. Once you log on, the process is essentially a computer-assisted interview. You're asked basic questions about your background and work experience, and the computer generates a report for the recruiter. Companies like this because it's a big time-saver, but it also benefits job seekers, since travel expenses for interviews are usually paid for only the most high-level executives or most highly sought college recruits.

Computerized Telephone Interview

Job interviews via the telephone are nothing new to job seeking. The telephone interview is often the first contact a job seeker has with a potential employer: A human resources person or hiring manager will call up a candidate, ask a few basic questions, and, if those questions are answered satisfactorily, invite the candidate in for a face-to-face interview.

A computerized telephone interview is similar to a regular telephone interview. It's designed to get a better sense of a candidate's background, to help determine suitability for a particular position. With the ApView interview from SHL Aspen Tree Software, an applicant calls a phone number and—using a touch-tone phone—answers some basic questions regarding his or her qualifications. If the candidate meets the position's requirements, the candidate can schedule a more in-depth interview. SHL Aspen Tree reports that this system is especially helpful to companies that are planning to hire workers in large numbers, as for site openings or seasonal employment.

Pinkerton Services Group designs computerized structured interviews for client companies. Offered as part of their pre-employment assessment services, the IntelliView Structured Interview System is a hundred-question interview about an applicant's employment background. These questions are of the yes/no variety, which makes it easier on the applicants, because they have less information to remember before they respond. This system, which can be administered either over the telephone or on a computer, is constructed for a particular industry rather than for a company or position. Each interview contains about one hundred generic questions regarding the industry (like retail, health care, or child care) or the work area (like customer service). For instance, someone taking the child-care interview may be asked if he or she likes to work in an orderly, quiet environment. A candidate who answers yes would probably not last long in a day-care center.

Scenario-Based Interview

As the name implies, a scenario-based interview involves more situational interviewing than the structured, computerized multiple-choice interviews discussed above. Scenario-based interviews are used to see how candidates behave in simulated work situations. Learning Systems Sciences, a leader in this type of computerized interview, reports that their clientele consists primarily of banks and retail establishments, including many large department store chains. Like the structured, computerized job interviews, these interviews are most often used to screen candidates for entry-level positions that traditionally have high turnover rates. Candidates who pass these simulations are brought in for a face-to-face interview.

Many companies prefer this type of interviewing, because instead of asking someone, for instance, how he or she feels about customer service, the employer can see how a candidate will perform in tough situations. For instance, the computer screen might show an irate customer yelling about a product he bought that he believes is faulty, and the candidate must try to placate the customer.

Advantages of Scenario-Based Interviews

Scenario-based interviews help give candidates a realistic idea of what to expect when they're on the job. For instance, many people say they like working with people, but that doesn't always include rude and unpleasant people. If someone is unable to handle a tough situation on a computer, chances are he or she won't be able to handle one in real life. It's better to find this out before accepting a position and beginning work.

Since these types of systems assess how well someone can read a situation and act appropriately, companies that use them report lower turnover rates than those that still use traditional methods. Like users of the computerized, structured job interviews, companies that use these systems also report an improvement in the overall quality of employees.

Instead of having a candidate key in one of a set of preformulated answers, the computer records the candidate's voice, allowing the recruiter to hear how he or she handled the situation. Did the candidate remain calm and polite, or did he or she sound harried and rude? Candidates are usually graded on a decided-upon scale. For instance, a candidate might get extra points for apologizing to a customer but could lose points for not sounding sincere.

Computerized Assessment Tests

Assessment tests are nothing new to the world of job hunting. For years, applicants have been asked to take all kinds of tests to evaluate their suitability. The reasoning behind these tests is simple: hiring new employees is time-consuming and expensive. By carefully screening applicants with both structured, computer-assisted interviews and computerized assessment tests, recruiters can greatly reduce the chances that a new hire will leave after only a few months.

Types of Computerized Assessment Tests

Employers generally use three main types of assessment tests: skills, integrity, and personality. The purpose of each of these tests is pretty basic. Skills tests determine if you have the ability to do a particular job, integrity tests help determine whether you'll be a trustworthy employee, and personality tests tell the interviewer if your disposition is suited for a particular position. Depending on the nature of the position, you may be asked to take one, two, or all three tests.

Most positions require some type of skills test—for example, a math test for accountants and a typing test for administrative assistants. Some computer programmers are even asked to write a short program as part of their pre-employment testing. If you're applying for a position where you'll be dealing with goods or money, you'll probably be required to take an integrity test. Personality or psychological tests can be used in virtually any situation but are especially common if you're interviewing for a management position or one where you'd be working with sensitive material.

Pinkerton Services Group stresses that prevention—by using pre-employment screening like personality and integrity testing—is the best way to reduce or eliminate serious workplace issues like theft, drug use, or even employee violence.

What to Expect

Skills tests can often be part of the initial screening process, but personality and integrity tests are usually one of the last steps of the interviewing process. If you're asked to take a computerized assessment test, your interviewer will likely take you to a room with a computer. After you receive instructions on how to use the program, the test will be administered, usually with a time limit. Depending on the nature of the test, you may answer multiple-choice or true/false questions or transcribe written information into a computer program. Integrity and personality tests typically contain upwards of one hundred questions. Most are of the multiple-choice, yes/no, true/false, always/sometimes/never variety. Once your time is up, the computer will score your work and, if applicable, compare your answers to a specified profile. It then generates a report that tells the recruiter how a candidate fits in relation to other candidates.

Computerized Skills Tests

Skills tests are the most straightforward types of computerized assessment tests. Basically, they measure your aptitude for performing a specific task or duty. Anyone who has done any temporary work will be familiar with many computerized skills tests. These tests determine your proficiency in word processing, spreadsheet, and database programs. You're asked to do some basic exercises using the various applications and are tested on your accuracy. With some tests, especially those for word processing programs, you have a certain amount of time to format and write a document, for example. Then the computer tests not only your accuracy but how much you managed to accomplish in that time. Similarly, a spreadsheet test might judge you on how quickly and accurately you can enter data and perform different functions.

An accountant or engineer might be tested on his or her mathematical or logical reasoning skills. A computer programmer might need to write a few lines of code or debug a problematic program. A test may measure the applicant's reaction time or memory.

Scoring

Computerized skills assessment tests are measured on your raw score, which is then compared to a mean, or average score, of everyone who has taken the test. For instance, if you scored a seventy-five and the mean is sixty-eight, this will show the employer that you have above-average skills.

Strategy

Unfortunately, there's no real way to prepare for skills tests. The best you can do is prepare for the type of test, like a typing or math test, by brushing up on those skills.

Computerized Integrity Tests

Integrity tests measure your honesty and morals. The Pinkerton Stanton Survey, for instance, is designed to measure the moral standard by which you live. This doesn't just mean whether someone is likely to embezzle company funds or steal from the cash register. An applicant's level of honesty and moral standard can also help determine whether someone is likely to be tardy, socialize excessively during work hours, leave early, take long lunches, "borrow" office equipment, and so forth.

Integrity tests allow employers to measure a candidate's reliability, work ethic, and trustworthiness. These traits are important indicators of performance. For instance, a recruiter might question the candidacy of an applicant who, on his integrity test, stated that it's all right to steal sometimes.

Strategy

When taking an integrity test, try to avoid absolutes, like always or never. No one is likely to believe you if you say you've never in your whole life lied or have never gotten so much as a parking ticket. Simply be honest, but don't reveal more than you have to.

Computerized Personality Tests

Personality tests are the most complex of all computerized assessment tests. They're generally used to see if a candidate's personality is suited to the job. Tests like Pinkerton's Adult Personality Survey measure traits like work motivation, adaptability, and trustworthiness. The results of a personality test are then compared against a standard, or norm, developed from those who have previously taken the test. For instance, if you're applying for a position as an insurance underwriter, your scores will be measured against a norm group of successful underwriters.

Companies like personality tests because they allow them to see if you'll fit in. This benefits both you and the employer, because if you're not happy with your job, it hurts both you and the company. The company has wasted time and money to train you only to have you quit in a few months, and you've wasted time in a job you didn't like.

Another Pinkerton test, the Stanton Profile, is a hybrid personality/skills test that measures work preferences to determine general employability. The score is measured against the minimum requirements of a particular job. For instance, the test will ask you a question regarding your adaptability. This is a good trait for an administrative assistant but less important for someone working in a stockroom, who will likely be doing the same tasks day after day.

Strategy

While preparing for skills and integrity tests is difficult, preparing for personality tests is nearly impossible. First, many people aren't sure whether they should let their "true" selves answer questions or should answer based on the kind of personality they think the company is looking for. Experts differ on the subject. Some suggest you use your work personality; others say you should just be yourself. Still others suggest coming up with a "character" based on successful friends and colleagues.

While it's good to look at traits that have made others successful, first look at what's gotten you where you are. If you've spent any time in the workforce, you know that your work personality differs from your personality outside work. Therefore, use what you've learned in the workplace—what is and isn't acceptable workplace behavior—to answer the questions.

As with the integrity tests, try to avoid using absolutes like "always" and "never." A large number of "always" and "never" answers might make it look as if you're lying—or, worse, be a signal of extreme behavior. Employers look for moderation and tend to stay away from extremists.

CALL HEAD HUNTER

AD'S
FAX RESUMES

LL HEAD HUNTER

PICK UP Suit at
Dry Clean
Thank y
Note

SEND THANKS
Note

9 A.M.
INTERVIEW WITH THOM TANI
AT NARD INC.

8 A.M.
MEET WITH BILL MacNEILL
DIRECTOR OF CAREER PLANNING
AT BIG RED UNIVERSITY

NFORMATIO
URNS RES
UR OF

RVIE
URN

TO DO

ACTION LIST   DATE:

Get Sunday Newspaper
WANT-ADS
Mail/Fax Resumes ✓

Call Head Hunter ✓

Pick up Suit at
Dry Cleaners ✓

Send Thank You
Notes

ACTION LIST

YEAR

HEAD HUNTER

11 INFORMATIONAL MEETING
    BURNS RESEARCH AGENCY
12 TOUR OF FACILITY

1   INTERVIEW WITH KARA FORR
    AT BURNS RESEARCH AGEN

2

3   Commute Home
    * SEND THANK YOU NOT
    GO TO CAREER FAIR

4

5

6

TOUR, IN
ARCH AGE.

WITH THOM TANI
NC.

VW.CAREERCITY.COM

11 INFORMATIONAL M
BURNS RESEARCH A
12 TOUR OF FACILITY

1 INTERVIEW WITH KARA H
AT BURNS RESEARCH AGE

2

3 Commute Home
* SEND THANK YOU NOTE
4 GO TO CAREER FAIR

5

WWW.CAREERCITY.COM

9

HEAD HUNTE

INFORMATIONAL MEE
URNS RESEARCH AGE
R OF FACILITY

EW WITH KARA
RESEARCH

11 A.M. – 3 P.M.
NFO. MEETING, TO
T BURNS RESEARCH

9 A.M.   WEDNESDAY
INTERVIEW WITH
AT NARD INC.

THURSDA

8 A.M.   FRIDAY
MEET WITH BILL
DIRECTOR OF CAREER
AT BIG RED UNIV

SATURDAY

DATE:

TO DO   ACTION LIST

CHAPTER 16

The Job Offer

In today's tough economy, one of the most nerve-racking steps on the trail to a new job is near the end of the path: deciding whether to accept an offer. On the one hand, if you've been in the job market for some time, your instinct may scream, "I'll take it, I'll take it," before the last syllables of the offer are out of the recruiter's mouth. On the other hand, you may also be worrying that the salary being offered won't be enough.

Faced with these conflicting emotions, it's easy to see how many job seekers can make unnecessary, costly mistakes during this final, vitally important stage. Far too many job seekers sell themselves short without even exploring their options. Others have wildly unrealistic expectations of what level of compensation they should expect. Still others get so wrapped up in money questions that they forget to consider any other issues, which is a big mistake.

Do You Want This Job?

If you're going to consider a job offer seriously, be confident that it is a job you really want. Are you willing to live and work in the area in question? Is the work schedule and way of life one you'd enjoy? If you're just graduating, is the job in the field you'd like to pursue?

Will It Help Your Career?

Whether or not a job will help your career progress is ultimately a much more important question than what your starting salary will be. In some organizations, you may be given a lot of responsibility right away but then find your progress blocked. Make sure you know if there are opportunities for advancement. Ask about performance reviews—how often are they conducted?

Do You Like the Environment?

Another important factor to consider is the kind of environment in which you'll be working. Is the company's atmosphere comfortable, challenging, and exciting? Consider specifics, including office or workstation setting, privacy, proximity to other staff, amount of space, noise level, and lighting. What is the level of interaction among coworkers? Some organizations strongly encourage teamwork and dialogue among staff, while others emphasize individual accomplishment. Which approach works better for you? Remember: If you don't like the work environment before you accept the job, you probably won't like it as an employee.

The Money Questions

The questions of salary and benefits strike fear into the hearts of job seekers young and old. But handling the inevitable money questions doesn't have to be difficult, and the more you think about them in advance, the easier they'll be to answer.

First, never try to negotiate salary or benefits until you've gotten an offer. At that point, don't worry about the recruiter withdrawing his or her handshake and showing you the door if you dare ask about flexibility in the company's offer. The worst case might be that the salary is set by company policy and the recruiter has no power to negotiate. Or else the recruiter may not be able to give you an immediate answer and will have to get back to you.

Negotiating a Salary

According to David G. Jensen, of Search Masters International, companies come in two types—those that won't negotiate salaries and those that will. He refers to these philosophies as "First offer, best offer" and "Negotiation is OK and expected." It's necessary to find out which type your company is before attempting to negotiate. You can determine this from their response to an appropriately phrased question about more money or benefits. The idea is to first assure them of your interest, then give reasons for your proposed increase rather than just saying you need it or want it. For example, explain why their offer doesn't sufficiently cover your living expenses or moving expenses or the cost of maintaining a wardrobe if your position requires you to dress up. Their response to this will indicate whether they're willing to negotiate or not. David Jensen's Web page, at *www.bio.com/hr/search/search_1.html* discusses these two approaches in greater detail, along with other aspects of job searching.

If you do negotiate, this doesn't mean you name a figure and the employer either matches it or doesn't. It means you're ready to listen to what the recruiter has to offer and give it consideration. To succeed in negotiation, both parties have to reach an agreement with which they're happy. If you succeed at winning yourself a bigger paycheck but antagonize your future boss in doing so, trouble lies ahead. If, on the other hand, you set realistic expectations and realize you may not get everything you want, you'll probably do just fine.

How Much Should You Expect?

Just how do you know how much you should expect? The answer is the same as in every other step of your job search: Do your homework. Read the trade journals for your industry. Read the newspaper help-wanted ads. If possible, talk to current employees. The *Occupational Outlook Handbook,* mentioned in Chapter 2 and available in libraries, lists salaries and other information about a variety of jobs.

Try to get objective comments. Alumni of your college or university in similar positions (or employed by the same organization) may be an excellent source of information. Doing this research will give you an idea of the salary level you can realistically expect.

Your Expectations

Setting realistic expectations is especially important for the entry-level job seeker or recent graduate. If you don't have a lot of professional experience, you don't leave the recruiter with much hard evidence on which to base a decision. Instead, you're asking him or her to take a leap of faith based on potential you've demonstrated in classes, internships, volunteering, or extracurricular activities. Without a track record of professional experience, your arsenal is missing a powerful weapon. This is why entry-level salaries are often determined by the marketplace, which leaves you with little leverage. Even so, that doesn't mean you can't give it a try.

On the other hand, if you have some experience under your belt and are looking for a mid-level or executive position, your negotiating power might be much greater. For a lucky (or unlucky) few at the top of the heap, salary and benefit negotiations can be as complex and painstakingly slow as watching the grass grow. Whatever your level of experience, your task is to try to figure out just how high the employer is likely to go.

Don't Mention It

If, after listening politely to the specifics of the offer, you're left hoping for a higher salary, greater health coverage, or something else, it's okay to (calmly) say so. Find out if the offer is firm. If it seems there may be some room to negotiate, make sure you have a figure in mind, because if the recruiter does have the freedom to barter, he or she will probably ask you point blank to supply a figure.

When you're asked that question, rule number one is as follows: *Don't tip your hand by giving the interviewer a specific number for which you're willing to settle.* You don't want to take yourself out of the running by naming a figure that's absurdly optimistic, and you certainly don't want to risk naming a figure lower than what the employer is ready to offer. Instead of naming your price, say something like, "Based on my experience and skills and the demands of the position, I'd expect I'd earn an appropriate figure. Can you give me some idea what kind of range you have in mind?"

Of course, the recruiter may come back with "Well, how much were you interested in?" There's a limit to how far you can take this without antagonizing the other person, so if you can't get him or her to name a range, give in graciously and name your own. Be sure not to make the bottom number too low (because you may be stuck with it) or the range too large, and give yourself enough room at the top without being unrealistic. If you name a range of, say, $25,000–30,000, it may be that the company was considering a range of $22,000–28,000. Therefore, you should receive an offer in the mid-to-upper end of your range, depending on your experience and qualifications.

The Salary Question

Tell me about your salary expectations.
"Based on salary information published by our national association, the market price for someone with my experience and educational background is in the broad range of thirty to forty thousand dollars per year. Although I'm not certain how your salaries compare to the national norms, my feeling is that my value would certainly be in the upper half of this national range."

A well-prepared candidate can effectively turn this question around. Ask first for the company's salary range, then answer in general terms based on your qualifications in relation to the job requirements.

The Five-Year Outlook

What do you reasonably expect to earn within five years?
"My expectation is that my contributions will be recognized and appropriately rewarded. I realize that salary levels are based on many factors, including the company's profitability and the general business cycle that affects our industry, but I would expect to take on greater responsibility each year and to be appropriately compensated."

Turn this question around and ask what's typical for the career path. Convey, based on your skills, the areas you'll excel in. Leave it to the interviewer to determine the appropriate "time frames" for promotions. Don't speculate, or you'll risk sounding arrogant.

Get It in Writing

If you're somewhat content with the distribution of funds but haven't discussed health insurance and other benefits, like a 401(k) plan and vacation time, do so immediately. Then request that everything be outlined in writing, especially if you'll be leaving a job to take the new position. You have rights, and if something looks amiss, it's time to go back to the bargaining table—that is, if you're still interested. Regard with suspicion an employer who won't give you confirmation of the position in writing.

It's about Job Satisfaction

The point of your job search is not salary negotiation; it's finding a job you'll be happy with, that you'll grow with, and that will allow you to be yourself. If your starting salary isn't the one you dreamed about but the job presents the right opportunity, think about how much easier it'll be once you've had a chance to make yourself invaluable to the organization.

On the other hand, if the salary or benefits fall far short of your realistic expectations, despite all your efforts to negotiate, nothing says you have to take the job. Don't make the mistake of accepting a position with which you're fundamentally unhappy. Trust your instincts—if you're dissatisfied with the employer before your start date, don't bet the situation will get better.

Index

Your Job Search—Your Questions

During your job search you may have a question that you are not sure how to answer concerning some aspect of your resume, cover letter, etc. If this book does not provide the answer, perhaps we can help. Please email your question to *reference@adamsmedia.com*, include your phone number, and we will put our career resources to work to try to make your job search easier.

– No question is too small (or too strange) –

Small details can make a big difference in landing a job!

We Have

EVERYTHING

More Bestselling Everything Titles Available From Your Local Bookseller:

Everything **After College Book**
$12.95, 1-55850-847-3

Everything **Astrology Book**
$12.95, 1-58062-062-0

Everything **Baby Names Book**
$12.95, 1-55850-655-1

Everything **Baby Shower Book**
$12.95, 1-58062-305-0

Everything **Barbeque Cookbook**
$12.95, 1-58062-316-6

Everything® **Bartender's Book**
$9.95, 1-55850-536-9

Everything **Bedtime Story Book**
$12.95, 1-58062-147-3

Everything **Beer Book**
$12.95, 1-55850-843-0

Everything **Bicycle Book**
$12.95, 1-55850-706-X

Everything **Build Your Own Home Page**
$12.95, 1-58062-339-5

Everything **Casino Gambling Book**
$12.95, 1-55850-762-0

Everything **Cat Book**
$12.95, 1-55850-710-8

Everything® **Christmas Book**
$15.00, 1-55850-697-7

Everything **College Survival Book**
$12.95, 1-55850-720-5

Everything **Cover Letter Book**
$12.95, 1-58062-312-3

Everything **Crossword and Puzzle Book**
$12.95, 1-55850-764-7

Everything **Dating Book**
$12.95, 1-58062-185-6

Everything **Dessert Book**
$12.95, 1-55850-717-5

Everything **Dog Book**
$12.95, 1-58062-144-9

Everything **Dreams Book**
$12.95, 1-55850-806-6

Everything **Etiquette Book**
$12.95, 1-55850-807-4

From the publishers of this book

CareerCity.com

Search *4 million* job openings at all the leading
career sites with just one click!

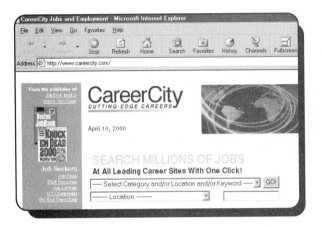

Find all the great job openings without having to spend hours surfing
from one career site to the next.

Now, with just one click you can simultaneously search all of the
leading career sites . . . at CareerCity.com!

You can also have jobs come to you! Enter your job search criteria
once and we automatically notify you of any new relevant job listings.

Plus! The most complete career center on the Web including . . .

- Descriptions and hot links to 27,000 U.S. companies
- Comprehensive salary surveys in all fields
- Expert advice on starting a job search, interviews, resumes and
  much more

You'll find more jobs at CareerCity.com!

Post your resume at CareerCity and have the job offers come to you!

It's fast, free, and easy to post your resume at CareerCity—and you'll
get noticed by hundreds of leading employers in all fields.